IMAGES
of America

DEADWOOD'S MOUNT MORIAH CEMETERY

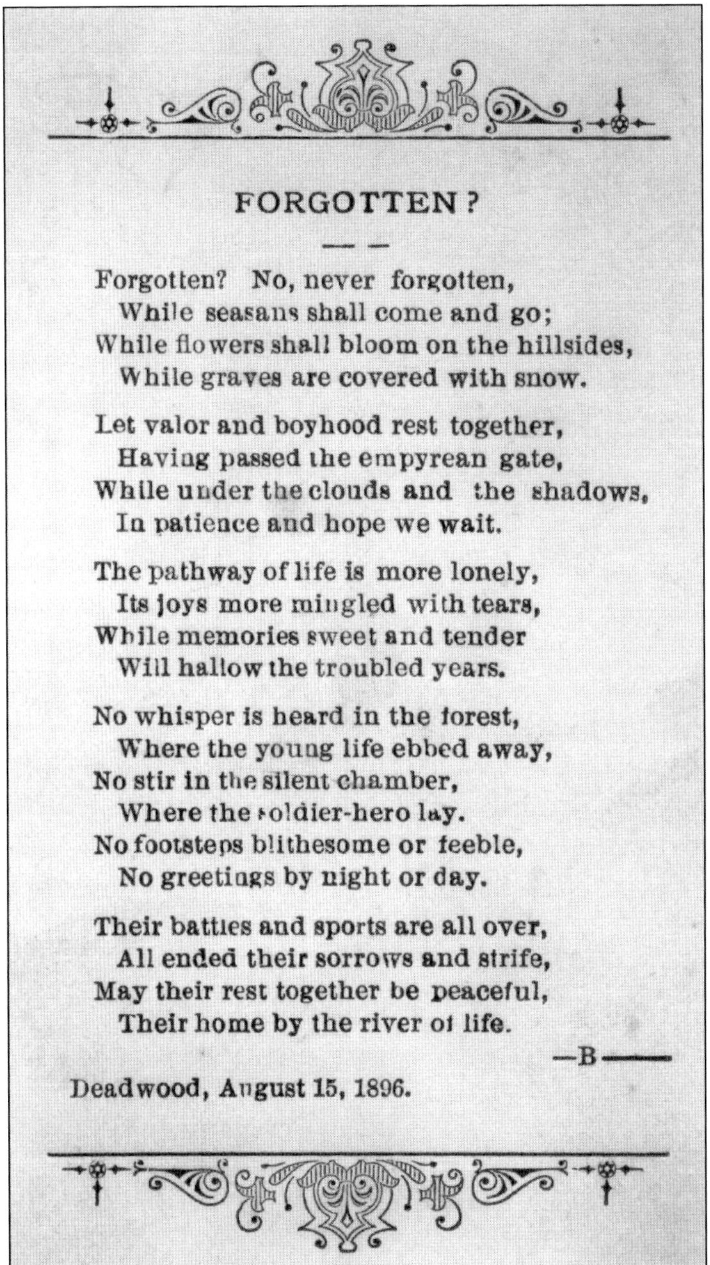

FORGOTTEN ?

Forgotten? No, never forgotten,
While seasans shall come and go;
While flowers shall bloom on the hillsides,
While graves are covered with snow.

Let valor and boyhood rest together,
Having passed the empyrean gate,
While under the clouds and the shadows,
In patience and hope we wait.

The pathway of life is more lonely,
Its joys more mingled with tears,
While memories sweet and tender
Will hallow the troubled years.

No whisper is heard in the forest,
Where the young life ebbed away,
No stir in the silent chamber,
Where the soldier-hero lay.
No footsteps blithesome or feeble,
No greetings by night or day.

Their battles and sports are all over,
All ended their sorrows and strife,
May their rest together be peaceful,
Their home by the river of life.

—B——

Deadwood, August 15, 1896.

At the beginning of this project, staff from the City of Deadwood Archives (CODA) accepted a donated scrapbook that belonged to the late Chambers Kellar, son-in-law of frontier lawman Seth Bullock. Loosely inserted among the pages was this funeral card with a poem titled "Forgotten?" and dated August 15, 1896. Though the poem, its writer, and the specific funeral are shrouded in mystery, the content exemplifies Mount Moriah Cemetery's role—to remember and honor those who came before us. (Courtesy of the Black Hills Mining Museum.)

On the Cover: On February 28, 1943, Deadwood celebrity John Eli "Potato Creek Johnny" Perrett was buried in Mount Moriah Cemetery under the sorrowful eyes of 17 witnesses. Perrett, like so many of those before and after him, would become part of the history that makes up Mount Moriah Cemetery. Several longtime residents of Deadwood reviewed this image and were able to identify the following people, from left to right: Albro Ayres, Lex Shostrom, unidentified, Charles Klein, Hilda Klein, two unidentified, Mart Morris, two unidentified, Margaret Smith, Rev. Zachary T. Vincent, unidentified, Cleo Wells, E.V. Cooper, Nel Perrigue, and unidentified. (Courtesy of the Minnilusa Historical Association.)

IMAGES
of America

DEADWOOD'S MOUNT MORIAH CEMETERY

Michael W. Runge

ARCADIA PUBLISHING

ISBN 978-1-4671-2644-1

Published by Arcadia Publishing
Charleston, South Carolina

Printed in the United States of America

Library of Congress Control Number: 2017946443

For all general information, please contact Arcadia Publishing:
Telephone 843-853-2070
Fax 843-853-0044
E-mail sales@arcadiapublishing.com
For customer service and orders:
Toll-Free 1-888-313-2665

Visit us on the Internet at www.arcadiapublishing.com

To those early pioneers who arrived, lived, died, and are buried in Mount Moriah Cemetery—may your memory never be forgotten.

Contents

ACKNOWLEDGMENTS

This book could not have been accomplished without the guidance of the Deadwood Historic Preservation Commission and the City of Deadwood Commission and their tireless efforts to preserve, protect, and promote Deadwood's history. Equally important are the city employees, many of whom work unnoticed, but who are just as dedicated in maintaining Mount Moriah Cemetery for its countless visitors every year. I would like to thank David and Greg Akrop of the Deadwood Granite and Marble Works for the use of their images and the brothers' knowledge of and longtime family connection with the cemetery. A thank-you goes to longtime volunteer Judy Farris, who reviewed this book and was a listening ear when needed. Thanks also to Lili Sjomeling and Carol Hauck at the Deadwood Public Library, who endured my constant requests for photographs and information, and to the staff at Deadwood History Inc. for helping locate photographs for this book. Thanks to Michael Bender, the project manager of the 1998–2003 Mount Moriah Cemetery restoration. His explanations helped me understand the dynamics of that grand project. I would also like to thank Katherine Lamie, the collections manager at the South Dakota Archaeological Research Center (SD-ARC), for her tireless effort in writing the final report pertaining to the unidentified 2012 burial. Thanks to Tom Loomis of Dakota Matrix Minerals Inc. for coming to Deadwood and helping identify the native rock and minerals used in the monuments at Mount Moriah Cemetery. Thanks also go to Jerry Klinger of the Jewish American Society for Historic Preservation for translating the Hebrew markers in Section 4 and explaining their meaning.

I would like to thank my loving and very patient wife, Brett, and my boys Jonas and Eli, who have been with me every step along the way. It has been many early mornings and one continuous, rolling conversation at the breakfast table. Finally, thanks to God, since there were many silent prayers that have been answered throughout this project. I have fought the good fight, I have finished the race, I have kept the faith.

INTRODUCTION

In December 2015, I received an unexpected phone call from Arcadia Publishing in Mount Pleasant, South Carolina, looking for someone to write a book on Deadwood's Mount Moriah Cemetery. After giving this some thought and consulting with the Deadwood Historic Preservation Commission and City of Deadwood Commission, I decided to embark on the project. Ever since I was small, cemeteries have fascinated me. They are one part mystery, one part creepy, and one part ancient. When combined, they are 100 percent fascinating to many adolescent boys. This childhood fascination turned into a full-time job in 2002 when I began working for the City of Deadwood as the city archivist. It turns out that a treasure trove of knowledge pertaining to Mount Moriah Cemetery is chiseled on the monuments, written in ledger books, and published in the local newspapers for those who are interested in researching the history of Deadwood.

Initially, the history surrounding Mount Moriah Cemetery can be compared to a jigsaw puzzle purchased in a secondhand store. The cover of the box provides a wonderful image of what awaits to be completed, but there is always the question of missing pieces. Thus is the case with information pertaining to Deadwood's first cemetery (1876–1878). Limited primary sources in the form of historic photographs, newspaper articles, and burial records written after the closing of this cemetery provide only a partial picture of it. In 2006 and again in 2012, two burials affiliated with this first cemetery provided the Deadwood Historic Preservation Office an opportunity to expand the collective knowledge pertaining to it. Historic record searches were conducted at the Lawrence County Register of Deeds, maps of the Ingleside Townsite (later the Presidential Neighborhood) were located and reviewed, and historic newspapers were reread. In unison with these efforts, forensic anthropologists and specialists from around the Unites States were hired by the Deadwood Historic Preservation Commission to analyze the unidentified remains. Their results, coupled with the historic record, have added to the overall understanding of this first cemetery.

Much of the early history surrounding Mount Moriah Cemetery has been preserved in the Deadwood Cemetery Association's Mount Moriah Ledger on file in the City of Deadwood Archives (CODA). In addition to recording the burials within the cemetery, the ledger also records the yearly activities of the Cemetery Association from its incorporation in December 1892 until this organization deeded the cemetery to the City of Deadwood in 1936. During this time, the association expanded the cemetery boundaries, the most noticeable being the Third Addition, Sections 1 and 2, in 1914. Numerous local fraternal organizations received permission to purchase ground in the cemetery for the burial of their dead, including Lodge No. 7 of the Deadwood Masons, Keogh Post No. 64 of the Grand Army of the Republic, and the Deadwood Fire Department. In 1908, representatives from the Deadwood Chinese community received permission to erect a brick altar and burner that were used in Chinese funerary rituals. One year later, the first automobile drove into the cemetery, ushering in a new era for both Deadwood and Mount Moriah.

After 1936, the City of Deadwood, in conjunction with the Deadwood Chamber of Commerce, was solely responsible for perpetual care and interpretation of the cemetery. In 1952, a devastating fire destroyed Deadwood City Hall along with written information pertaining to the city's involvement with the cemetery. Fortunately, the monthly minutes from the Deadwood Chamber of Commerce, on file in the City of Deadwood Archives, provided insight into the happenings within Mount Moriah Cemetery. This era also saw a rise in visitation to the cemetery, resulting in increased vandalism to the monuments and damage to the grounds caused by vehicular congestion and lack of parking.

Over the next five decades, Mount Moriah Cemetery, to use mining terminology, underwent a series of booms and busts that mirrored the local economy. In the late 1960s, three local women's organizations rallied together and formed the Tri-Club. Under their enthusiastic fervor, with the city's backing, the landscape architectural firm Theodore J. Wirth & Associates, of Billings, Montana, was hired to develop a master plan for the cemetery. Some of the recommendations proposed in this plan came to fruition, including a lockable gateway, the installation of a low retaining wall along David Street, offsite vehicular parking, and limited vehicular traffic in the cemetery. This last recommendation was to spur the development of a new motor coach industry that began in the 1970s and specialized in the transportation of tourists to and from the cemetery. This industry is still in existence today, with three separate companies operating during the summer months.

In 1989, Deadwood experienced yet another economic boom when limited stakes gaming was legalized within the city limits through a statewide vote. Funds generated through gaming revenues were in turn used for historic preservation projects throughout the city, including the restoration of Mount Moriah Cemetery. In 1997, the Deadwood Historic Preservation Commission hired the landscape architectural firm Wyss Associates, of Rapid City, South Dakota, to develop a multiphase master plan for the rehabilitation of the cemetery. Over the next six years, Mount Moriah Cemetery was rejuvenated. This included hillslope stabilization, drainage, monument and retaining wall repair, monument cleaning, the paving and curbing of the cemetery streets, and the complete overhaul of the celebrity graves in Section 1. August 2, 2002, marked the official completion of the restoration project with the dedication of the bronze Hickok monument created by Nebraska artist David Young.

Since the completion of the master plan, the Deadwood Historic Preservation Commission has continued to maintain the cemetery for the more than 80,000 visitors who come to Mount Moriah on an annual basis. In 2013, the Chinese burner and altar located in Section 6 was reconstructed using bricks from the Wing Tsue Building that once stood in Deadwood. The Deadwood Historic Preservation Commission has also placed outdoor interpretive signs commemorating the Chinese and Jewish communities that once existed in Deadwood and installed new street signs in the cemetery. Today, Mount Moriah Cemetery continues to be one of Deadwood's most beloved landmarks and a must-see on a visitor's list.

The information used for individual biographies was taken from several sources, including the Deadwood-based newspapers *Black Hills Daily Times*, the *Daily Deadwood Pioneer-Times*, and the *Deadwood Pioneer-Times* online through newspapers.com. In addition, the 1898 book *Memorial and Biographical Record of the Black Hills Region*, the 1904 *Black Hills Illustrated* by the Black Hills Mining Men's Association, Doane Robinson's *History of South Dakota*, the 1905 *Lead Daily Call Souvenir Edition*, and George W. Kingsbury's 1915 *South Dakota: Its History and its People*, volumes four and five, were also consulted.

One

Deadwood's First Cemetery

In the years following the American Civil War, the newly reunified United States plunged into a great recession. As the nation trudged through this murky time, rumors began to circulate about a great mineral wealth waiting to be discovered on the western edge of the Dakota Territory in an area known as the Black Hills. In 1874, the US government funded an exploratory expedition to the Black Hills under the leadership of Lt. Col. George Armstrong Custer and the 7th Cavalry. Accompanying the expedition were scientists, geologists, and prospectors. In August 1874, gold was discovered near present-day Custer, South Dakota.

Shortly after the discovery, the region surrounding the Black Hills began to buzz with anticipation. In less than a year, thousands of men and women from all walks of life converged upon the northern Black Hills, settling along Whitewood Creek in a series of makeshift mining camps. By June 1876, eight camps were established within Deadwood Gulch. Life within these camps was marginal at best. Lawlessness, overcrowded living quarters, dangerous working conditions, inadequate sanitary disposal, aggravated hostilities, and excessive debauchery were but a few of the problems that plagued the camps, and fatalities were inevitable.

It is unknown who was the first burial in Deadwood's mining camps, or when it happened. Land within Whitewood Gulch, approximately a quarter mile from the present-day downtown core district, was selected as a burial ground. From 1876 until 1878, an estimated 120 individuals were buried in this unnamed cemetery. In 1877, the newly formed Lawrence County purchased a tract of land for a new cemetery, Mount Moriah. This in turn led to the abandonment and removal of burials from the first cemetery. By 1900, the original cemetery land was opened for residential development. Over the next 100 years, occasional burials would be discovered during various construction projects. The most recent occurred in 2006 and 2012. Today, an outdoor interpretive panel, located at the corner of Taylor Avenue and Jackson Street, commemorates the location of Deadwood's first cemetery.

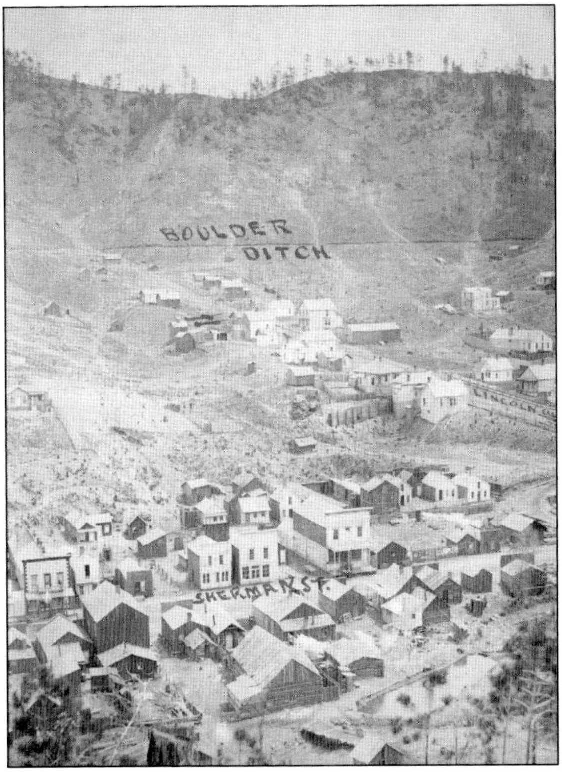

Deadwood's first cemetery was far enough removed from the daily hustle and bustle of the thriving mining camps in 1876. Within three years, residential development expanded beyond the 300-foot corridor along Whitewood Creek. The land that made up the Ingleside Townsite, located in Whitewood Gulch, provided ample space to expand beyond the tight confines of the steep-sided gulch walls. This photograph, taken after 1876, records Sherman Street and a portion of Lincoln Avenue's residential development. In contrast, the map below, created in 2006, highlights the 1879 property boundary of James Wilson's vineyard (solid line) and the boundary for the Ingleside Townsite (dashed line). In between these boundaries is a narrow strip of land (oval area). This was the location of Deadwood's first cemetery. (Both, courtesy of CODA.)

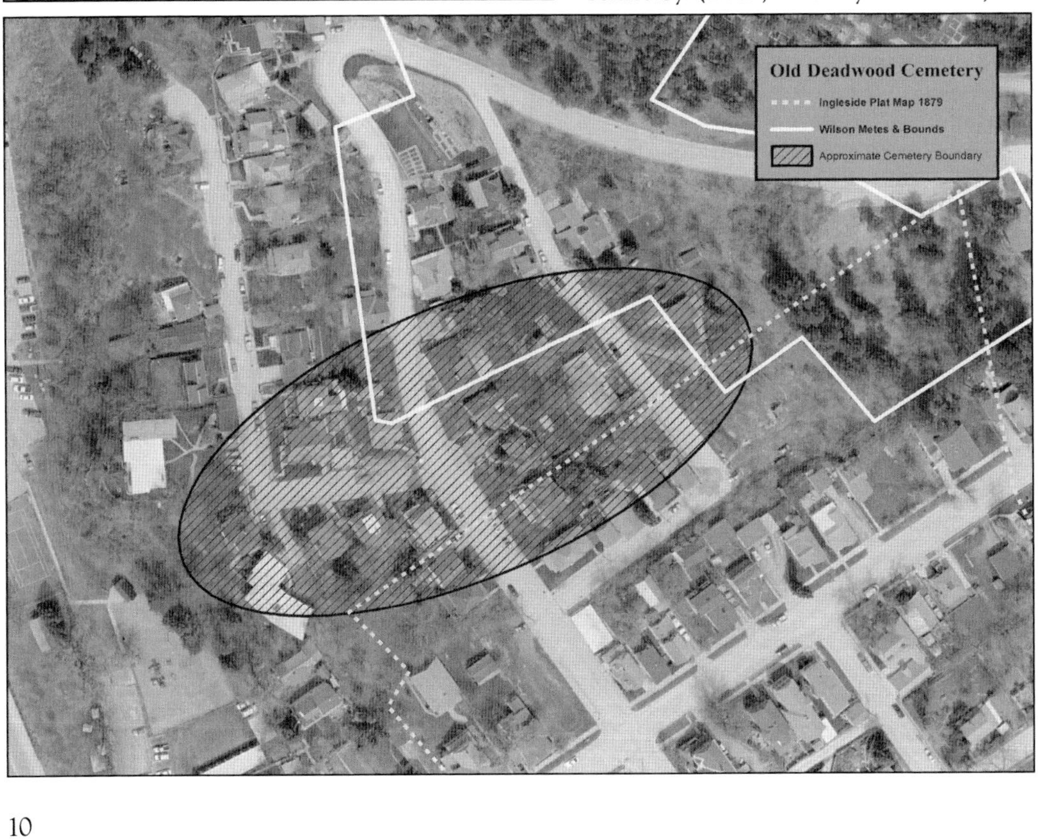

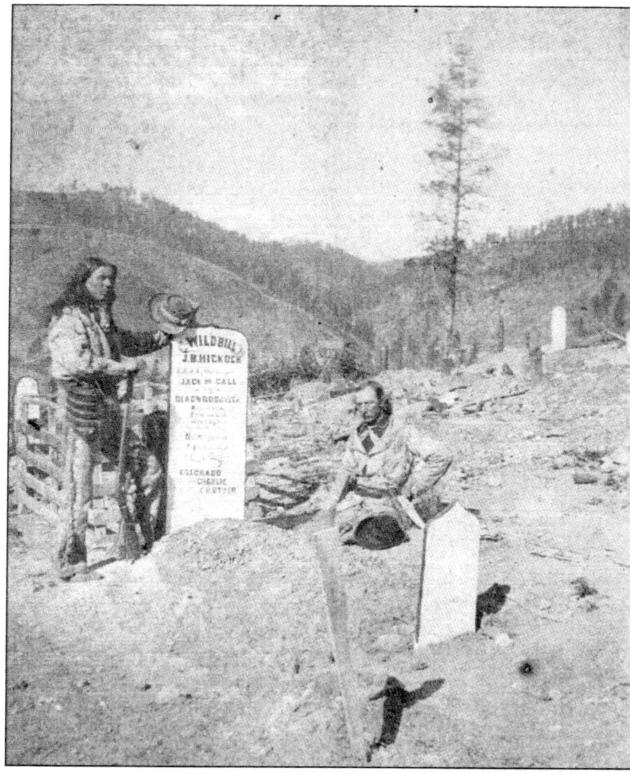

Of the 120 individuals buried in Deadwood's first cemetery, the most famous was western gunfighter James Butler "Wild Bill" Hickok. He was murdered in Nuttall & Mann's Saloon No. 10 on August 2, 1876, by Jack McCall. Because of his popularity both in life and death, two photographs were taken of his grave in 1877 and 1878. In August 1879, business partner Charles "Colorado Charlie" Utter exhumed Hickok's remains and reinterred them in Mount Moriah Cemetery. These are the only known photographs taken inside Deadwood's first cemetery. (Right, courtesy of CODA; below, courtesy of Deadwood History Inc., Adams Museum Collection.)

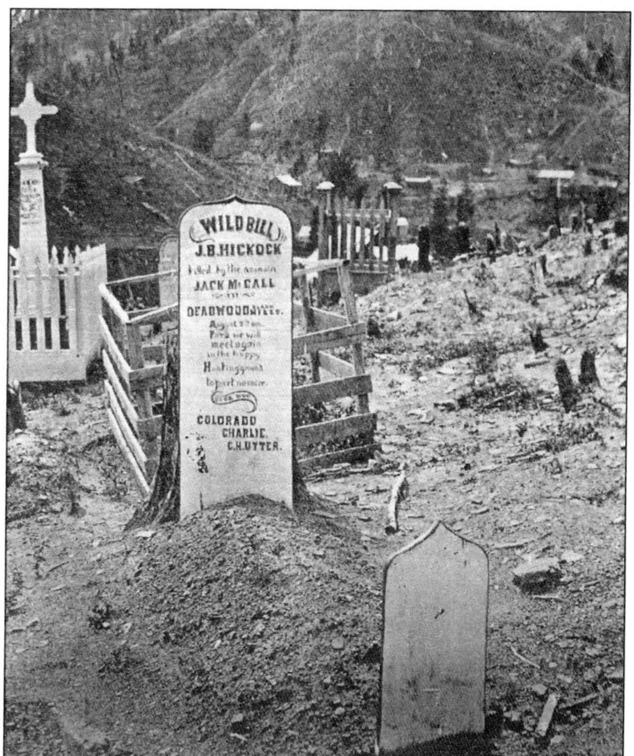

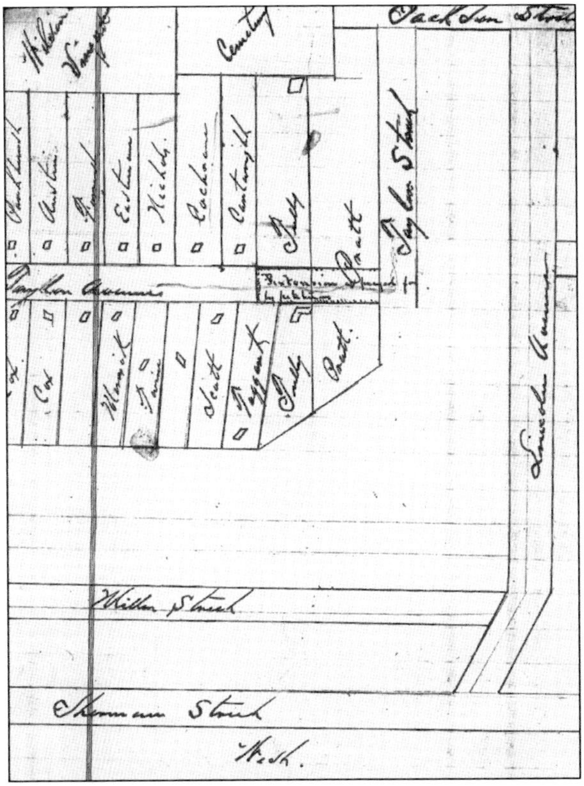

By the summer of 1878, Lawrence County established Mount Moriah Cemetery as the new municipal burial ground. One year later, 17 lots in the Ingleside Townsite bordering the old cemetery were purchased by James Wilson, owner of the Minnesota Bakery. According to a newspaper article, Wilson established a vineyard on this property. In April 1880, he was accused of encroaching upon the cemetery. Streets commissioner Patrick Early was instructed by the Lawrence County Commission to erect a wooden fence enclosing the old cemetery. Early also received permission to arrest anyone who further desecrated the graveyard. The 1880 hand-drawn map at left shows the location of Deadwood's first cemetery in relation to Wilson's Vineyard, Jackson Street, and Lincoln Avenue. The post-1880 photograph below shows the completed fence around the old cemetery. (Left, courtesy of CODA; below, courtesy of Deadwood Public Library.)

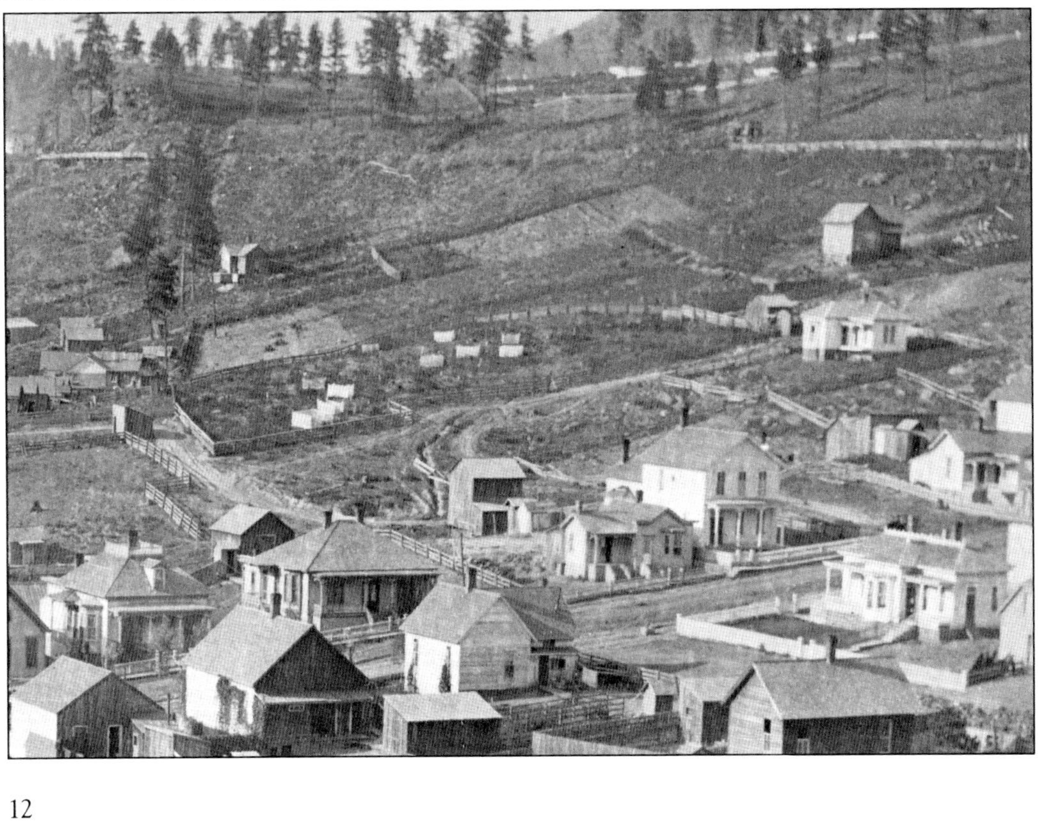

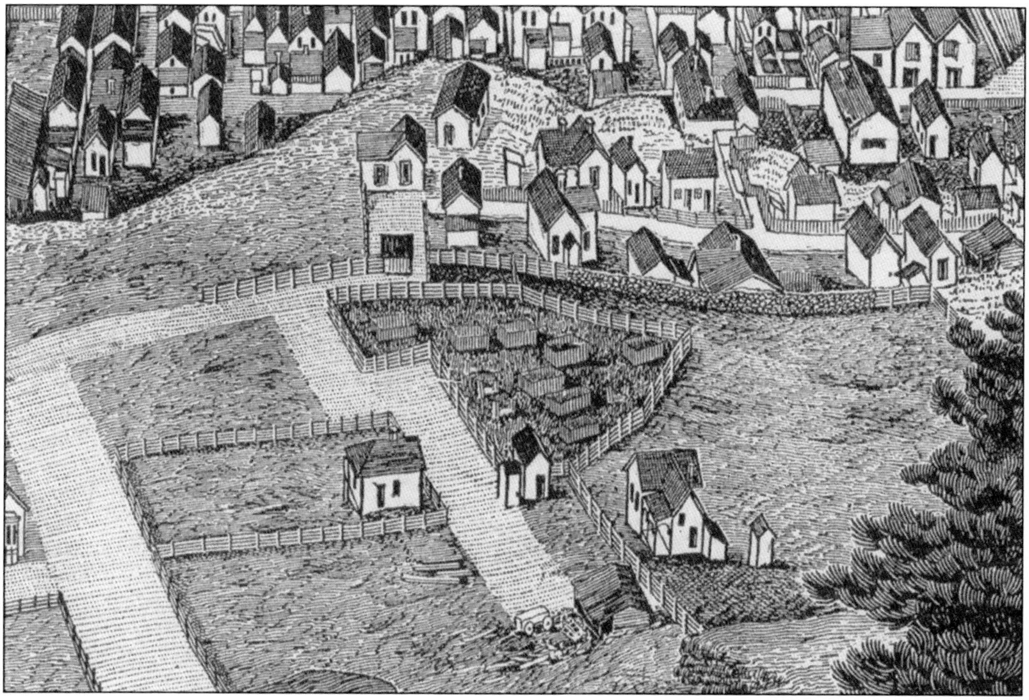

In 1883, nationally renowned illustrator William Valentine Herancourt arrived in the Black Hills and was commissioned to draw a bird's-eye view of Deadwood Gulch. Prominently featured in the center of his illustration was Deadwood's first cemetery. According to the local newspaper, longtime Deadwood residents John Treber and Jacob Goldberg were among the first to inspect and favorably comment on Herancourt's work. Six years later in 1889, amateur photographer Maud Stilwell photographed the Ingleside Townsite (Presidential Neighborhood) and Deadwood's first cemetery. By this time, much of the cemetery and fencing had fallen into disrepair. Only a few picket fences are visible marking individual burial plots. By 1900, all evidence of the cemetery was gone. (Above, courtesy of CODA; below, courtesy of Deadwood Public Library.)

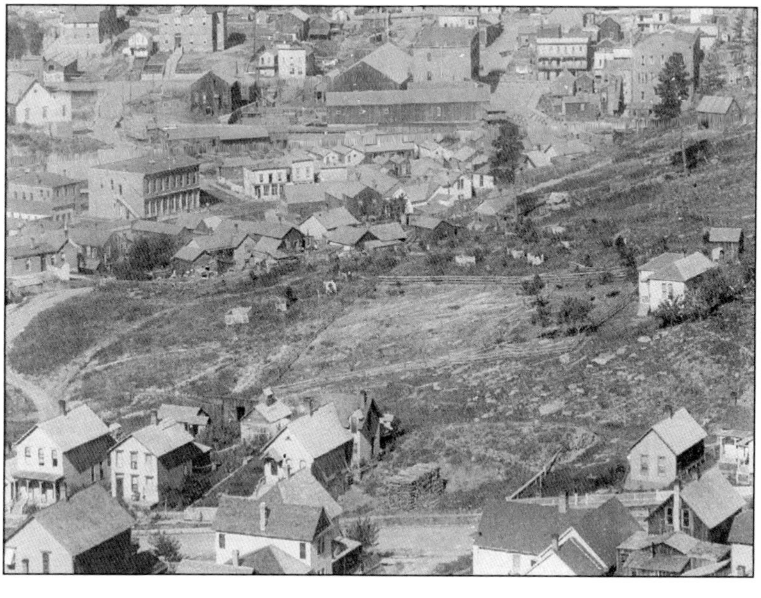

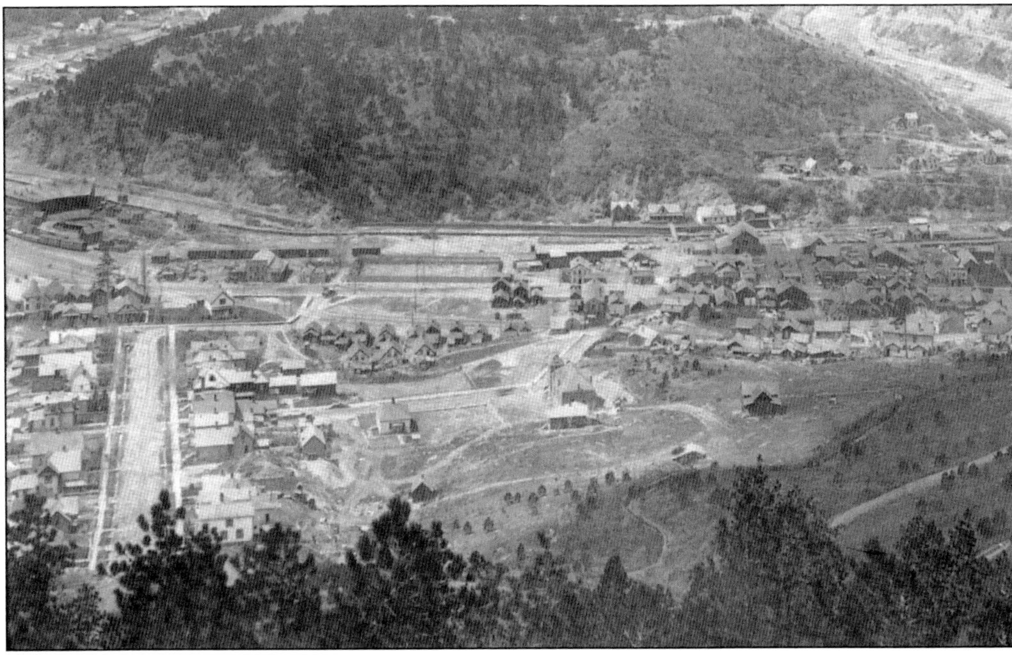

In 1892, Peter Kellar was awarded a City of Deadwood contract to install culvert pipe along Taylor Avenue. Kellar received 70¢ for every installed linear foot of pipe and $12.50 for every burial unearthed during the project. A total of 14 bodies were discovered and reinterred in Lots 329, 330, and 331 in North Potters Field. In 1893, construction began on the Fourth Ward School, located near the corner of Jackson Street and Taylor Avenue. An additional 38 burials were discovered during the project and reinterred in Lots 354 to 370 in North Potters Field. Entries for both of these projects were recorded in the Deadwood Cemetery Association's Mount Moriah Ledger. Above is an overview of Taylor Avenue and below is a close-up of the Fourth Ward School. (Above, courtesy of CODA; below, courtesy of Deadwood Public Library.)

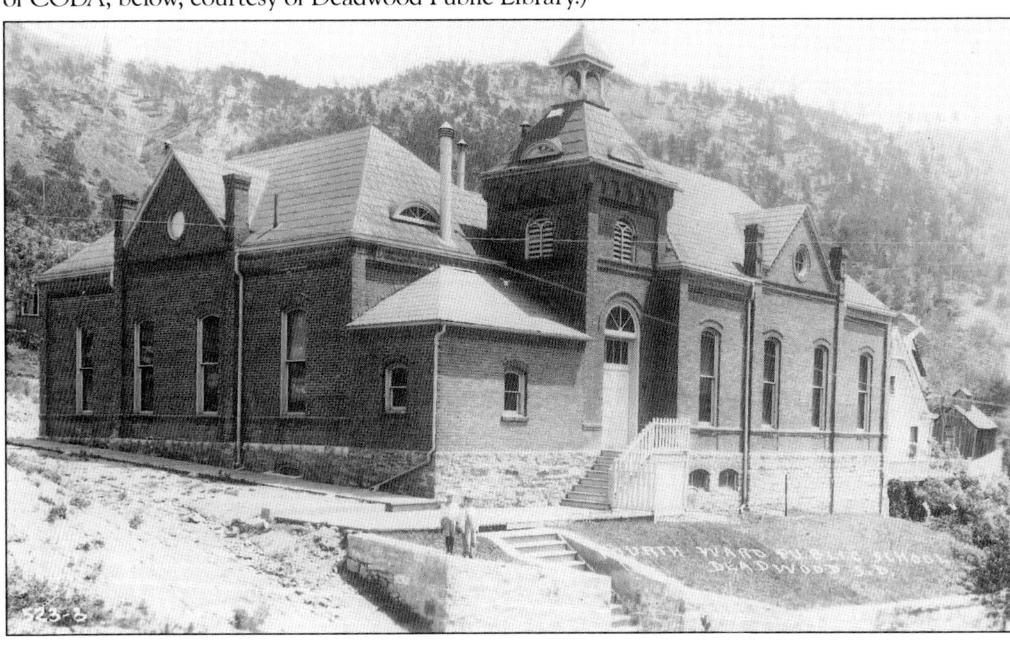

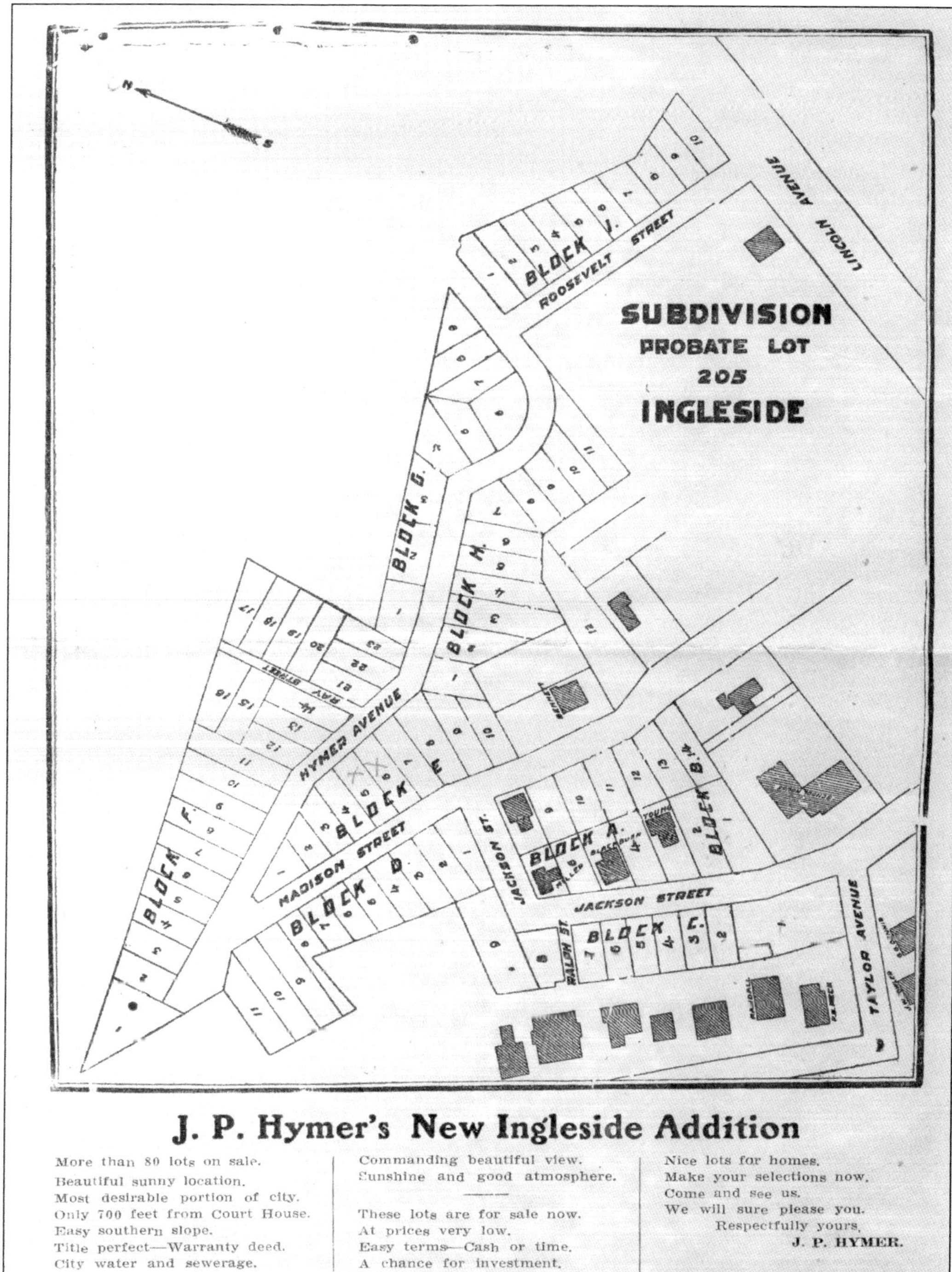

In 1904, the land that once made up the cemetery, more specifically Probate Lot 205, was finally opened for residential development by J.P. Hymer. The local newspapers ran this advertisement for the new subdivision boasting of the "Beautiful sunny location" and "good atmosphere." With the construction of new houses in this subdivision, burials were discovered over the next 100 years. (Courtesy of CODA.)

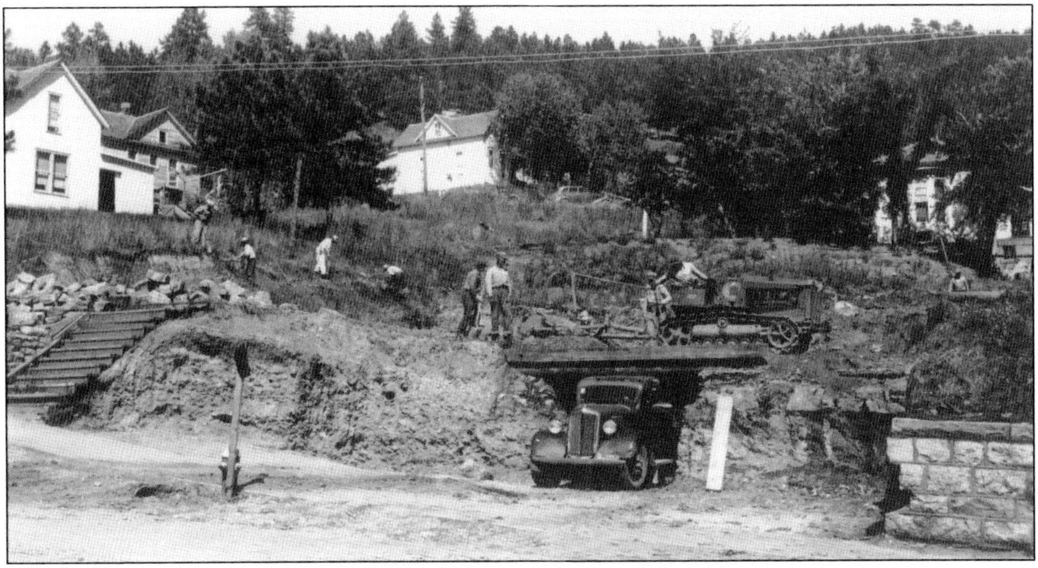

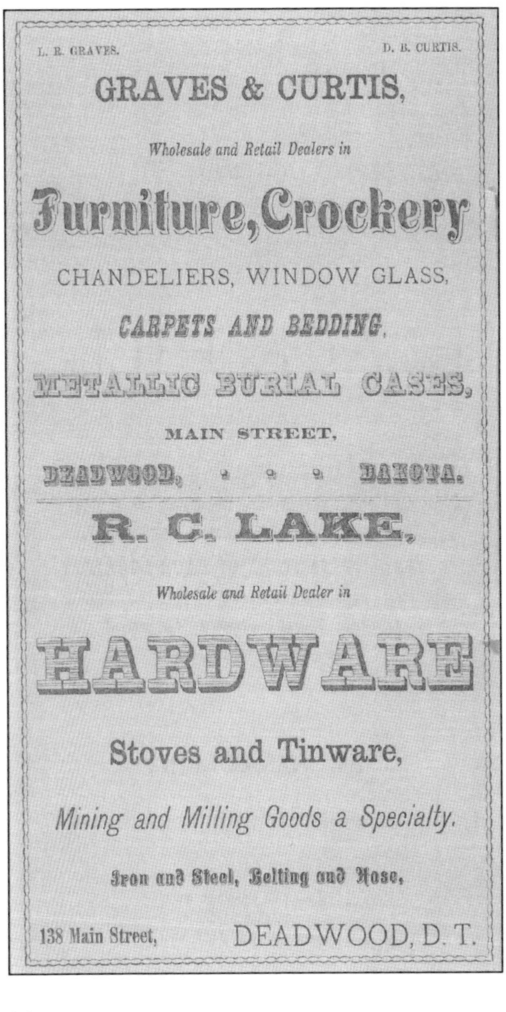

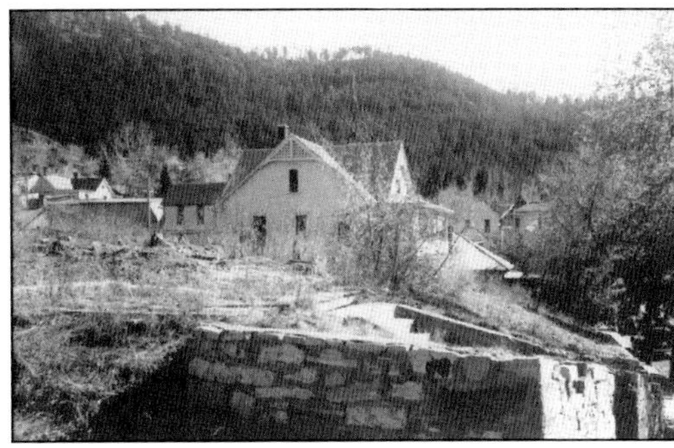

In 1930, the Deadwood School Board voted to sell the Fourth Ward School after 36 years of service. Seven years later, the brick schoolhouse was demolished, and the lots were purchased by the US Forest Service. In 1937, construction workers from the Civilian Conservation Corps began work on two houses for the Black Hills forest supervisor. During the excavation, construction workers unearthed a metal casket. After some research, it was found that metallic caskets were popular from the 1860s through the 1880s. It was believed that the caskets were airtight and would slow or stop the body from the natural decomposition process. Though hard to believe, metallic caskets found their way to Deadwood as early as 1878, based on this advertisement from the *Collins History and Directory of the Black Hills*. (Photographs courtesy of CODA; advertisement courtesy of Yale University Library.)

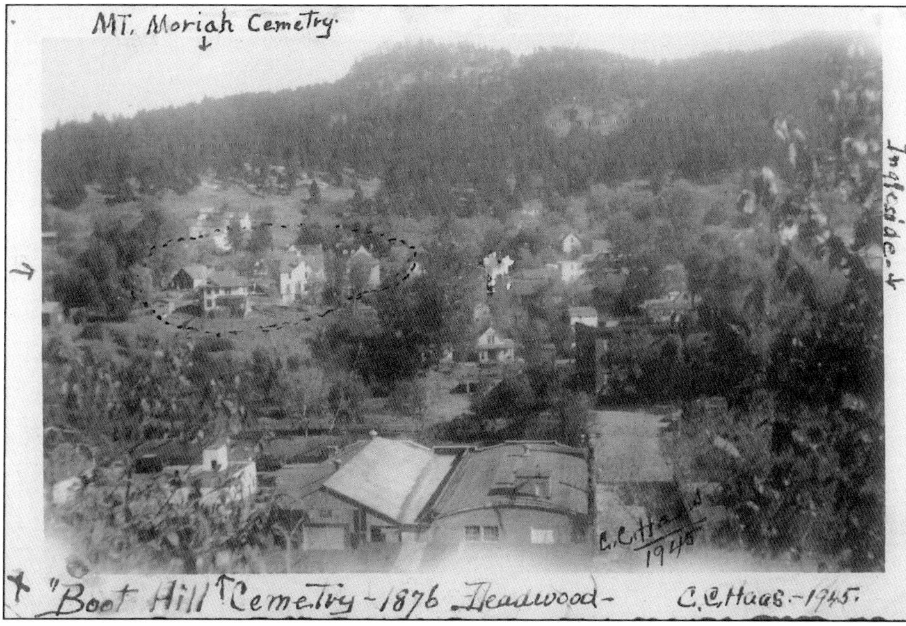

In the 1940s, Deadwood resident and amateur historian Charles C. Haas created a series of photographic scrapbooks chronicling the history of Deadwood and the northern Black Hills. In one of his scrapbooks, titled "Deadwood," Haas recorded the approximate location of Deadwood's first cemetery based on conversations with longtime residents. In some instances, Haas included notes and drew boundaries on his photographs, providing approximate locations of Deadwood's first cemetery as related to Mount Moriah Cemetery. In 2011, the Deadwood Historic Preservation Commission purchased this scrapbook from James Aplan of Piedmont, South Dakota. The Haas scrapbook has become a tremendous resource, helping city officials narrow down the original boundaries of the first cemetery. Haas also marked the approximate location of James Butler Hickok's original grave, behind the Forest Service houses. (Both, courtesy of James Aplan.)

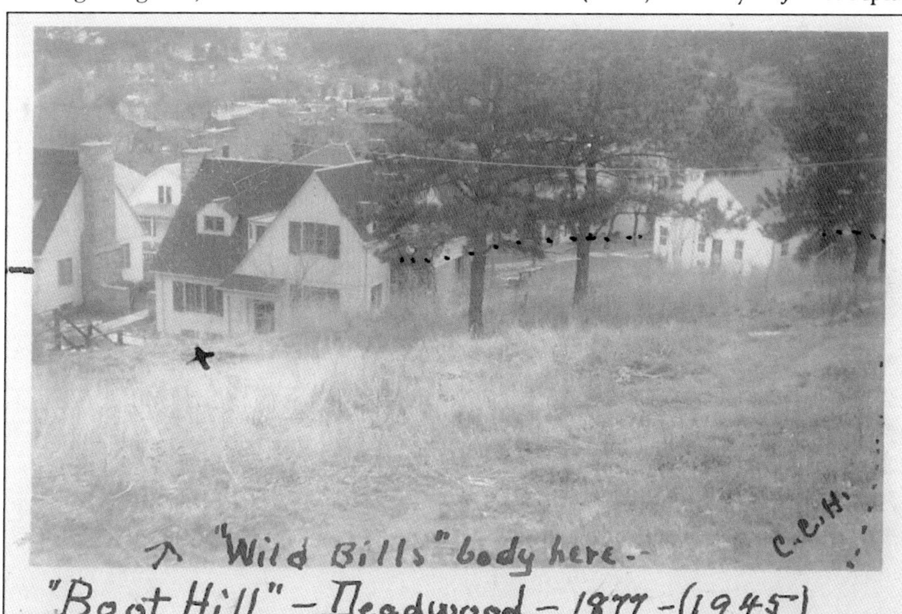

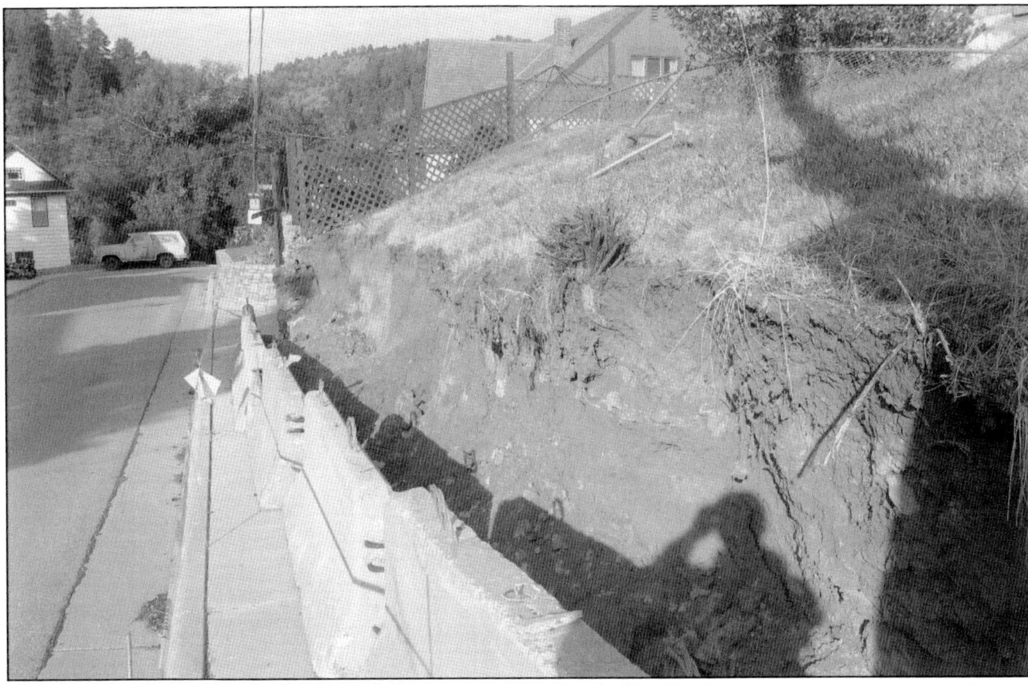

In 2006, a retaining wall along Taylor Avenue began to fail. After being reviewed by city officials, the wall was deemed unsafe and removed. Construction workers, while excavating the footing for the new wall, unearthed remnants of a wooden coffin in the wall scrape. Work was immediately stopped, and archaeologists from the South Dakota Archaeological Research Center (SD-ARC) were called in to excavate the burial. The remains were analyzed by a forensic anthropologist from Hamline University in St. Paul, Minnesota. The analysis identified the individual as a male who stood approximately 5 feet, 4 inches to 5 feet, 8 inches in height and was approximately 25 to 34 years old at the time of death. The ancestry was classified as "Mongoloid," or being from eastern Asia, southeast Asia, and/or indigenous tribes of North America. (Both, courtesy of CODA.)

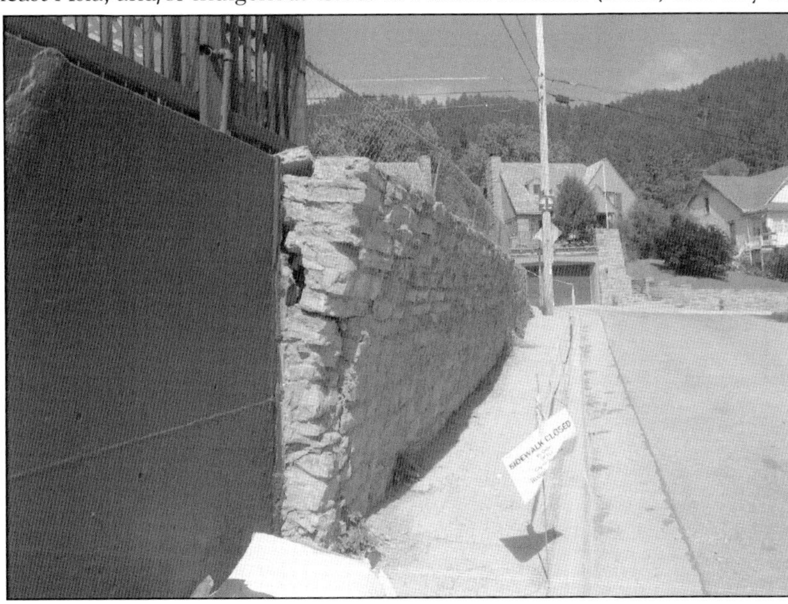

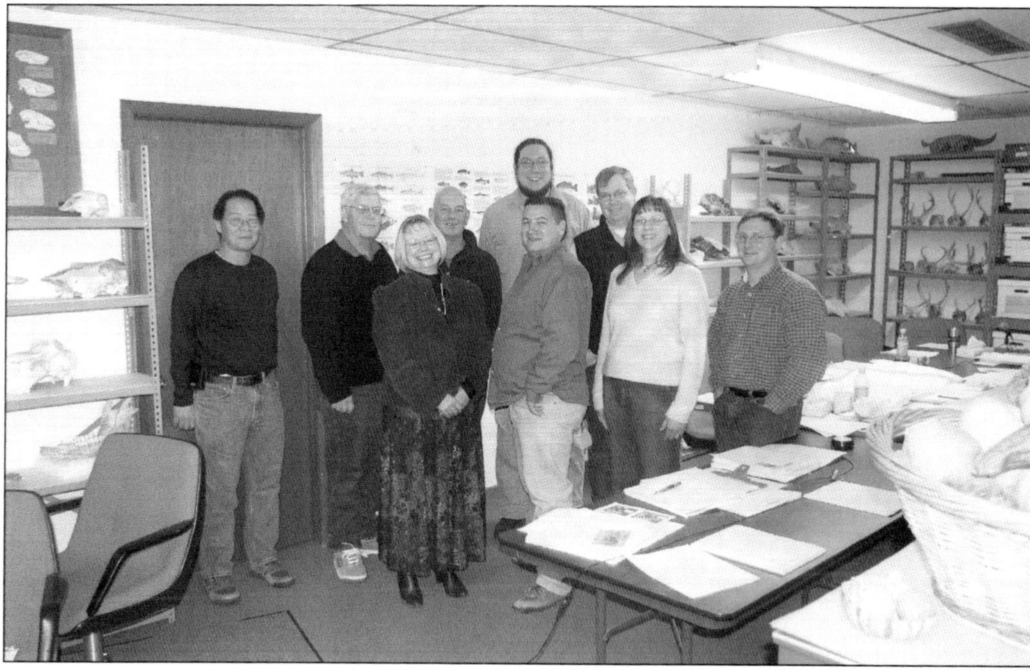

Based on the report, the City of Deadwood was obligated by federal law to comply with the Native American Graves Protection and Repatriation Act (NAGPRA). In December 2008, representatives from the Rosebud Sioux Tribe, Chinese Historical Society of Southern California, and the Deadwood Historic Preservation Commission met to discuss the repatriation of the remains. On July 28, 2010, representatives from these organizations jointly reinterred the unidentified remains in front of a large crowd of spectators. Fr. Kerry Prendiville of St. Ambrose Catholic Church in Deadwood, Master E-Man and his apprentice Sumo Liu from the First Taoism Foundation in Arcadia, California, and Oglala Lakota spiritual leader Wilmer Mesteth oversaw the funeral service. (Above, courtesy of SD-ARC; below, courtesy of CODA.)

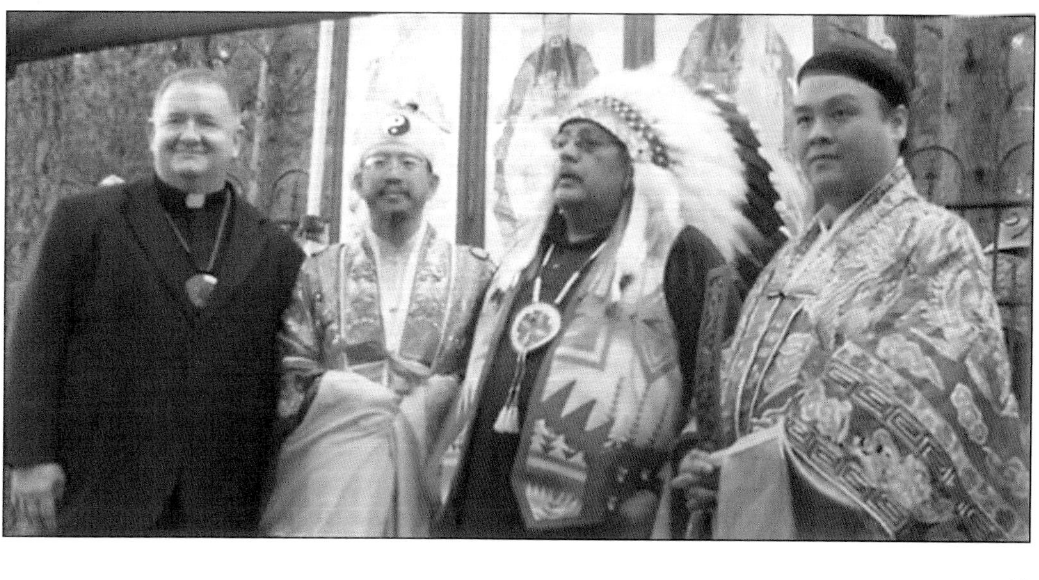

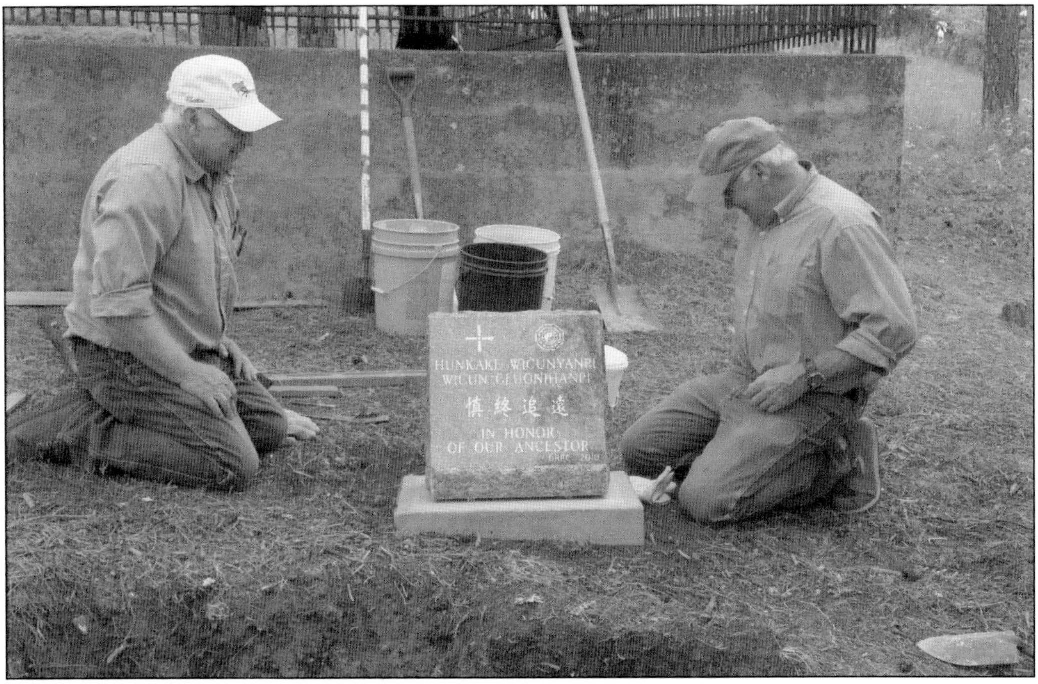

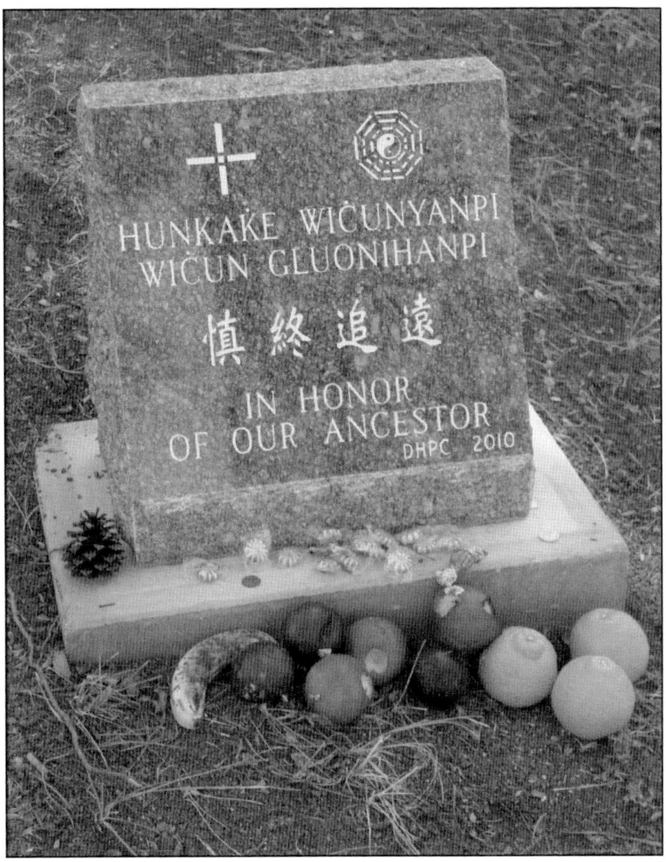

Since the identity of this individual will never be known, the spiritual leaders and the Deadwood Historic Preservation Commission agreed to incorporate symbols, characters, and words from Lakota Sioux, Chinese Taoism, and the English language. The phrase "In Honor of our Ancestor" appears in Lakota, Chinese, and English on the granite monument. David and Greg Akrop from Deadwood Granite and Marble Works were hired to prepare and install the monument in Mount Moriah Cemetery. City officials selected a 16-inch, wedged-shaped Bellingham granite monument from eastern South Dakota. Today, the monument is a tribute to an unidentified pioneer of Deadwood and also celebrates the partnerships that developed as a result of this burial. (Both, courtesy of CODA.)

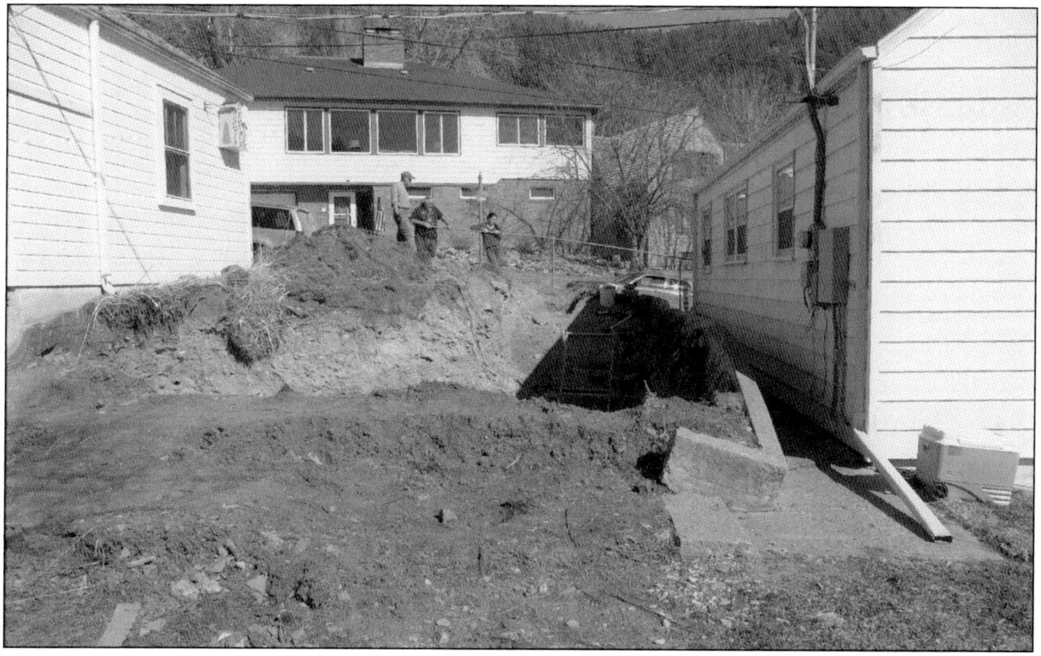

In 2012, a second burial was discovered during retaining wall replacement on the same property, on the opposite side of the house. Prior to the removal of the wall, city officials requested that an archaeologist from SD-ARC monitor the area. The backhoe operator unearthed a coffin, and all work was immediately stopped. Over the next two days, archaeologists and city officials excavated the burial. The remains were analyzed by a forensic anthropologist in Fort Collins, Colorado. Based on the final report, the individual was male, stood approximately 5 feet, 6 inches to 5 feet, 11 inches in height and was 18 to 24 years of age at the time of death. Based on the skeletal features, the ancestry of the individual was identified as "Caucasian." (Both, courtesy of SD-ARC.)

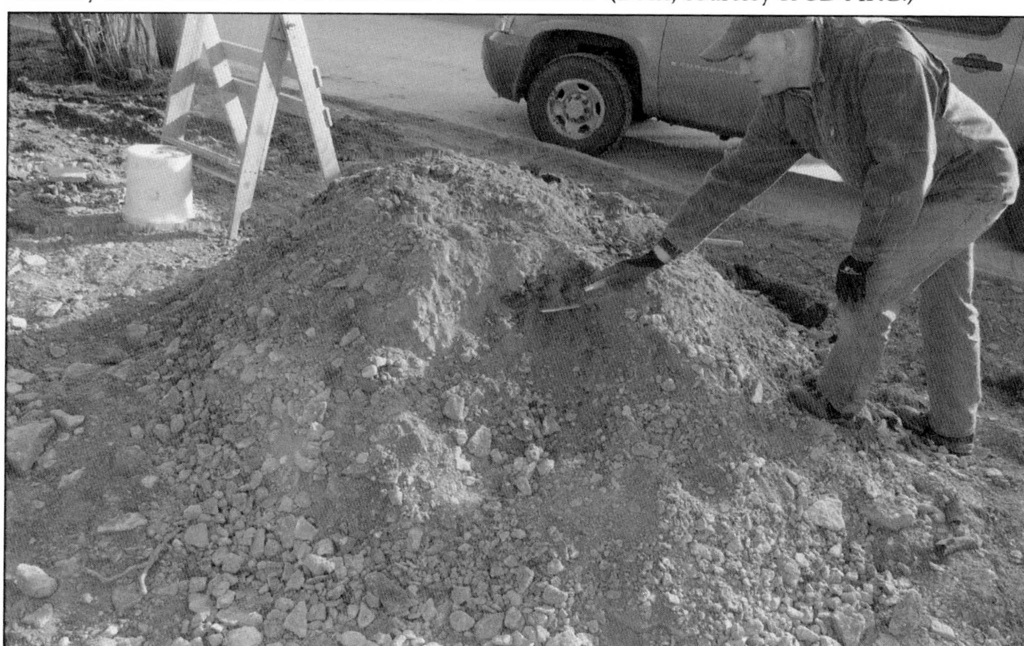

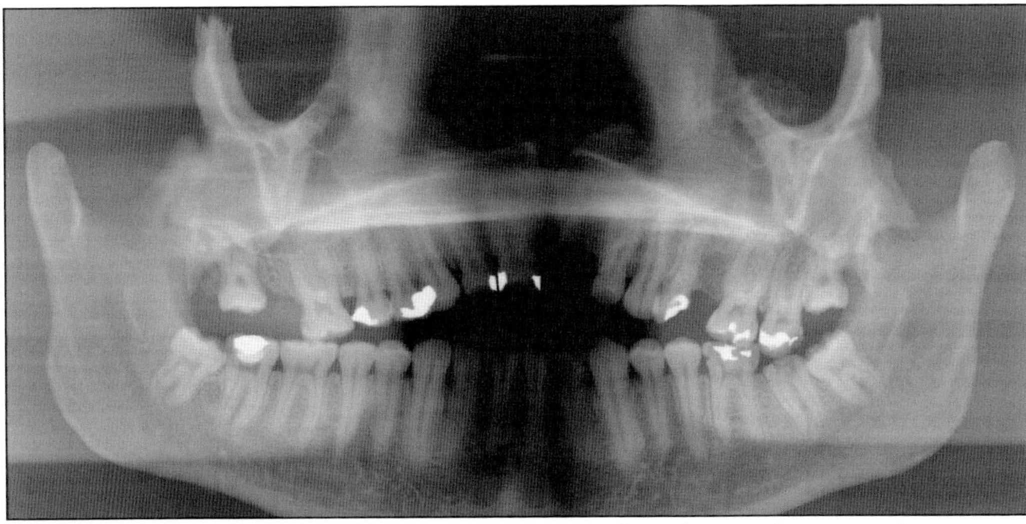

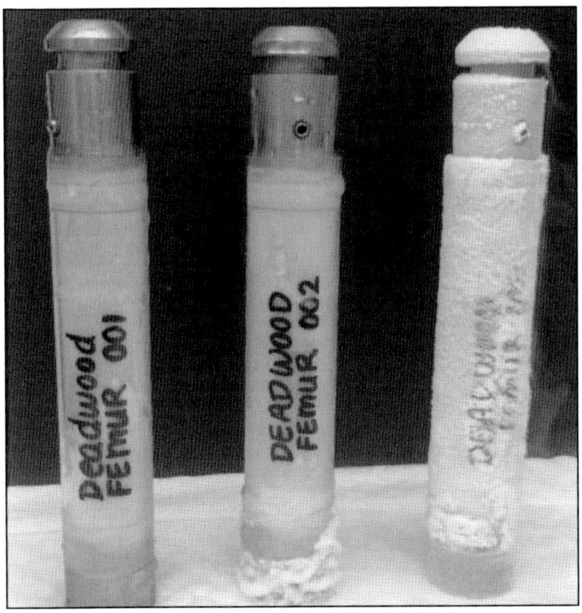

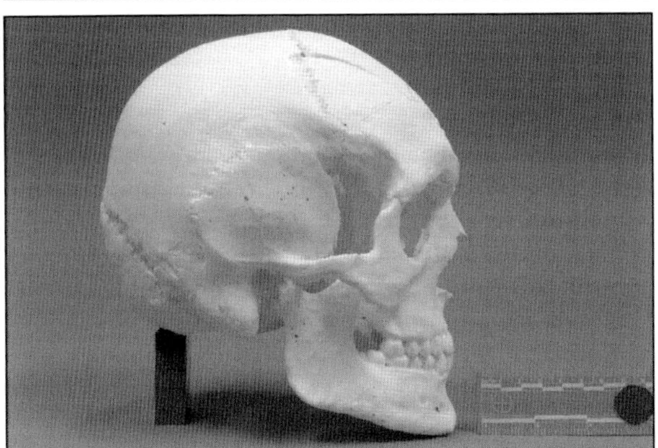

Over the next four years, the Deadwood Historic Preservation Office conducted a CSI-style investigation of the unidentified individual. Forensic specialists from around the United States analyzed the remains. The first examination focused on the individual's unique set of dental work. The results confirmed the individual underwent 13 dental restorations, including five gold foil and eight metal amalgam fillings. Other examinations determined the individual's ethic origin, DNA profile, eye and hair color, and personal habits. The preservation office also gained remarkable insight into late-19th-century dental procedures, burial apparel, and dietary practices. Once this segment of the project was completed, the specialist reports and plastic casting of the cranium and mandible were sent to a forensic artist to develop a two-dimensional drawing of the individual. (Top, courtesy of Deadwood Dental; center, courtesy of Dr. Angie Ambers; bottom, courtesy of Dr. Diane L. France.)

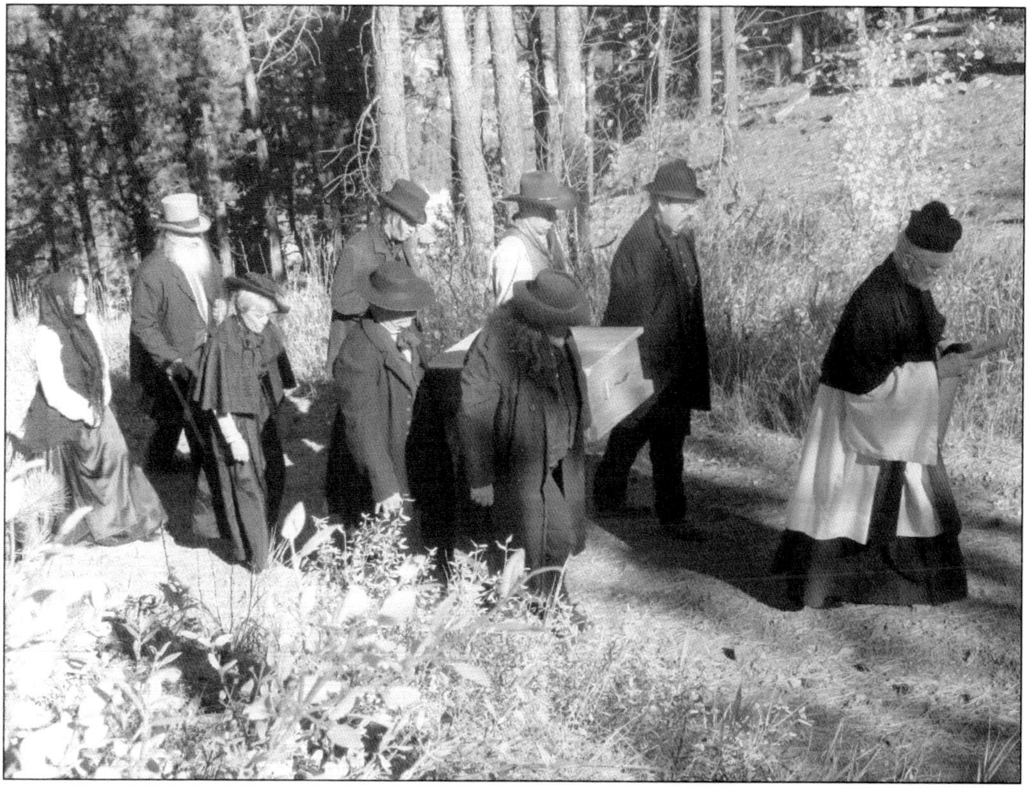

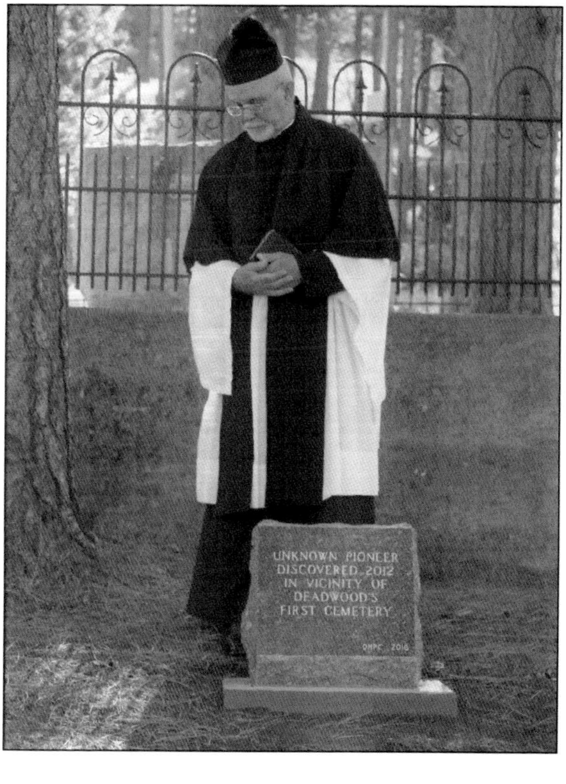

On September 29, 2016, the remains of the unidentified individual were reinterred in Mount Moriah Cemetery. The Rev. Michael Johnson from St. John's Episcopal Church in Deadwood conducted the funeral service, and members from the acting guild known as Deadwood Alive dressed in period attire to assist with the burial. Deadwood Granite and Marble Works was once again hired to prepare and install the monument. Dr. Angie Ambers, a forensic geneticist and DNA analyst from the Institute of Applied Genetics (University of North Texas Health Science Center in Fort Worth, Texas), and Katherine Lamie, archaeologist and repository manager for SD-ARC, provided a brief eulogy about their involvement in this project. A one-hour documentary chronicling the investigation was produced by South Dakota Public Broadcasting and aired in 2017. (Both, courtesy of CODA.)

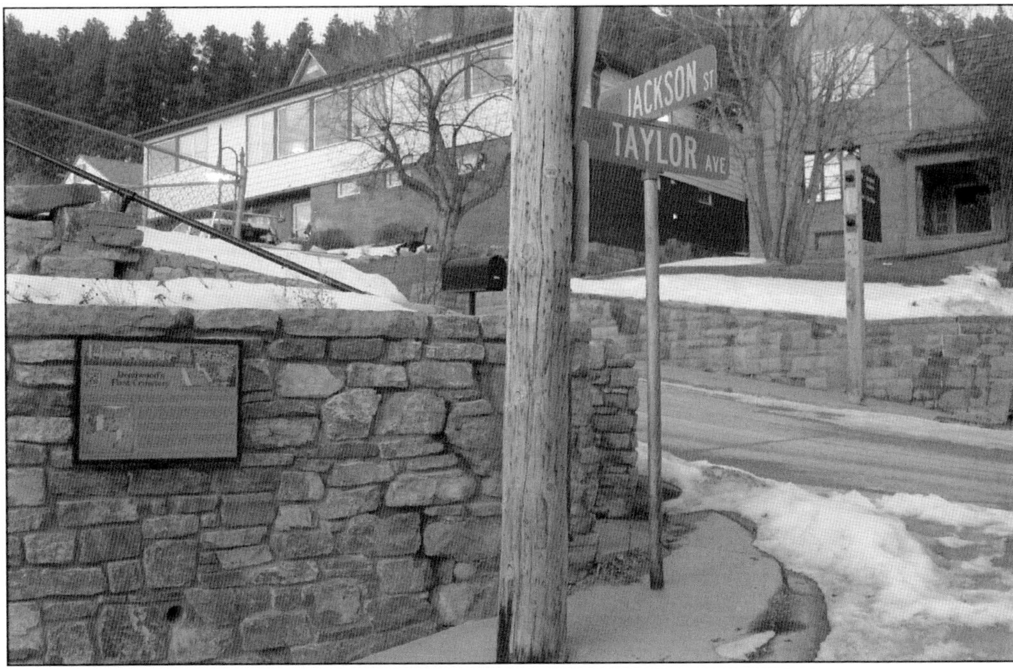

Today, an outdoor interpretive plaque is mounted to the retaining wall at the corner of Taylor Avenue and Jackson Street commemorating the location and history surrounding Deadwood's first cemetery. Visitors following the designated Mount Moriah Cemetery pedestrian route walk past the plaque as they navigate their way to Mount Moriah Cemetery. (Both, courtesy of CODA.)

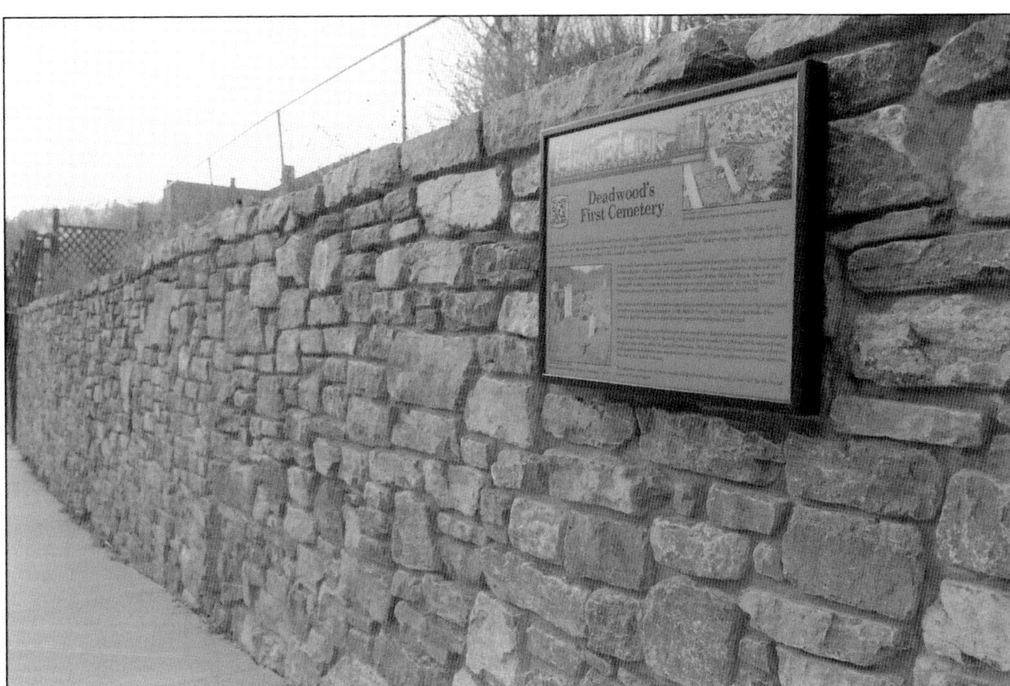

Two

Mount Moriah Cemetery

In the spring of 1878, the newly formed Lawrence County Commission purchased a tract of land on a plateau for the development of a new cemetery. Initially, the proposed cemetery consisted of approximately 4.6 acres and was mapped to resemble a large oval. The cemetery was then divided into four quadrants bordered by two potter's fields on the north and south. The cemetery name and streets within the necropolis correlate to Mount Moriah, a plateau located within the city of Jerusalem in Israel. The layout is indicative of a Victorian-era cemetery design, with a strong connection to Freemasonry, based on its orientation and selection of street names. For 71 years, Mount Moriah Cemetery served as the municipal cemetery for Deadwood and Lawrence County. Over the years, land was added to the cemetery several times, the two most significant additions being Sections 5 through 9 on the west side of the oval in 1893 and the Third Addition Sections 1 and 2 on the eastern side in 1914.

From its inception in 1878, over 3,600 recorded individuals have been buried in Mount Moriah Cemetery. James DeLong, who lost his life in a mining accident at the Pecacho Mine, became the first recorded burial on June 1, 1878. By the close of the year, an additional 44 burials were recorded. In 1892, a group of Deadwood citizens, concerned about the welfare and overall condition of the cemetery, incorporated the Deadwood Cemetery Association. Under their leadership, the cemetery expanded, standardized its record keeping, and began to beautify the grounds. By the late 1920s, funds needed for the perpetual care of the cemetery began to dwindle. In 1936, the Deadwood Cemetery Association deeded Mount Moriah to the City of Deadwood. From this point forward, the cemetery has been under the stewardship of the city. From the 1950s through the 1980s, the Deadwood Chamber of Commerce partnered with the City of Deadwood on several ventures to raise funds to rehabilitate the cemetery. With the advent of gaming in the 1990s, Mount Moriah Cemetery, under the direction of the Deadwood Historic Preservation Commission, underwent a $4.8 million restoration. These efforts in recent years have preserved the cemetery yet maintained its historic appearance. Today, Mount Moriah Cemetery continues to serve as a cemetery and a tourist attraction.

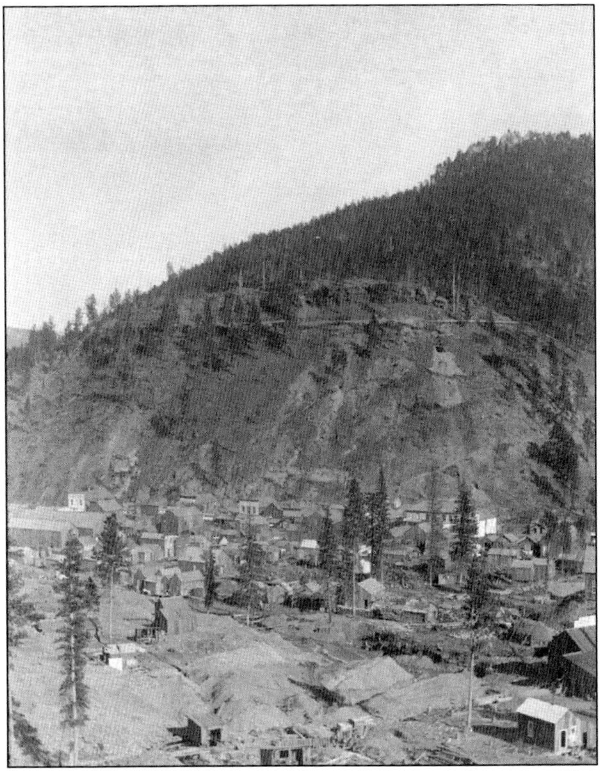

F. Jay Haynes came to the Black Hills in 1877 and photographed the Deadwood Gulch mining camps. The photograph at left shows the upper part of Main Street in the foreground. In the background, the horizontal flume of the Boulder Ditch and the plateau that would become Mount Moriah Cemetery can be seen. On April 11, 1878, Lawrence County acquired ground east of the old cemetery for a new cemetery. Jerome Hollenbeck was awarded the contract to clear the ground and erect a fence around the cemetery. The land was mapped in an oval configuration and orientated on an east/west axis. The first cemetery map was lost during the September 26, 1879, fire that destroyed Deadwood's downtown district. In 1880, William L. Smith redrew the cemetery map (below) for the Lawrence County commissioners. (Left, courtesy of CODA; below, courtesy of Lawrence County Register of Deeds.)

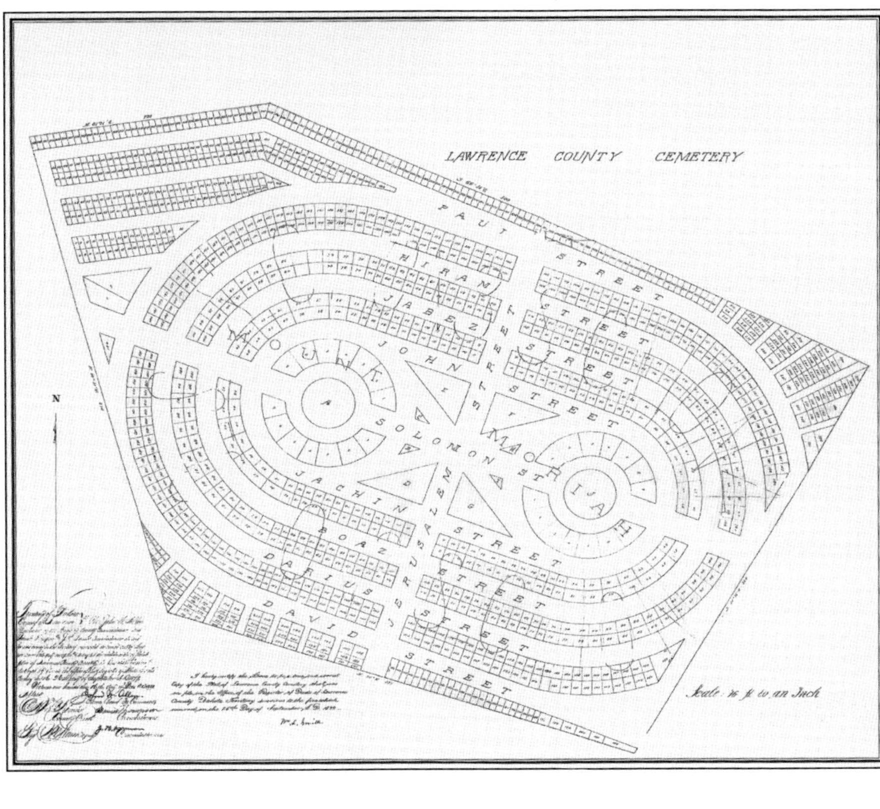

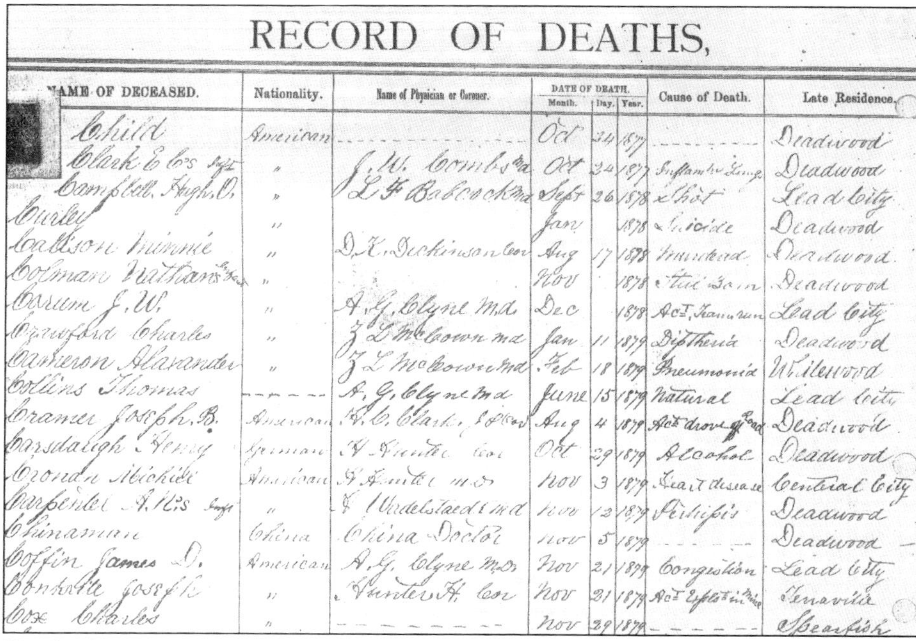

RECORD OF DEATHS,

Name of Deceased.	Nationality.	Name of Physician or Coroner.	Date of Death. Month.	Day.	Year.	Cause of Death.	Late Residence.
Child	American	----------	Oct	24	1877	----------	Deadwood
Clark E. C's Infant	"	J. W. Combs Md	Oct	24	1877	Inflamation Lung	Deadwood
Campbell, Hugh O.	"	L. F. Babcock Md	Sept	26	1878	Shot	Lead City
Curley	"		Jan		1878	Suicide	Deadwood
Callson Minnie	"	D. K. Dickinson Cor	Aug	17	1878	Murdered	Deadwood
Colman Nathan Infant	"		Nov		1878	Still born	Deadwood
Corrum J. W.	"	A. G. Clyne M.D.	Dec		1878	Acc. Tramway	Lead City
Crawford Charles	"	Z. L. McGown Md	Jan	11	1879	Diptheria	Deadwood
Cameron Alaxander	"	Z. L. McGown Md	Feb	18	1879	Pneumonia	Whitewood
Collins Thomas	------	A. G. Clyne Md	June	15	1879	Natural	Lead City
Cramer Joseph B.	American	H. C. Clark, [illegible]	Aug	4	1879	Acc. drowned	Deadwood
Carsdaugh Henry	German	H. Hunter Cor	Oct	29	1879	Alcohol	Deadwood
Cronin Michael	American	H. Hunter M.D.	Nov	3	1879	Heart disease	Central City
Carpenter A. H's Infant	"	F. Underlstaed M.D.	Nov	12	1879	Erisipelas	Deadwood
Chinaman	China	China Doctor	Nov	5	1879	------	Deadwood
Coffin James D.	American	A. G. Clyne M.D.	Nov	21	1879	Congestion	Lead City
Conkrite Joseph	"	Hunter H. Cor	Nov	21	1879	Acc. [illegible]	Terraville
Cox Charles	"	----------	Nov	29	1879	------	Spearfish

In 1879, the Lawrence County commissioners requested that a written record be kept of the burials within the cemetery. Cemetery superintendent Barclay P. Smith created the Lawrence County Death Record, a ledger that recorded the name, age, cause of death, attending physician, and burial location in Mount Moriah Cemetery. This information was then presented in an annual report to the county commission outlining the death statistics and overall health of the community. The first of these annual reports is recorded in the Lawrence County Commission minutes dated January 24, 1880. The death statistics for 1879 were broken down by month and cause of death, including natural death, murder, suicide, and accidents. (Above, courtesy of CODA; below, courtesy of Lawrence County Commission.)

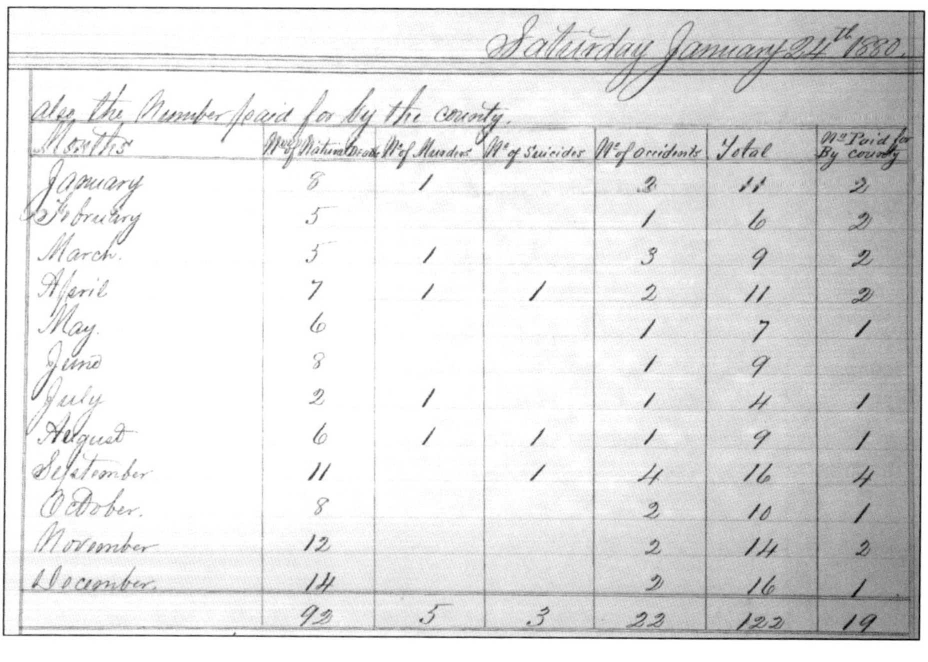

Saturday January 24th 1880.

also the Number paid for by the county.

Months	No. of Natural Deaths	No. of Murders	No. of Suicides	No. of accidents	Total	No. Paid for By county
January	8	1		2	11	2
February	5			1	6	2
March	5	1		3	9	2
April	7	1	1	2	11	2
May	6			1	7	1
June	8			1	9	
July	2	1		1	4	1
August	6	1	1	1	9	1
September	11		1	4	16	4
October	8			2	10	1
November	12			2	14	2
December	14			2	16	1
	92	5	3	22	122	19

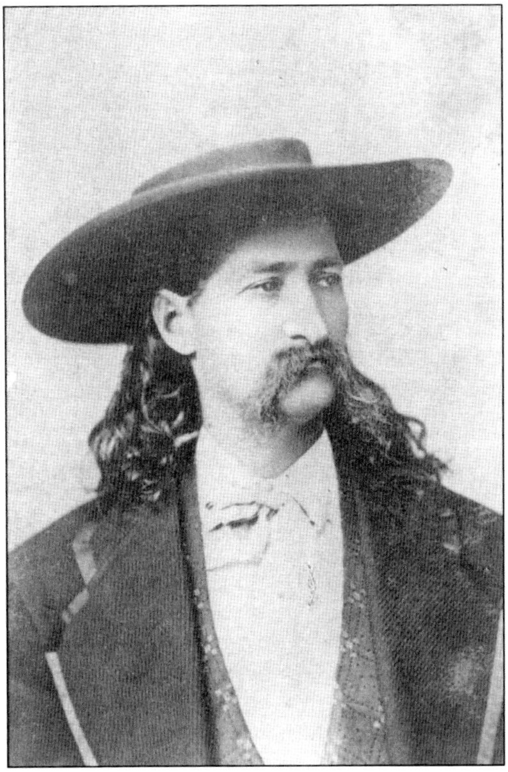

James Butler Hickok (May 27, 1837–August 2, 1876) is one of the most recognized gunfighters on the American West. In 1861, Hickok joined the US Army and served as a teamster, scout, and spy during the Civil War. In July 1876, Hickok arrived in Deadwood Gulch. On August 2, he was murdered by Jack McCall in Nuttall & Mann's Saloon No. 10 and buried in Deadwood's first cemetery. In 1879, Louis Shoenfield, John McClintock, and Charles "Colorado Charlie" Utter exhumed and reinterred Hickok in Section 1, Lot 71 of Mount Moriah Cemetery. Years later, McClintock wrote a detailed account of this event in his book *Pioneer Days of the Black Hills*. The photograph below, taken after 1880, most likely shows the first of Hickok's graves in Mount Moriah Cemetery. (Both, courtesy of CODA.)

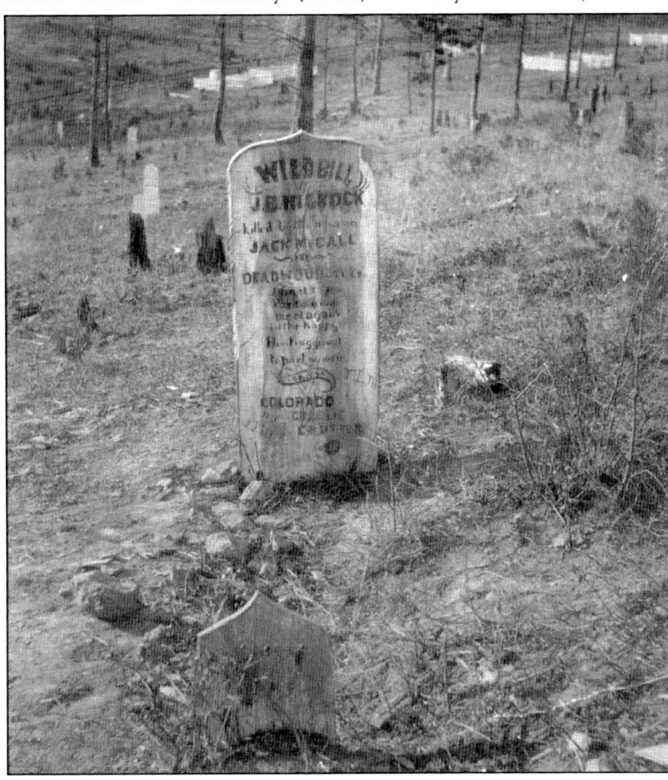

Hickok's grave became a popular attraction and was subject to repeated vandalism. In 1890, the citizens of Deadwood commissioned New York artist James H. Riordan to sculpt a memorial using native Black Hills sandstone. On September 27, 1891, this memorial was placed on Hickok's grave and local photographers recorded the artist next to the completed memorial. Unfortunately, this monument also succumbed to repeated vandalism. In 1902, artist Alvin Smith began sculpting a life-size sandstone statue of Hickok at Black Hills Marble and Granite Works. One year later, through popular subscription, the completed statue was purchased and installed on Hickok's grave. For the next 52 years, the statue would remain on Hickok's grave before it was destroyed by vandals. The pieces of the statuary were removed and stored at the Adams Museum. (Right, courtesy of CODA; below, courtesy of Historic Black Hills Studios.)

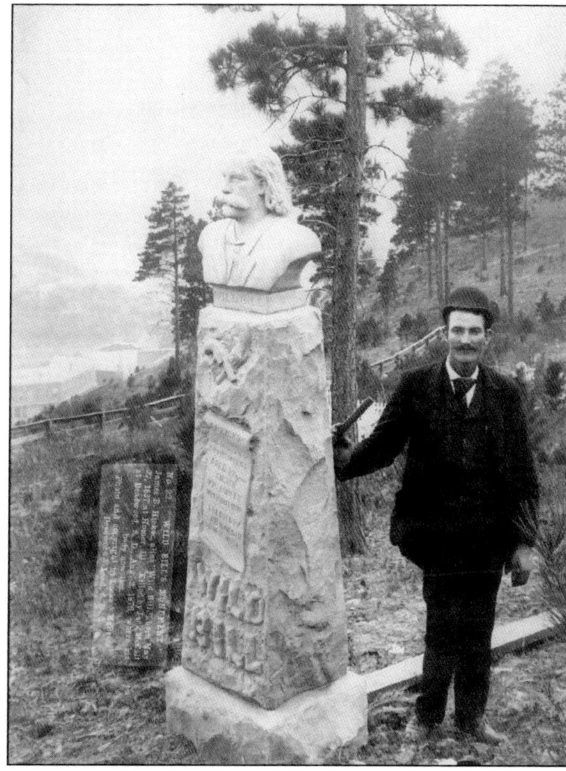

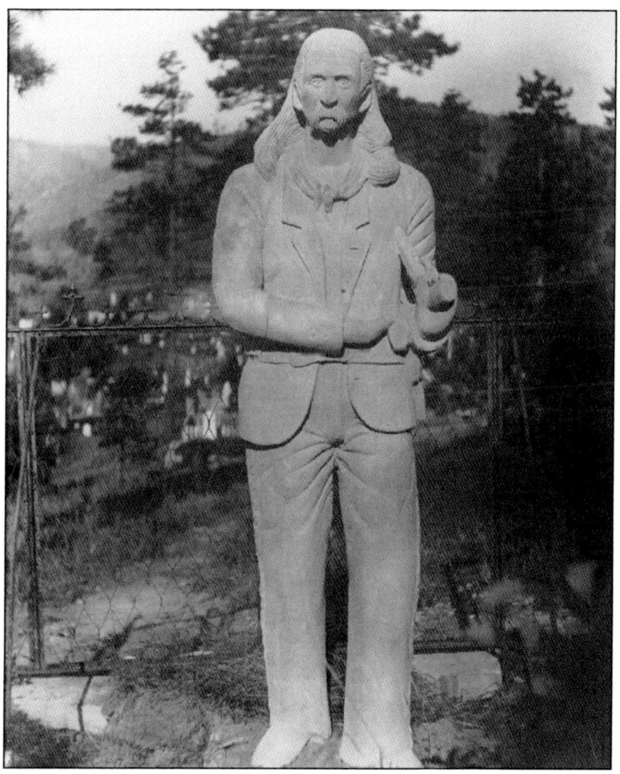

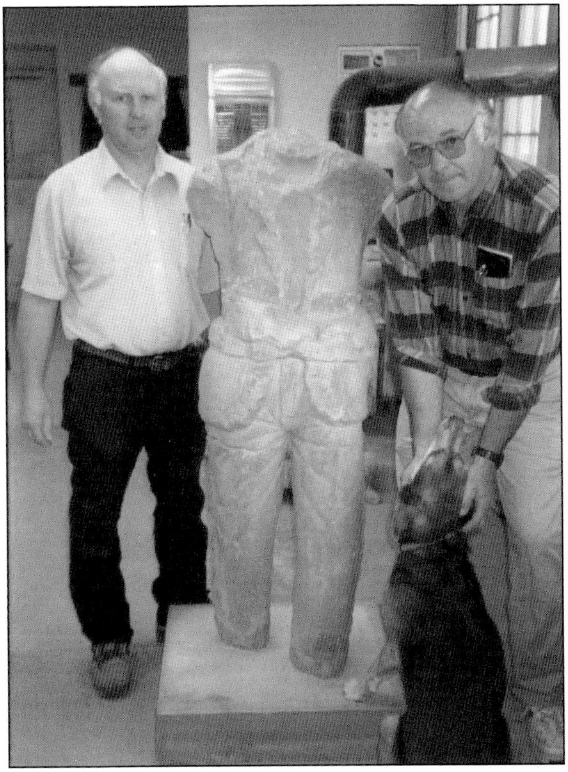

In 1996, the Adams Memorial Museum in Deadwood hired David and Greg Akrop, owners of Deadwood Granite and Marble Works, to reassemble the Hickok sculpture for public display. The Akrops are the grandsons of Albert Louis Duchene, one of the original proprietors of Deadwood Granite and Marble Works. Their father, Paul John Akrop, with their mother, Genevieve (Duchene) Akrop, owned and managed the business from 1946 to 1966. After Paul's unexpected death in 1966, sons David and Greg Akrop and their sister Mary Ann (Akrop) Oberlander operated the business, which has now been in continuous operation for over 110 years. Upon completion, the Alvin Smith statue, locally known as the *Venus de Hickok,* is on permanent display in the Legends Section at the Adams Museum. (Left, courtesy of David Akrop; below, courtesy of CODA.)

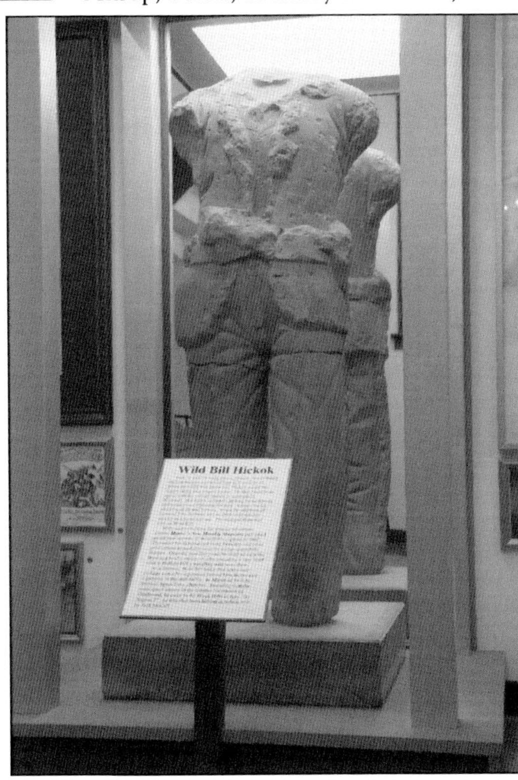

Rev. Henry Weston Smith came to Deadwood Gulch on his own accord to spread the word of God. Smith was born on January 10, 1828, in Ellington, Connecticut. In 1852, he was ordained in the Methodist Episcopal Church and served the Providence, Rhode Island, Methodist Conference for 10 years. In 1862, Smith enlisted in the 52nd Massachusetts Infantry during the Civil War. After the war, he and his family moved to Kentucky. In 1876, he left for the Black Hills to spread the gospel in the mining camps. On Sunday, August 20, 1876, Smith was murdered en route to the mining camp of Crook City and was buried in the first cemetery without a Christian service. The painting below by Charles Hargens depicts Smith's date with destiny. In 1883, Smith's body was exhumed and given a Christian burial in Mount Moriah. (Right, courtesy of Dakota Wesleyan University Archives; below, courtesy of Dakota Discovery Museum.)

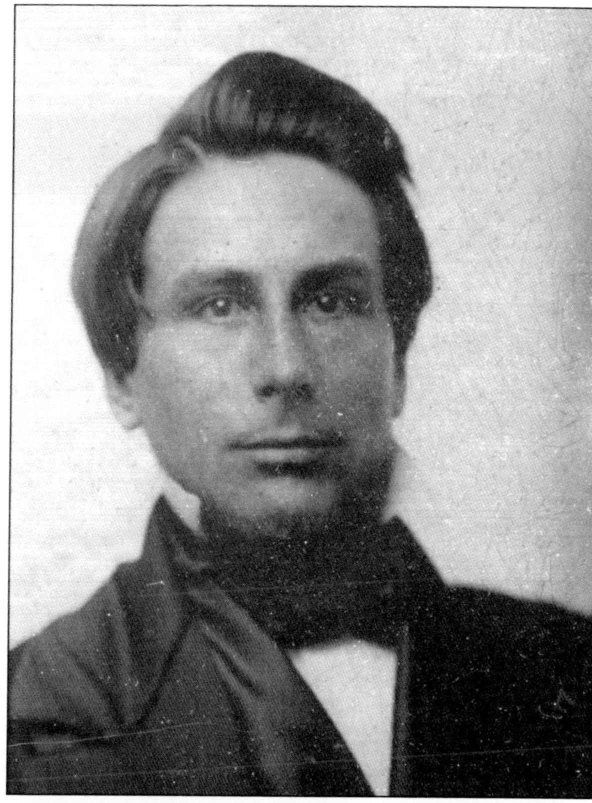

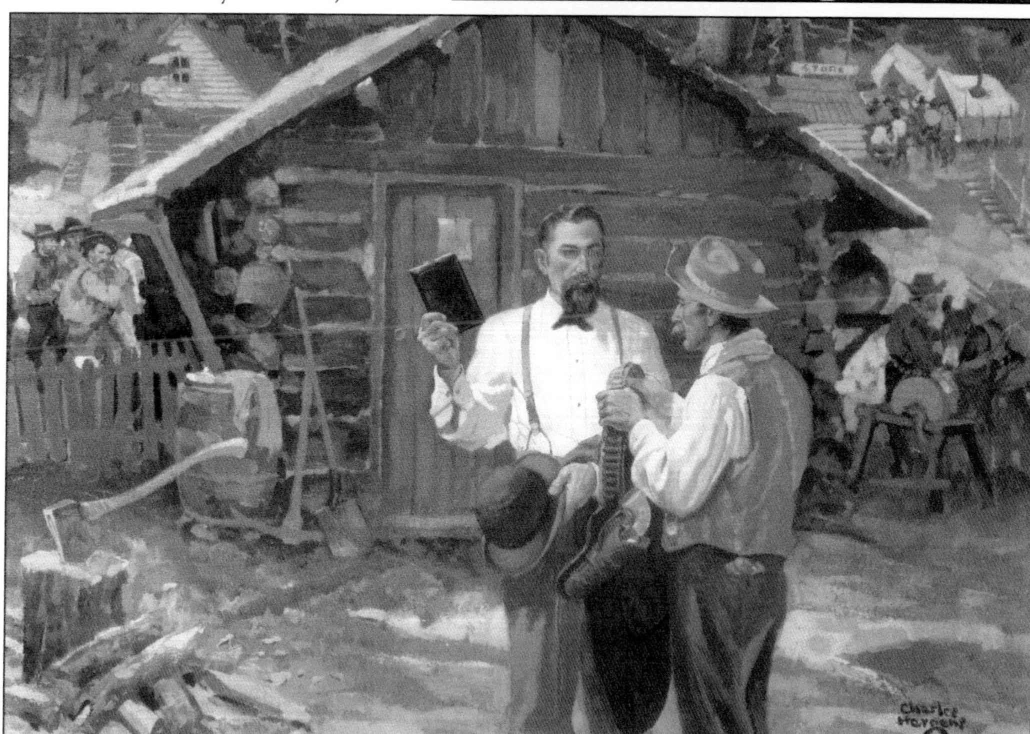

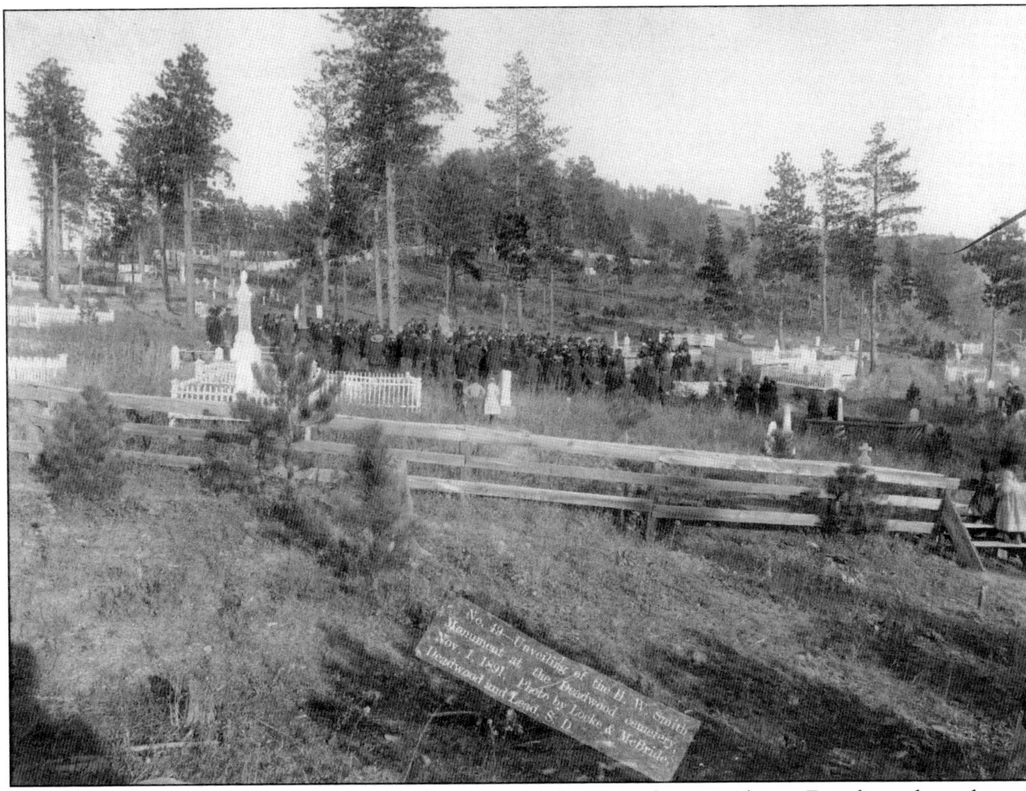

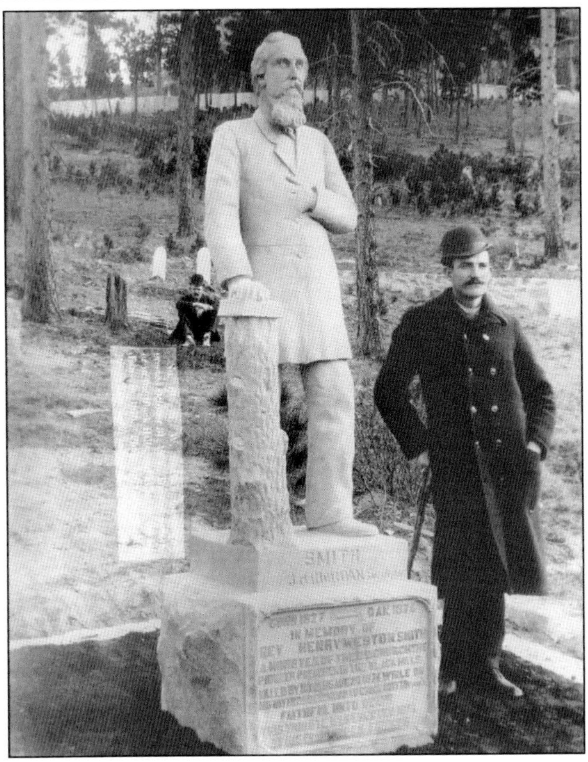

Eight years later, Deadwood resident Lucien Stilwell began a capital campaign to raise funds to place a suitable monument on Preacher Smith's grave. In 1891, New York sculptor James H. Riordan was hired again to carve a monument for the grave. Upon its completion, the monument portrayed a stoic, life-sized statue of Henry Weston "Preacher" Smith delivering a sermon. The new monument was unveiled and dedicated on Sunday, November 1, 1891, in front of a large crowd. Sculptor James H. Riordan posed beside the completed statue after the dedication. (Above, courtesy of Deadwood Public Library; left, courtesy of Historic Black Hills Studios).

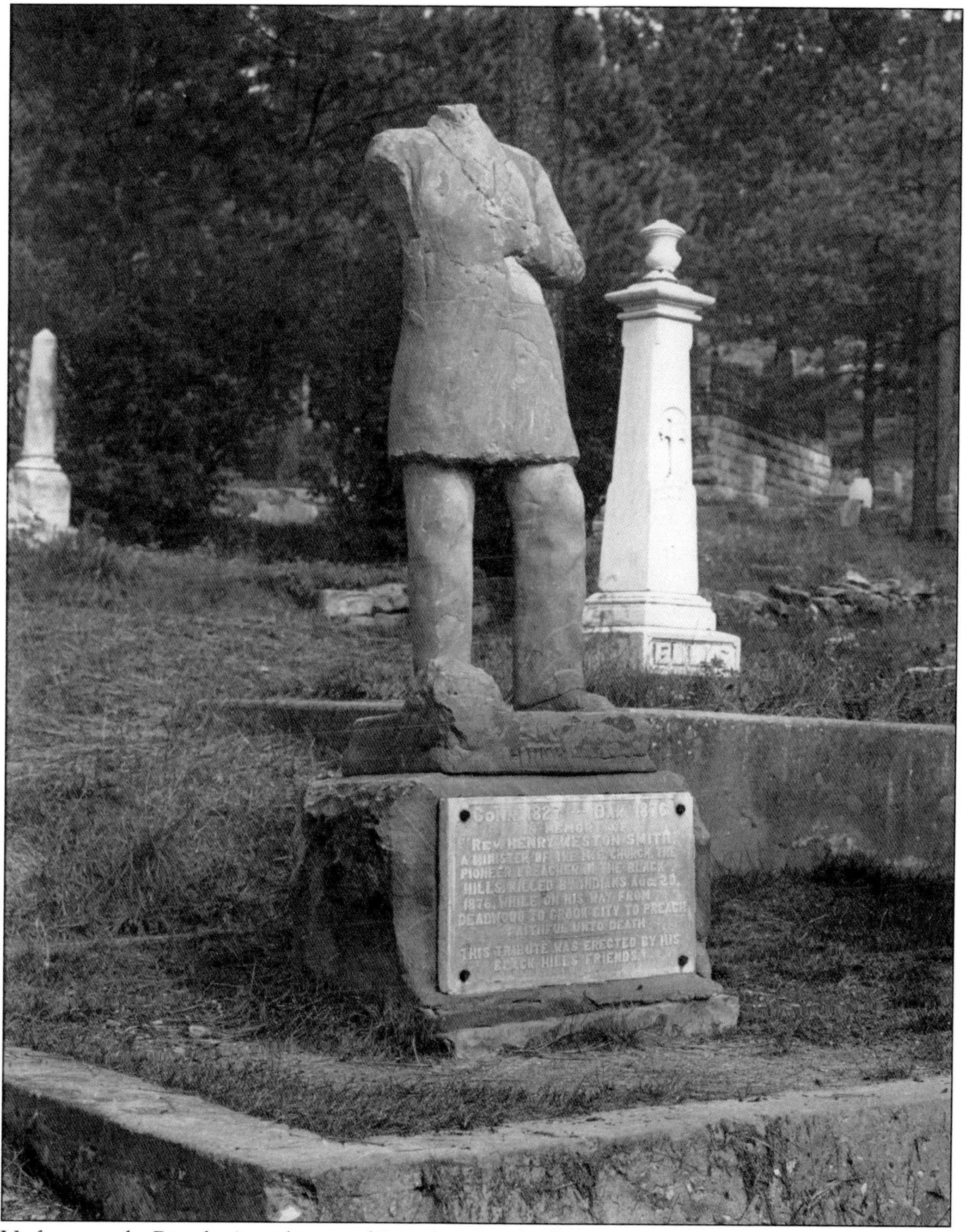

Unfortunately, Riordan's sculpture of Preacher Smith also succumbed to repeated vandalism by tourists, including the removal of Smith's head in 1945. Some tourists then began the practice of climbing on the back of the statue and posing with their heads in place of Preacher Smith's. Three years later, on July 22, 1948, the monument finally toppled when a careless tourist climbed behind the statue to have a picture taken. (Courtesy of Historic Black Hills Studios.)

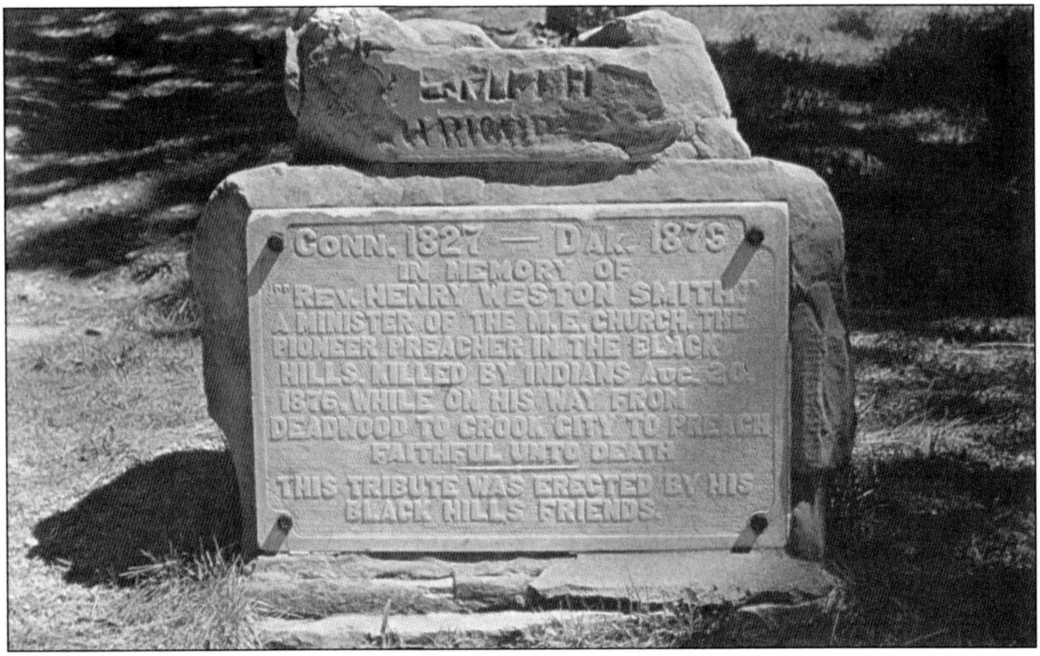

For the next 39 years, a carved marble plaque was bolted to the sandstone base of Smith's grave. On August 23, 1987, members of the Black Hills Regional United Methodist Historical Society (BHRUMHS) placed a new granite marker on his grave. BHRUMHS members Rev. Dwayne Knight and Marjorie Pontius, South Dakota UMC bishop Edwin C. Boulton, and Deadwood mayor Tom Blair helped in the dedication of the new monument. (Both, courtesy of CODA.)

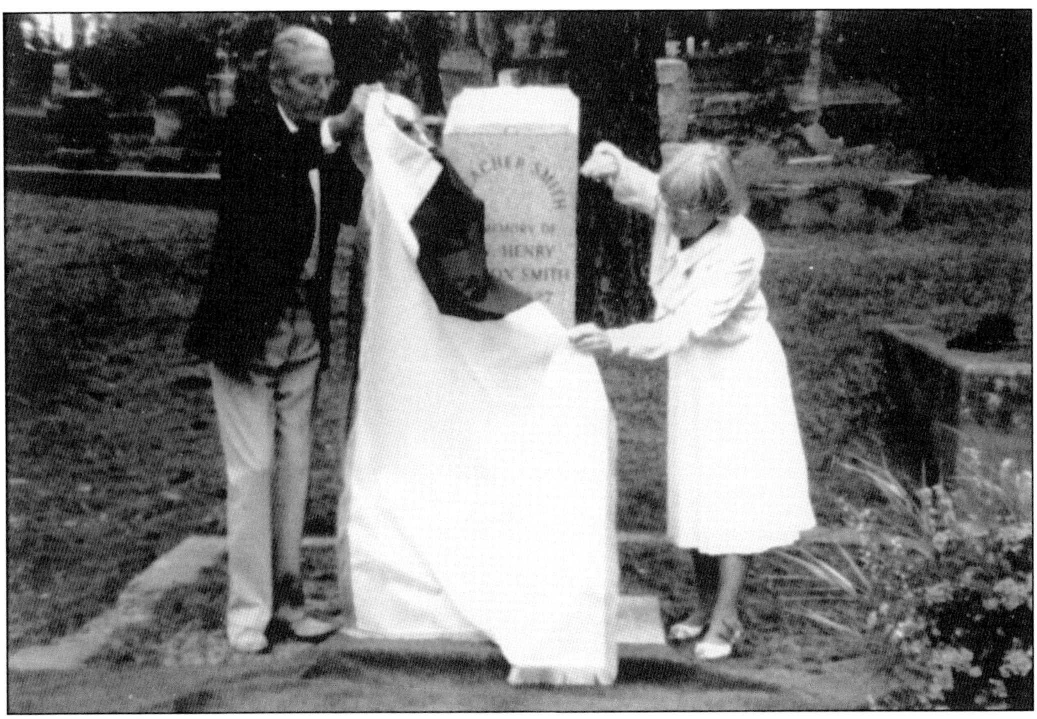

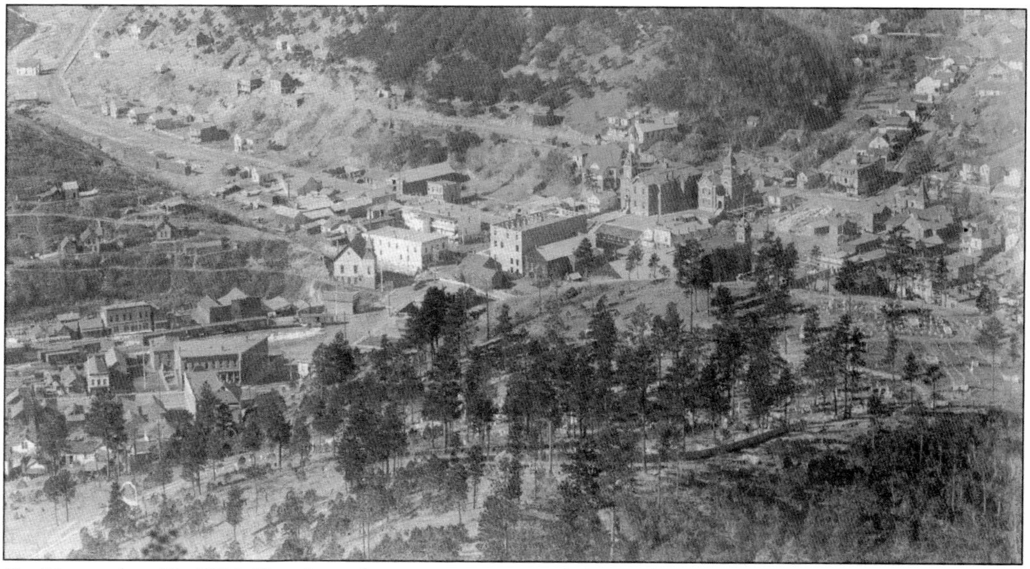

On December 10, 1892, Deadwood citizens concerned about the welfare and overall management of Mount Moriah Cemetery incorporated the Deadwood Cemetery Association, thereby releasing Lawrence County from the management of the cemetery. The first board of directors included Porter Warner, Frank L. Brown, Lucien W. Stilwell, H.B. Wardman, and Byron P. Dague. During their 44-year tenure, the association expanded the cemetery, standardized its record keeping, and beautified the grounds through the planting of nonnative plant species, including Siberian (Chinese) elm, poplars, maples, boxelder maple, bluegrass, and clover. In 1895, the association hired land surveyor P.L. Rogers to draw a new map of the cemetery. Two years later, the association installed a water pumping plant/irrigation system, and in 1911 purchased a wrought iron gateway. (Above, courtesy of Deadwood Public Library; below, courtesy of CODA.)

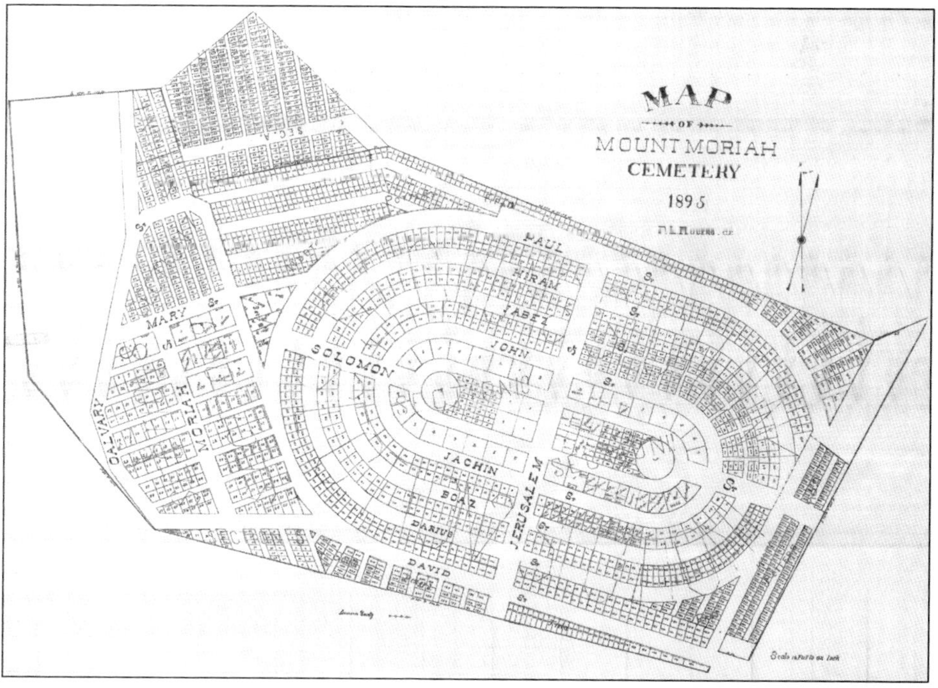

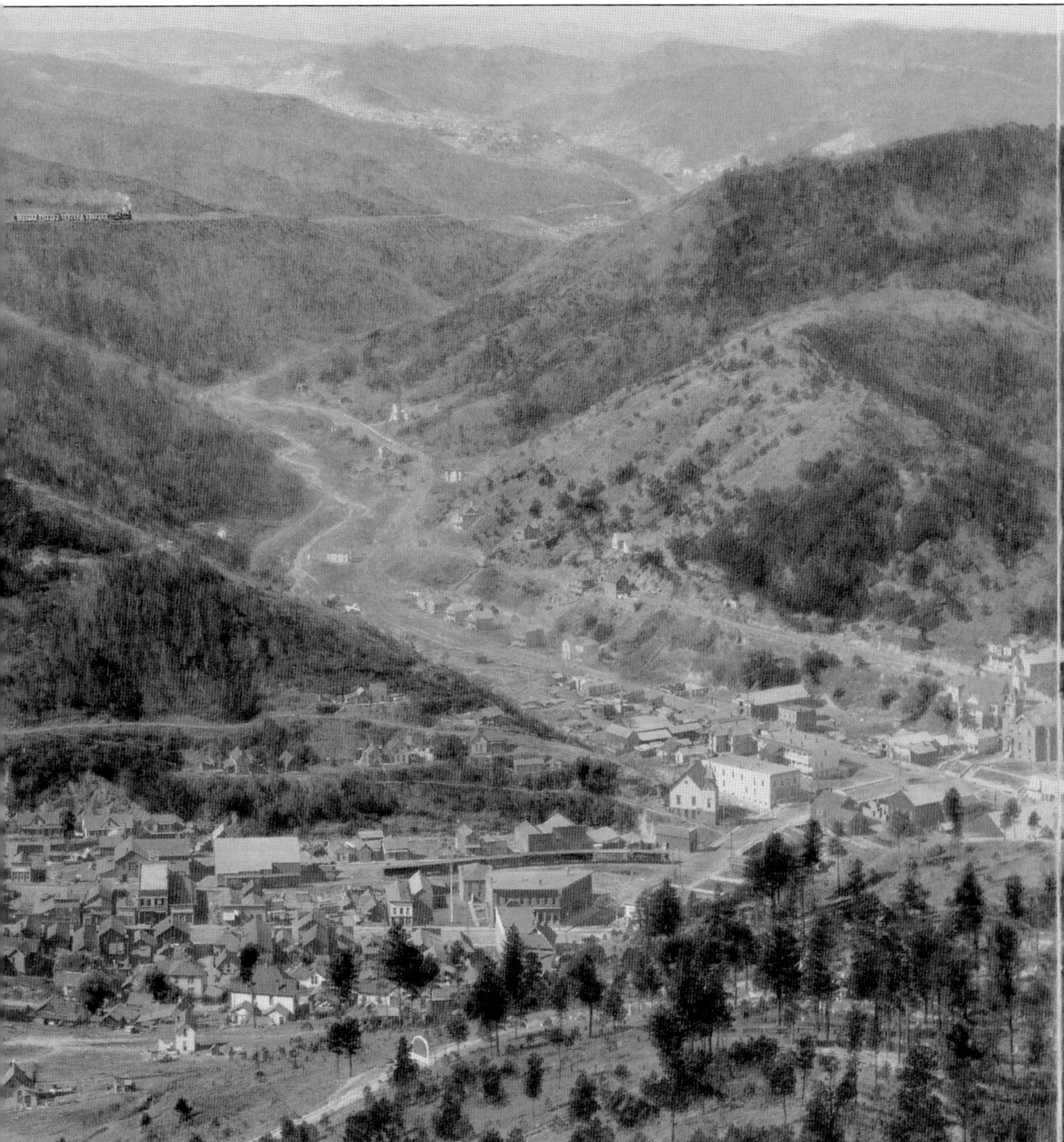

In July 1899, Clarence Jackson, son of the nationally renowned photographer William Henry Jackson, photographed Deadwood Gulch from White Rocks (looking north) and Centennial Avenue (looking south). Jackson's images were then combined to create two panoramic views of the city of Deadwood. Four years later, the Deadwood Business Club purchased Jackson's photographs and placed them in the South Dakota Exhibit at the 1904 St. Louis World's Fair. Two of the eight images looking north provided a wonderful overview of the Presidential Neighborhood and

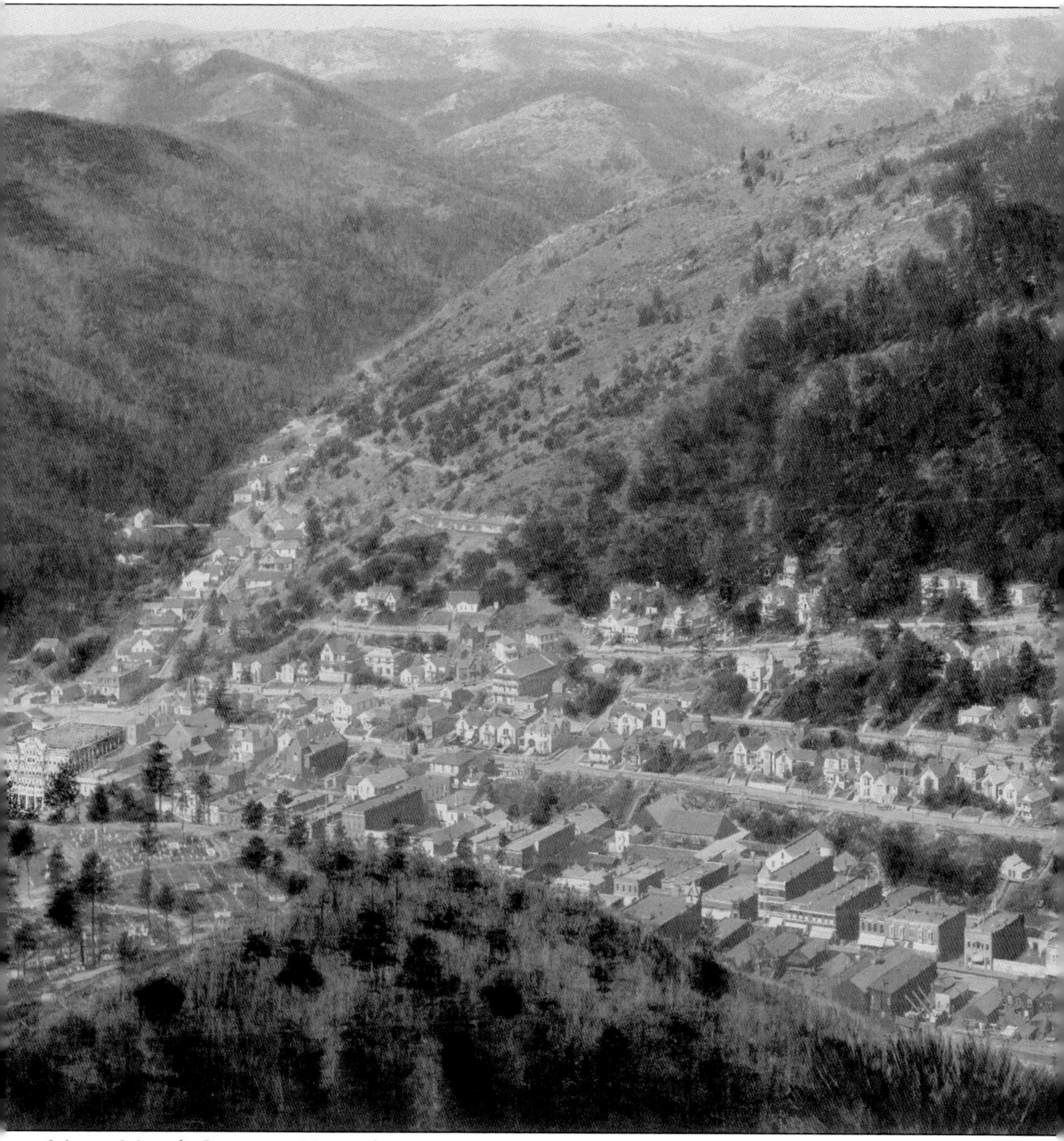

Mount Moriah Cemetery. Upon close inspection, the cemetery entrance, James Butler Hickok's monument, and the openness of Sections 5 through 9 are visible. The Deadwood Business Club requested that the newly completed Franklin Hotel be added into the image. This is an early example of photograph editing. (Courtesy of CODA.)

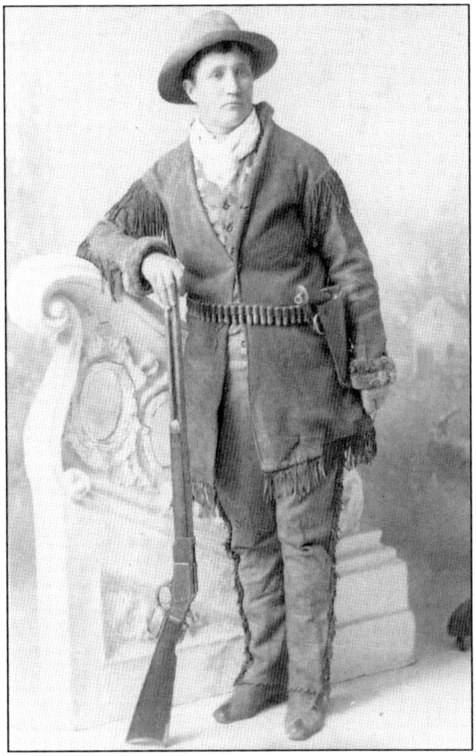

On August 1, 1903, another Deadwood celebrity joined Hickok in Section 1, Lot 70—Martha "Calamity Jane" Canary. Canary was born on May 1, 1856, in Mercer County, Missouri. In 1866, the Canary family moved to Virginia City, Montana Territory. Within two years, Canary and her siblings lost both parents. Canary relocated herself to Wyoming Territory in 1868, where she worked in railroad camps and military posts along the Union Pacific. It was most likely during this time that Canary began her transformation into a Western legend through her rabble rousing, drinking, carousing, and dressing in men's clothes to infiltrate the railroad camps. On the East Coast, Canary's life became one of legend as many of her fabricated exploits were recorded in the Western dime novels of the day. (Left, courtesy of Deadwood Public Library; below, courtesy of Johannsen Collection, Rare Book and Special Collections, Northern Illinois University Libraries.)

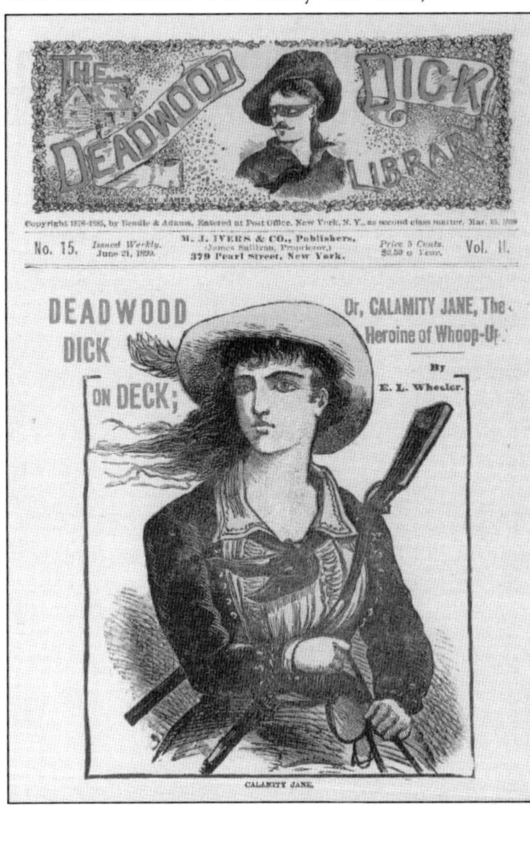

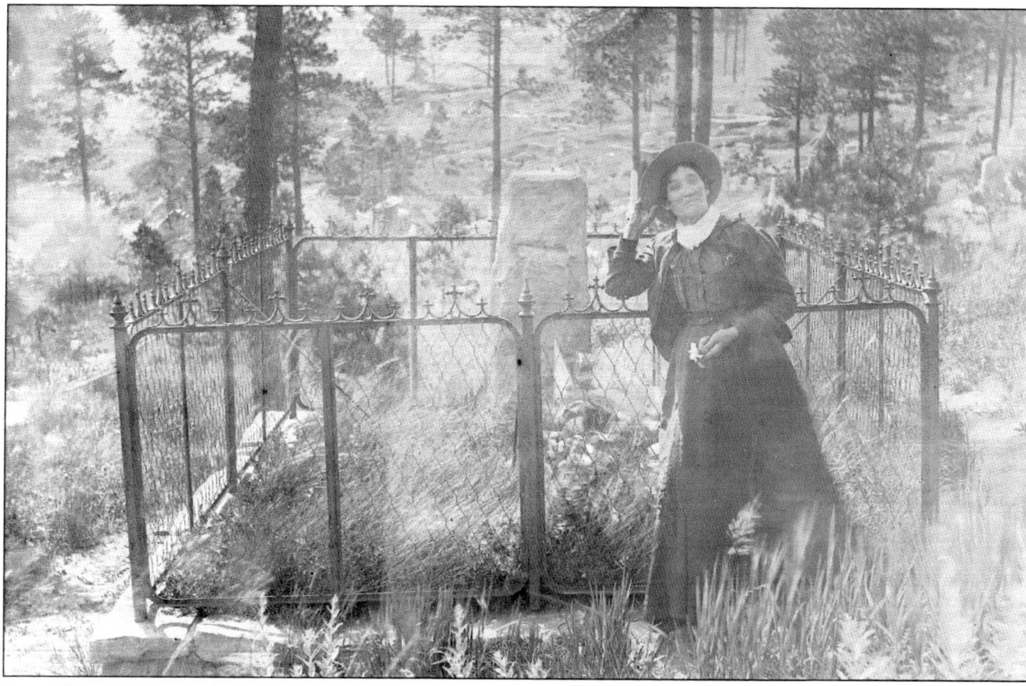

In reality, Canary's life was less than glamorous. She was an acute alcoholic, which caused many problems throughout her life and led to her death at 47. In 1903, she came back to the Black Hills and briefly worked as a cook and laundress in Dora Dufran's Belle Fourche brothel. In July, John B. Mayo photographed Canary in front of James Butler Hickok's grave in Mount Moriah Cemetery. This was to become one of the last photographs of Canary before her death. Several weeks later, she boarded a train in Deadwood and traveled to the mining camp of Terry, South Dakota, and died at the Calloway Hotel on August 1, 1903. Her body was brought back to Deadwood for burial adjacent to Hickok, forever solidifying her mark in the American West. (Above, courtesy of Library of Congress; below, courtesy of Denver Public Library.)

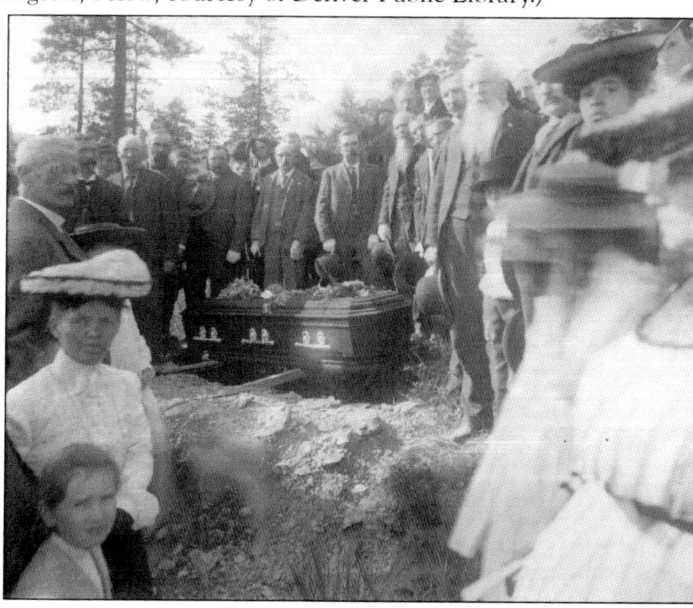

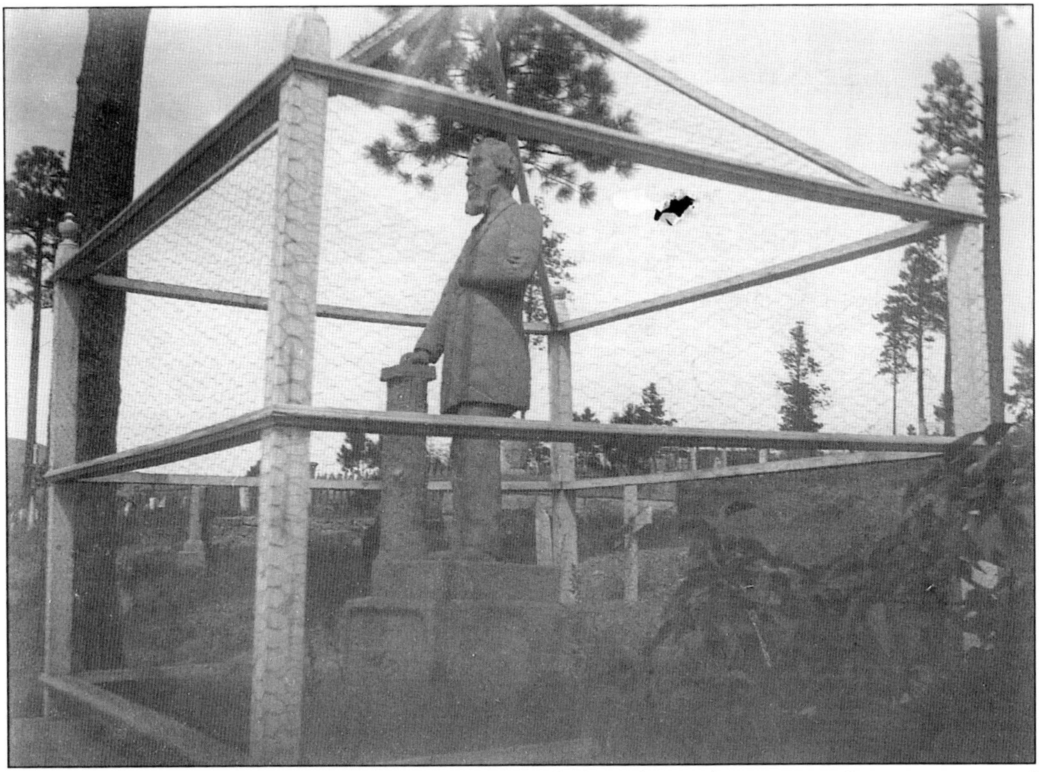

After 1903, the sandstone sculptures on the Hickok and Smith graves underwent repeated vandalism caused by tourists chipping away at the monuments. To combat this problem, the Deadwood Cemetery Association erected chicken wire cages around the plots to protect them against further vandalism. This proved to be a fruitless endeavor as tourists were able to enter the cages, and on occasion, have their photographs taken beside the statues. (Above, courtesy of Deadwood Public Library; below, courtesy of CODA.)

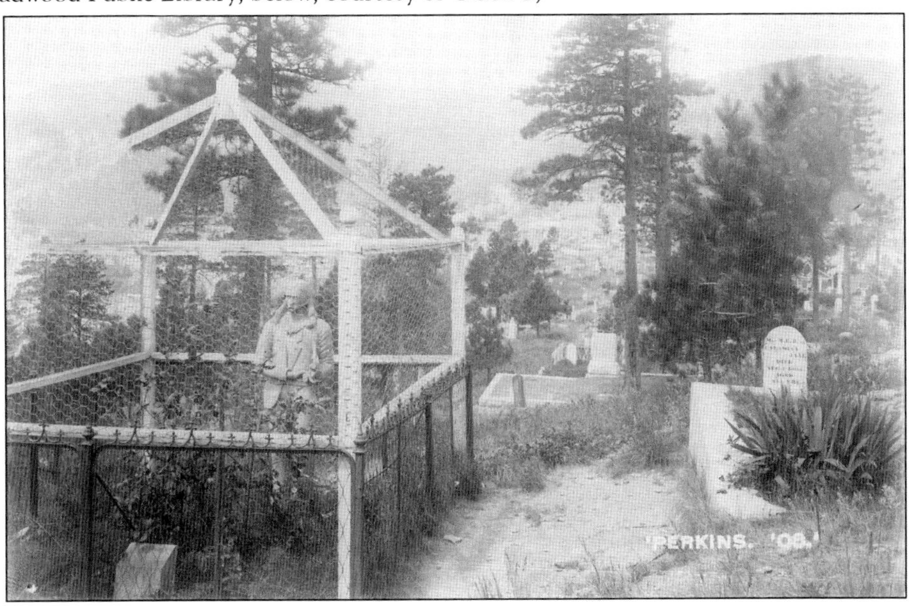

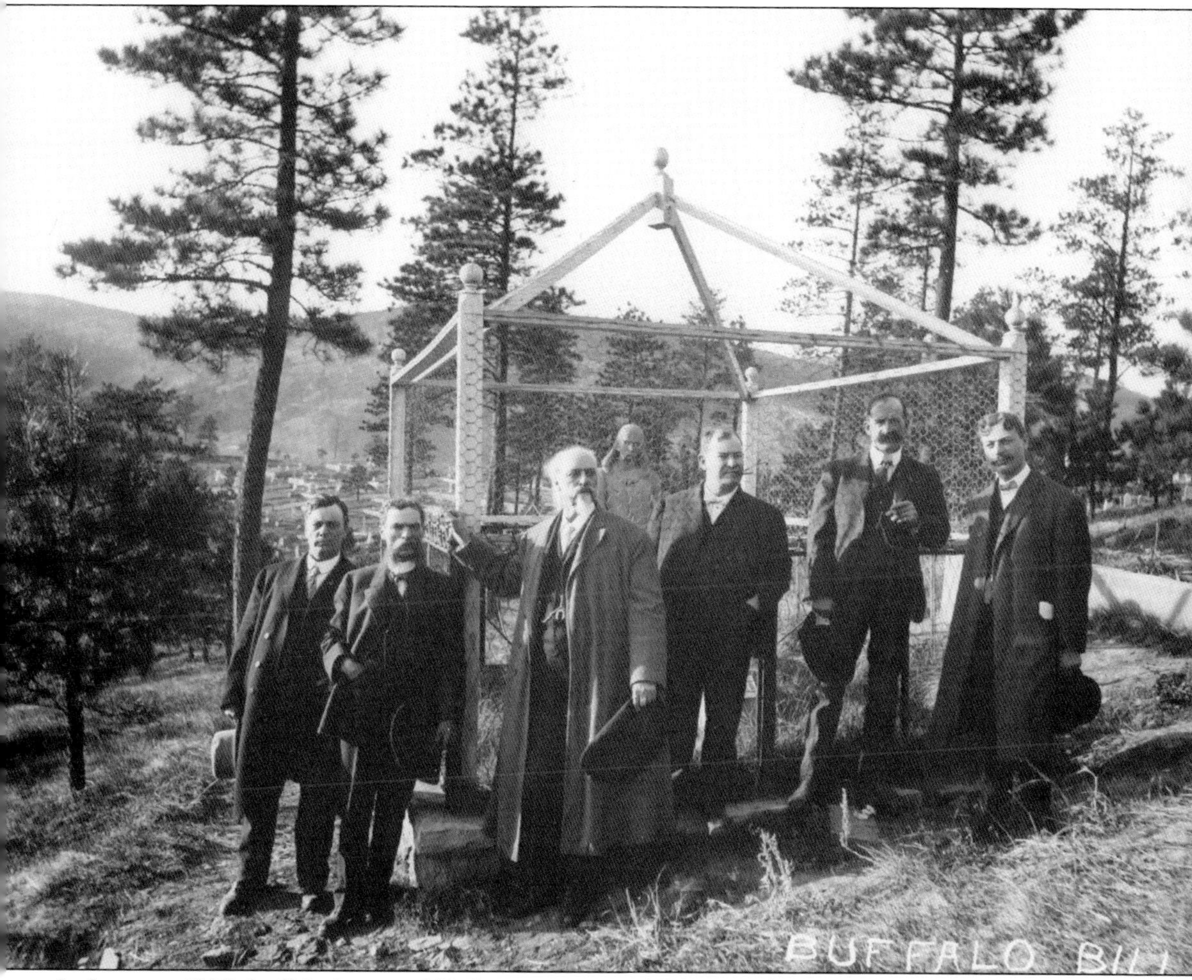

In January 1908, buffalo hunter, US Army scout, and Western showman William F. "Buffalo Bill" Cody came to Deadwood to visit longtime friend Mike Russell, the proprietor of the Buffalo Bar on Main Street. During this visit, from left to right, Col. William J. Thornby, Russell, Cody, Judge C.E. McHugh, Hank Fulton, and John R. Russell posed in front of James Butler Hickok's grave in Mount Moriah Cemetery. During the 1860s, William Cody met Mike Russell and James Butler Hickok while in Kansas. It was during this time that Cody and Russell forged a friendship that lasted for the rest of their lives. In the fall of 1873, Hickok became part of William Cody's theatrical troupe but became quickly disillusioned by the stage and returned to the West several months later. (Courtesy of Historic Black Hills Studios.)

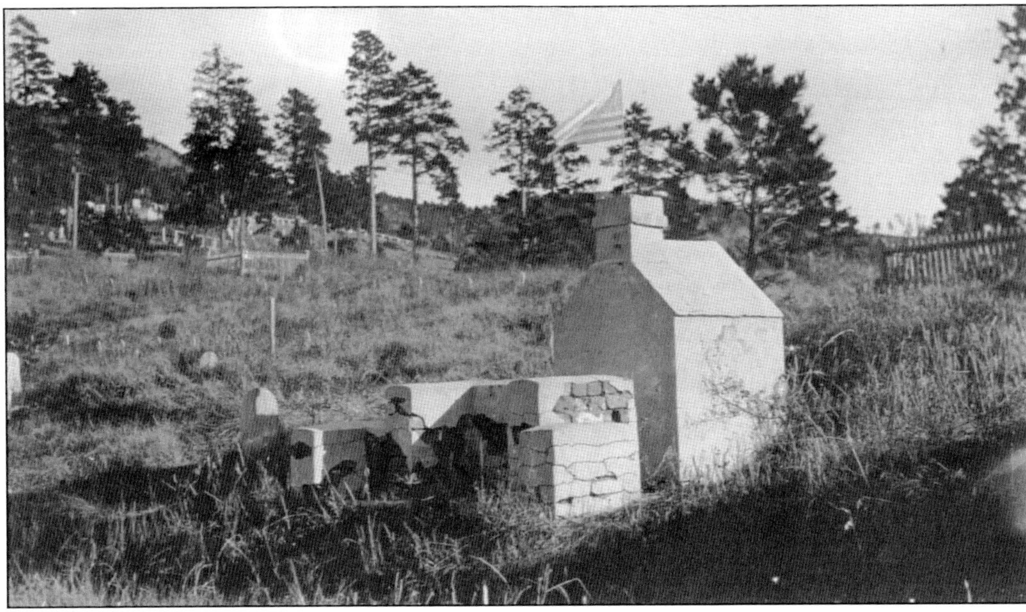

During the Deadwood Cemetery Association's tenure, several unique features were added to Mount Moriah Cemetery, including a Chinese altar and burner. In 1908, Lee Tang, representing Deadwood's Chinese community, received permission from the association to erect a brick altar and burner in Section 6, Lots 53–55. Upon completion, these features were used in conjunction with burial rituals and ancestor worship. By the 1930s, Deadwood's Chinese community was nonexistent, and the altar and burner fell into disrepair and were subject to random acts of vandalism. These two photographs, taken after 1920, provide a detailed view of the altar and burner. By 1945, both brick features had been destroyed. (Above, courtesy of Deadwood History Inc., Adams Museum Collection; below, courtesy of Deadwood Public Library.)

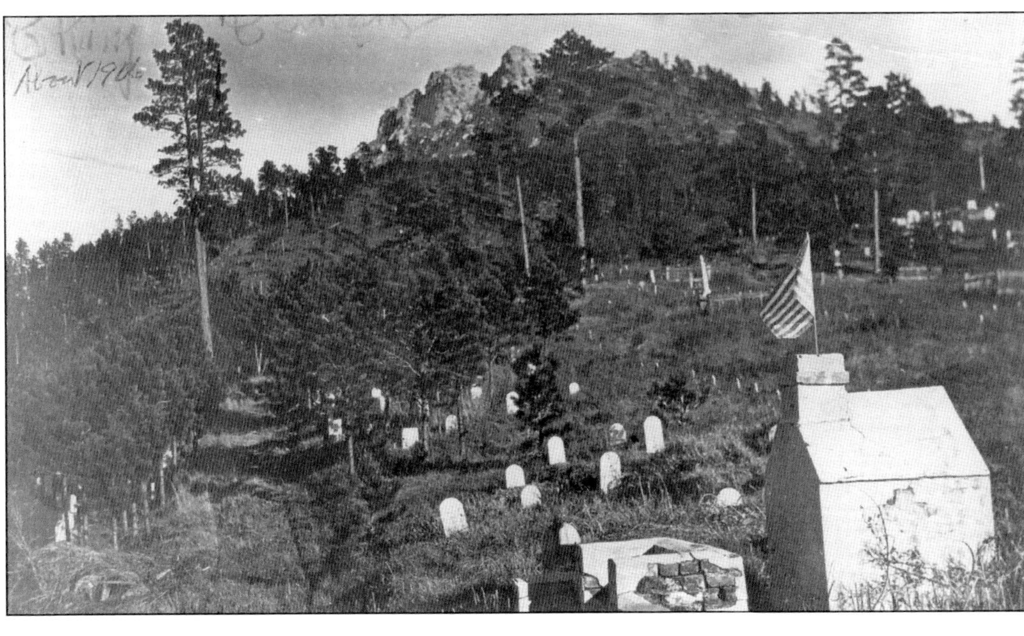

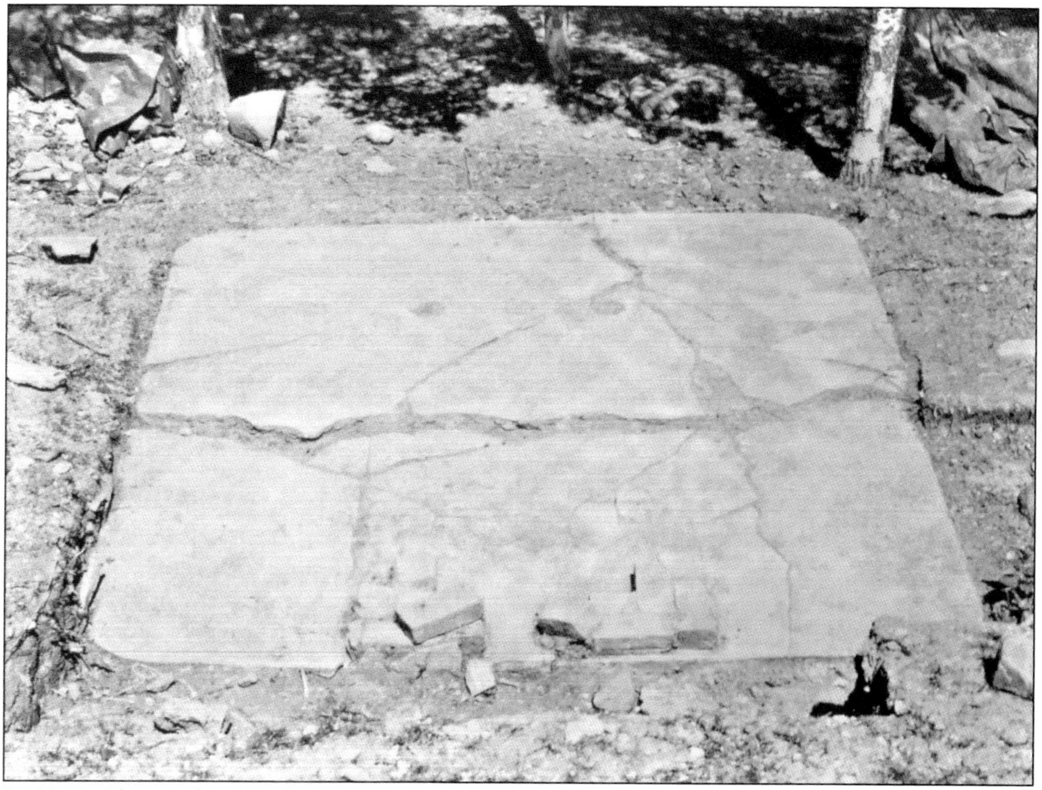

In 2003, Christopher Leatherman, a graduate student from the University of South Dakota, was hired by the Deadwood Historic Preservation Commission to excavate the concrete platform associated with the Chinese altar and burner. A total of seven test excavation units were opened to expose the concrete platform that measured 2.4 meters square. After being exposed, Leatherman observed bits of concrete and mortar embedded in the platform. This helped determine the size and orientation of the brick altar and burner. A total of 500 artifacts associated with these features were collected during the excavation. Later analysis of the artifacts provided insight into the funerary objects once used by the Chinese. The intact bricks collected from the excavation provided the necessary dimensions needed to reconstruct the altar and burner in 2013. (Both, courtesy of Chris Leatherman.)

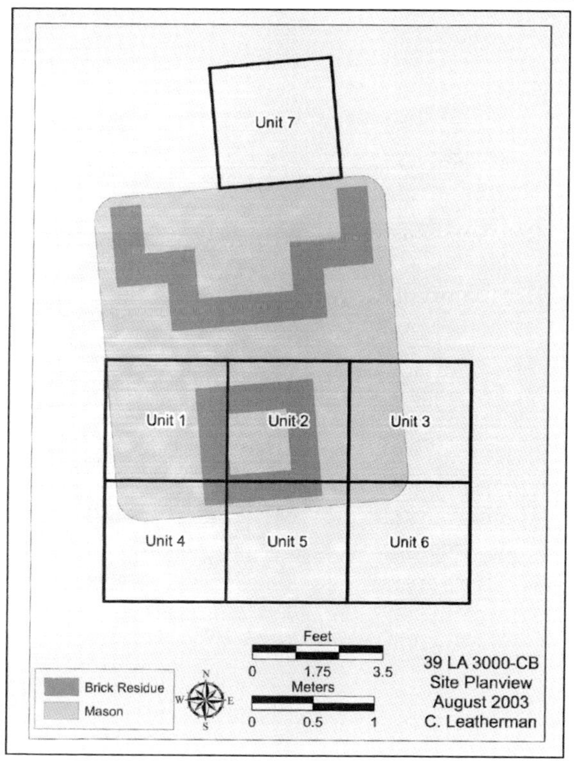

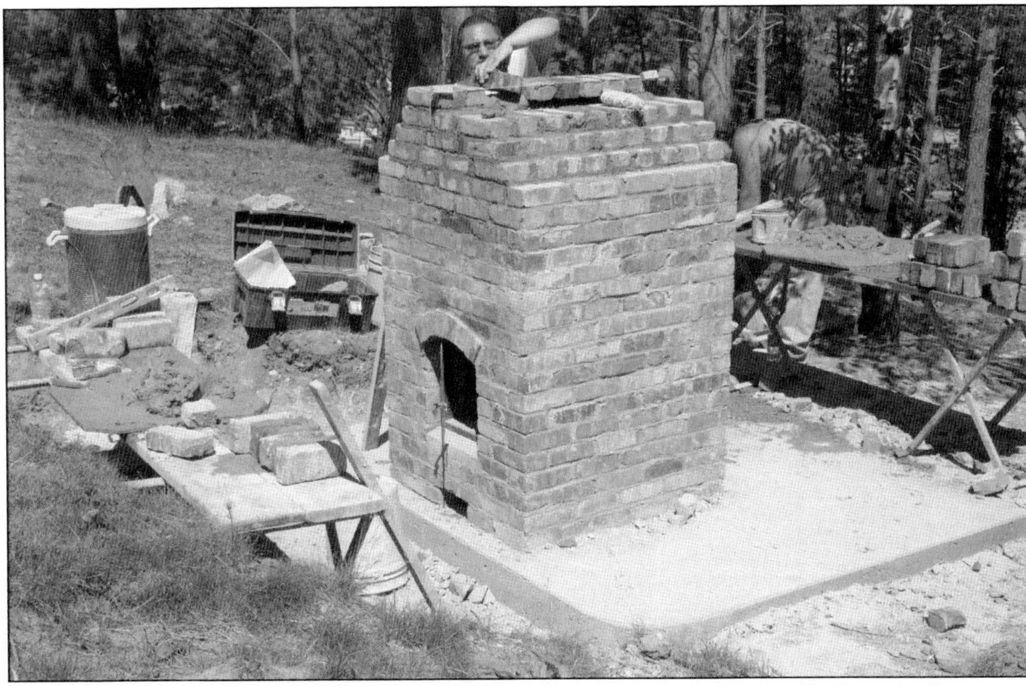

In 2012, the Deadwood Historic Preservation Commission hired Chamberlain Architects of Rapid City to develop plans for the construction of a new altar and burner in Section 6. The dimensions for these features were derived from the original brick dimensions unearthed during the archaeological excavation and number of courses of brick that appeared in the historic photographs. One year later, Competitive Masonry of Rapid City was hired by the Deadwood Historic Preservation Commission to reconstruct the altar and burner. Over 200 bricks salvaged from the Wing Tsue Building once located in Deadwood's Chinatown were integrated into the altar and burner. On July 23, 2013, the new altar and burner were dedicated by descendants of Fee Lee Wong, the original proprietor of the Wing Tsue Building. (Both, courtesy of CODA.)

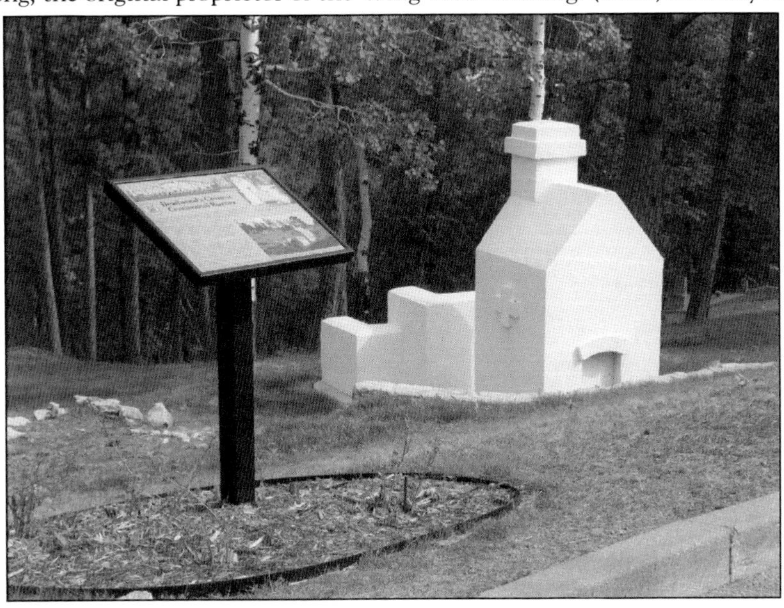

July 30, 1909, ushered in a new chapter in Mount Moriah's history—the arrival of the automobile in the cemetery. According to a local newspaper, C.J. Faehdrich and his White Steam automobile successfully traversed the steep grade of the Presidential Neighborhood and Mount Moriah Cemetery before stopping at the face of Black Rocks (today's scenic overlook area). By 1958, vehicular traffic and parking became an ever-growing problem in the cemetery. In order to combat this problem, the City of Deadwood and the Deadwood Chamber of Commerce decided to cut back the hillslope along David Street and erect a stacked rock retaining wall that allowed cars to parallel park in front of the celebrity graves. (Right, courtesy of Deadwood Public Library; below, courtesy of CODA.)

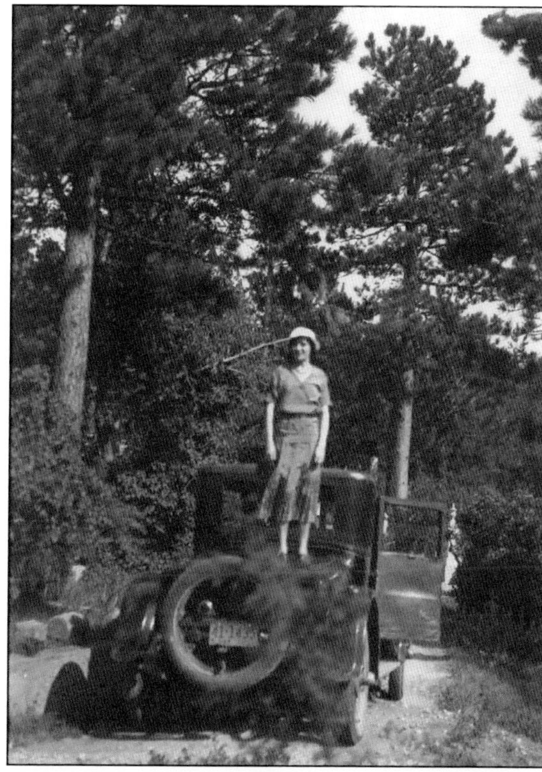

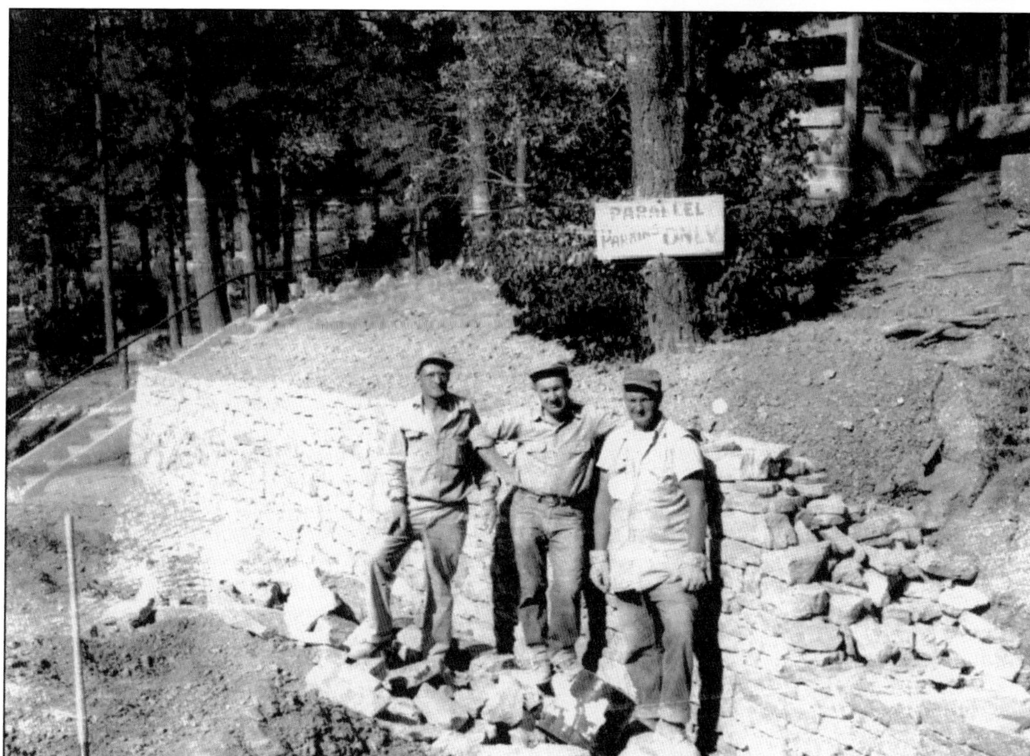

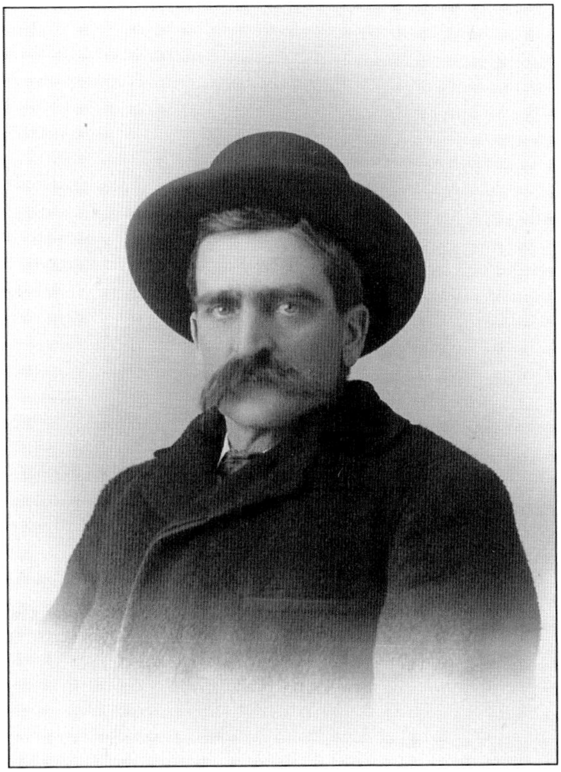

On September 23, 1919, Mount Moriah Cemetery received another nationally recognized celebrity, Capt. Seth Bullock. Born in Canada in 1847, Bullock moved to Montana and was elected to the Territorial Council in 1871. Two years later, he was elected sheriff of Lewis and Clark County, Montana. In 1876, Bullock and his business partner Solomon Star relocated to Deadwood Gulch and opened a hardware store at the corner of Wall and Main Streets. Immediately, Bullock became involved in the politics and law enforcement of the mining camps, being appointed the first sheriff of Lawrence County in March 1877. For 21 years, Bullock's business endeavors included retail hardware, mining, and ranching. In 1894, a fire destroyed Bullock's hardware store. Undeterred, he and several investors organized what became the Bullock Hotel. (Left, courtesy of Deadwood Public Library; below, courtesy of CODA.)

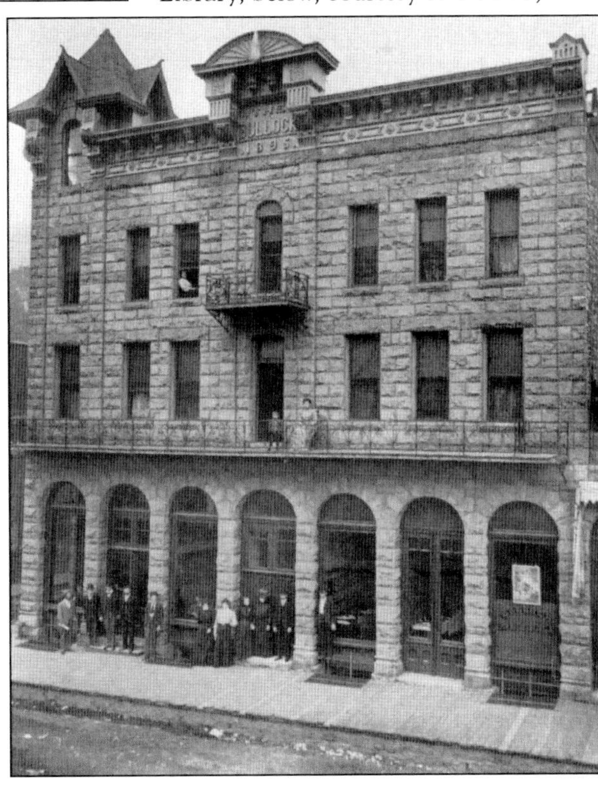

In 1898, Bullock enlisted in the US Army during the Spanish-American War. He was appointed captain of Troop A, 3rd US Volunteer Cavalry Regiment, under Melvin B. Grigsby. Though this regiment remained stateside, Bullock retained the title of captain for the remainder of his life. Prior to the war, Bullock became friends with Theodore Roosevelt. This connection helped him receive federal appointments as Black Hills forest supervisor in 1901 and US marshal in 1906. After Roosevelt's death in 1919, the Society of Black Hills Pioneers, under the direction of Bullock, erected the Friendship Tower to commemorate Roosevelt's legacy. The tower was dedicated on July 4, 1919. Two months later, Bullock died and was buried in a plot above Mount Moriah Cemetery. From Bullock's grave, Deadwood and Mount Roosevelt can be seen. (Right, courtesy of Deadwood Public Library; below, courtesy of CODA.)

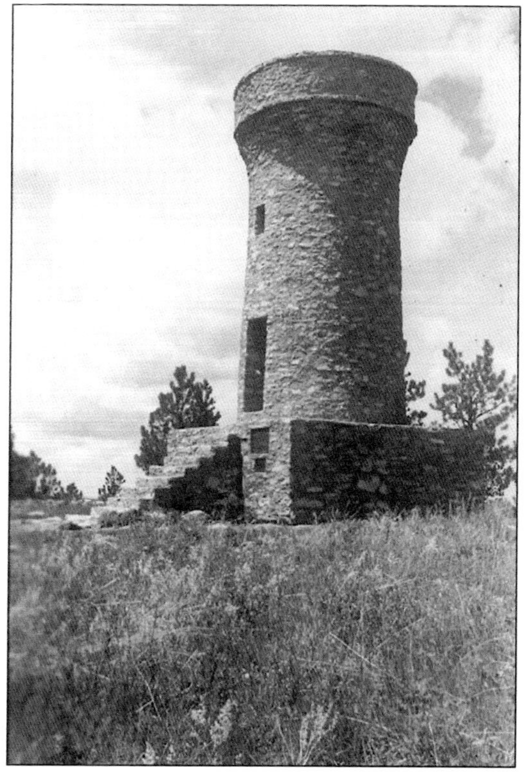

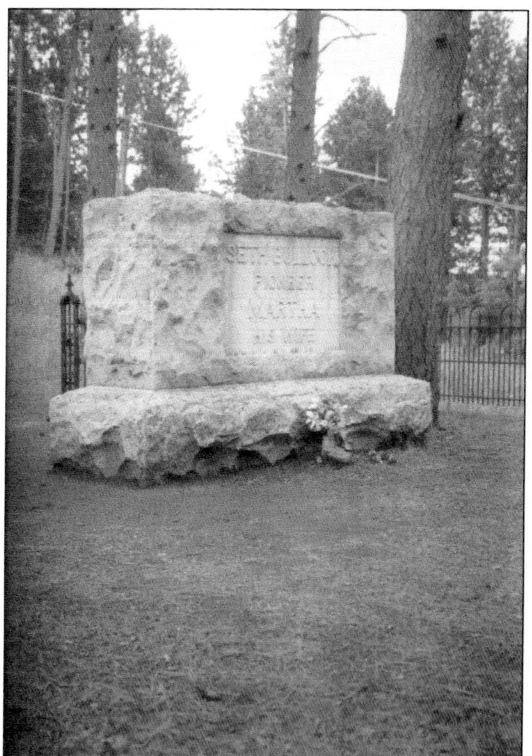

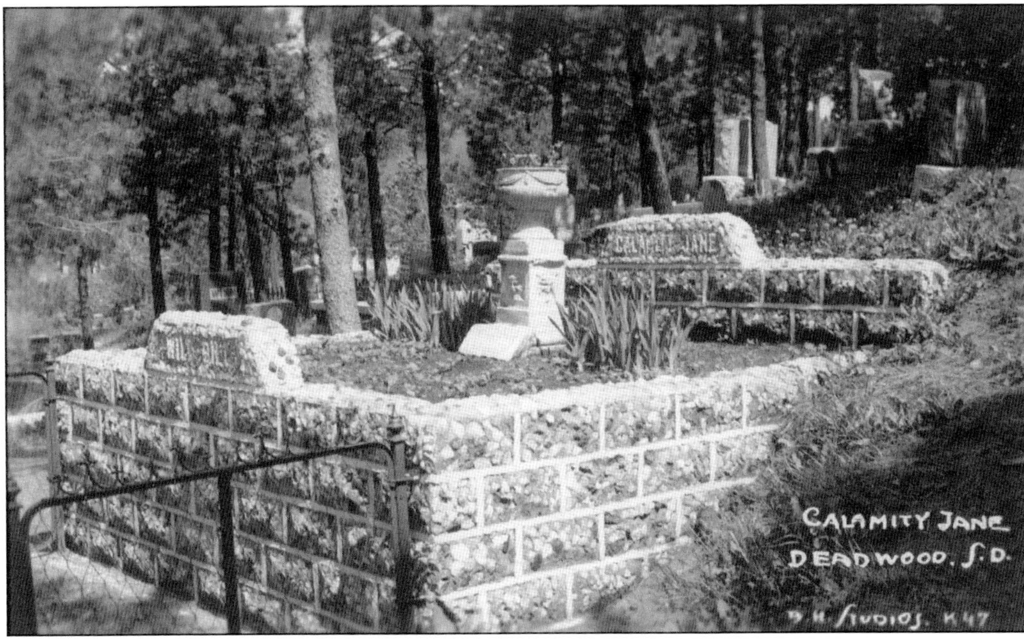

In June 1936, the Deadwood Chamber of Commerce hired local contractor J.B. Hill & Son to erect a retaining wall around the graves of Hickok and Canary. Upon its completion, the new retaining wall connected the celebrity graves together and was faced with native Black Hills stones. The names "Wild Bill" and "Calamity Jane" were spelled out on the outward facing veneer. (Both, courtesy of CODA.)

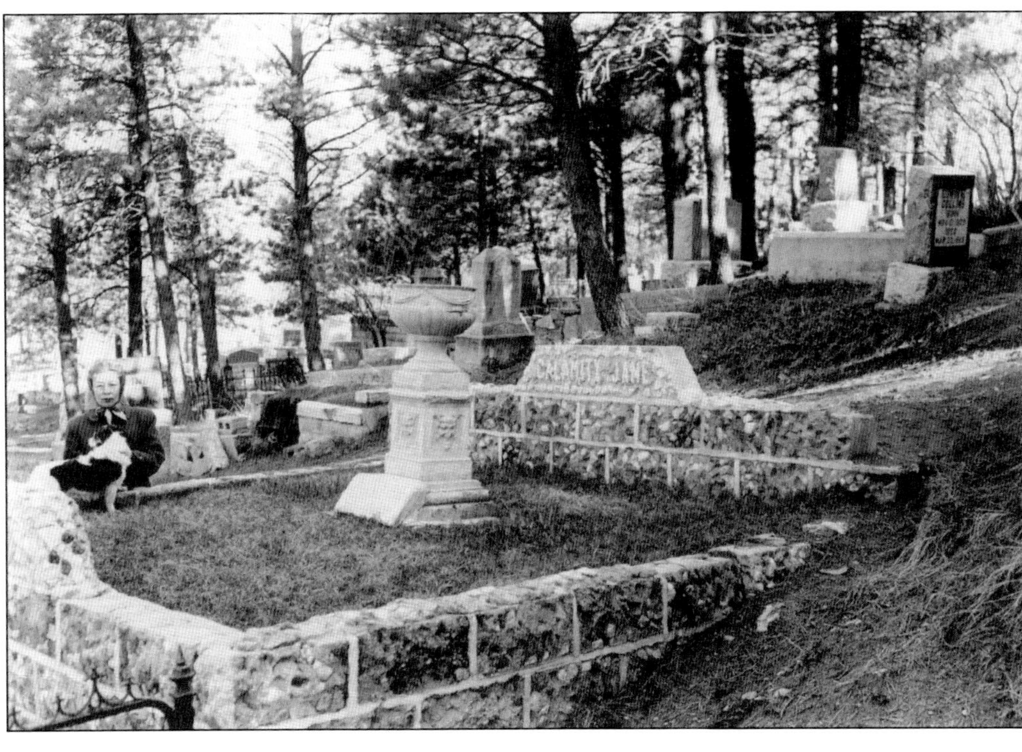

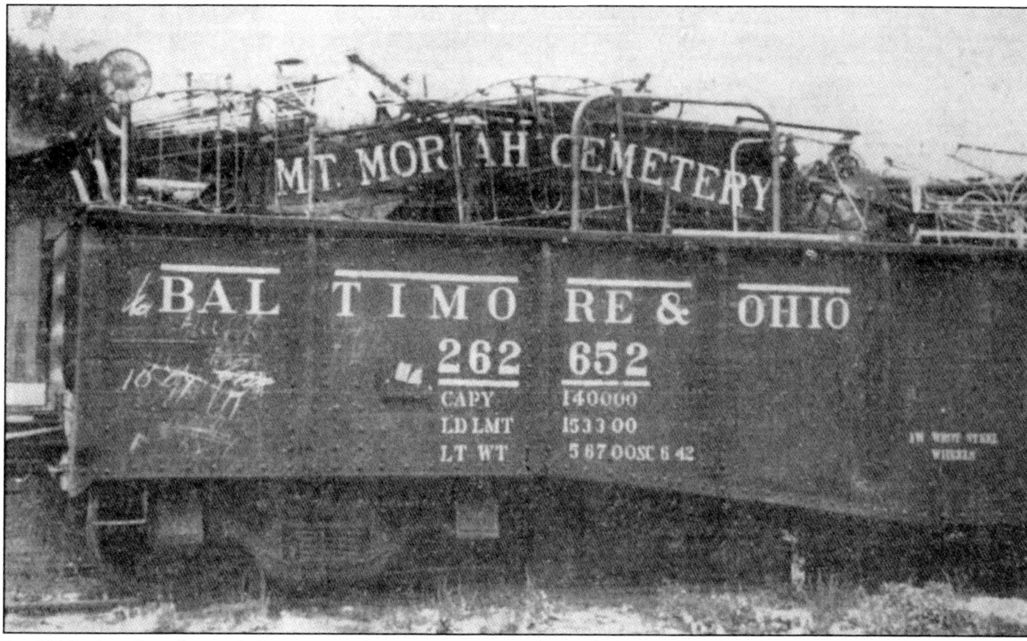

In 1911, the Deadwood Cemetery Association purchased an ornate wrought iron gateway from the E.T. Bormans Company of Detroit, Michigan, for $140 and installed it somewhere in the western side of the future Third Addition Sections 1 and 2. In November 1942, this gateway was removed as part of a Black Hills scrap drive organized by Norman S. Olson, the district representative of Special Projects Salvage. This photograph captured the Mount Moriah Cemetery's gateway loaded in a boxcar to be melted down as part of the national war effort. Through Olson's efforts, over 4,000 tons of salvaged metal were collected from the Black Hills. Olson, however, decided to leave the metal fencing around Hickok's grave. (Both, courtesy of CODA.)

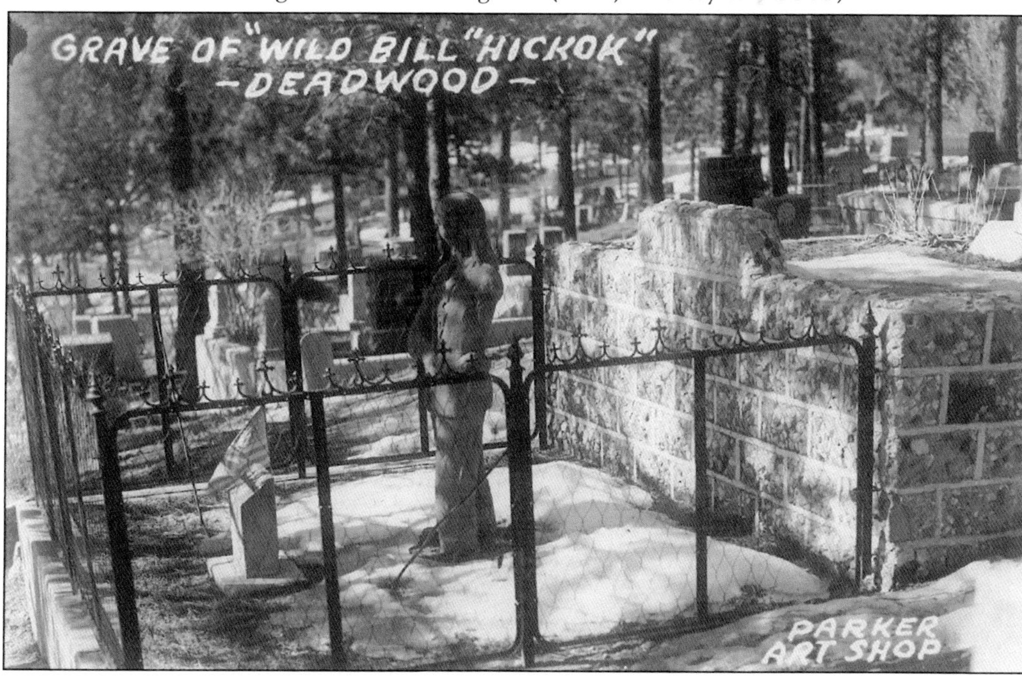

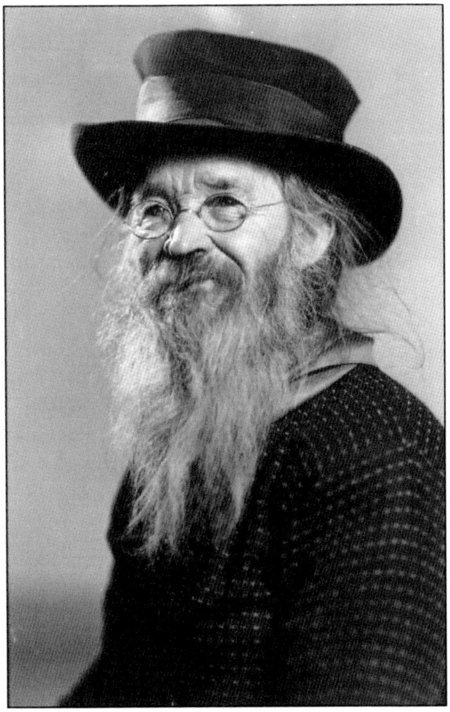

John Eli "Potato Creek Johnny" Perrett was born in Abergavenny, England, on February 9, 1866. In 1883, he immigrated and settled in Central City before staking a mining claim along Potato Creek near the mining town of Tinton. In 1929, Perrett discovered one of the largest gold nuggets ever found in the Black Hills, weighing 7¾ troy ounces and measuring five inches in length. After his discovery, Perrett worked for the Deadwood Chamber of Commerce, personifying the life of an early prospector during the annual Days of 76 Celebration and the Trial of Jack McCall. In 1941, Perrett traveled to New York and appeared on *We the People*, a national radio program sponsored by Sanka Coffee. On February 27, 1943, Perrett died and was buried beside the graves of James Butler Hickok and Martha Canary. (Left, courtesy of CODA; below, courtesy of Minnilusa Historical Association.)

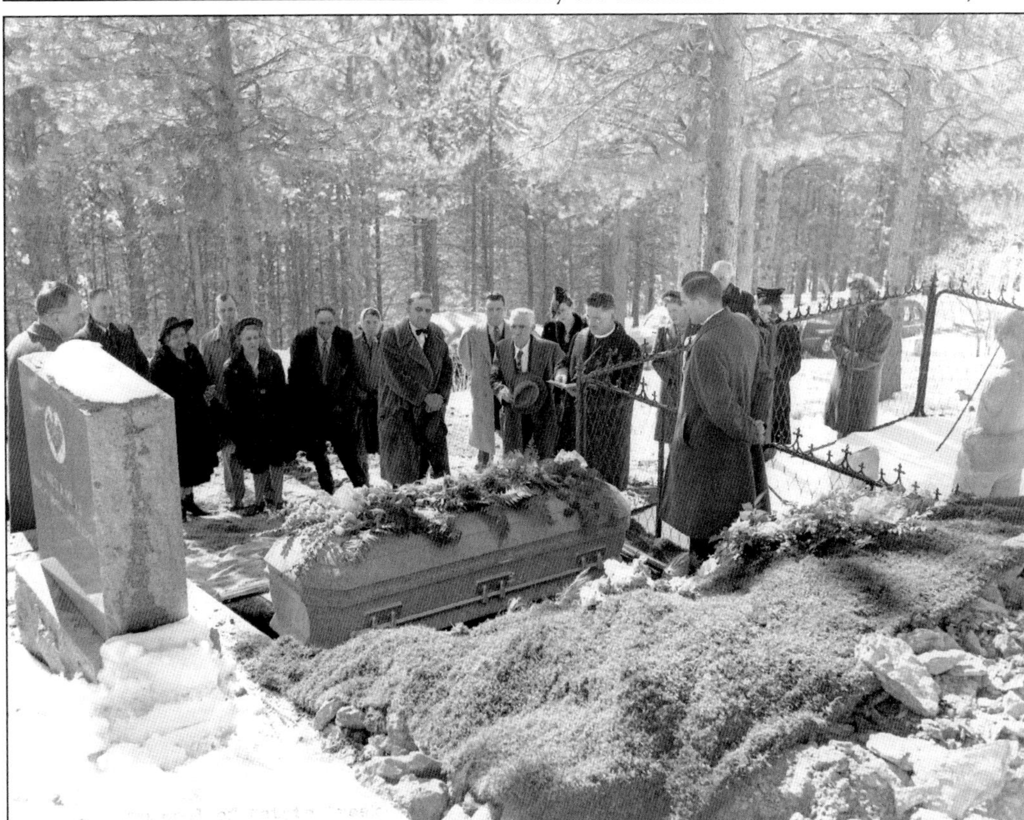

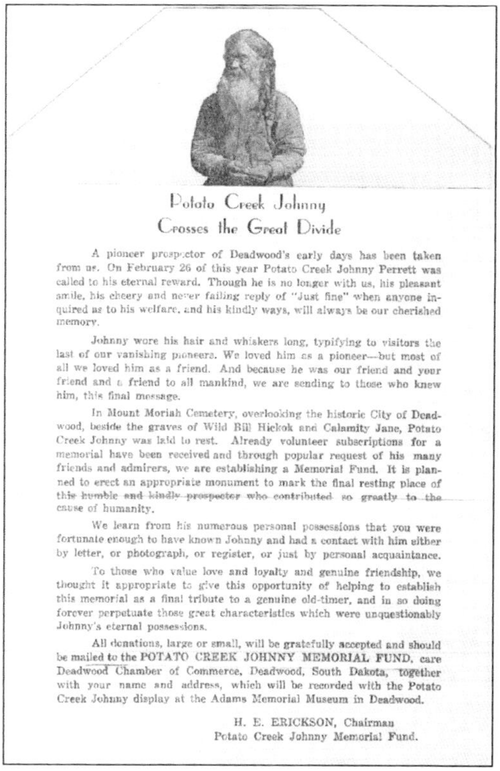

Potato Creek Johnny
Crosses the Great Divide

A pioneer prospector of Deadwood's early days has been taken from us. On February 26 of this year Potato Creek Johnny Perrett was called to his eternal reward. Though he is no longer with us, his pleasant smile, his cheery and never failing reply of "Just fine" when anyone inquired as to his welfare, and his kindly ways, will always be our cherished memory.

Johnny wore his hair and whiskers long, typifying to visitors the last of our vanishing pioneers. We loved him as a pioneer—but most of all we loved him as a friend. And because he was our friend and your friend and a friend to all mankind, we are sending to those who knew him, this final message.

In Mount Moriah Cemetery, overlooking the historic City of Deadwood, beside the graves of Wild Bill Hickok and Calamity Jane, Potato Creek Johnny was laid to rest. Already volunteer subscriptions for a memorial have been received and through popular request of his many friends and admirers, we are establishing a Memorial Fund. It is planned to erect an appropriate monument to mark the final resting place of this humble and kindly prospector who contributed so greatly to the cause of humanity.

We learn from his numerous personal possessions that you were fortunate enough to have known Johnny and had a contact with him either by letter, or photograph, or register, or just by personal acquaintance.

To those who value love and loyalty and genuine friendship, we thought it appropriate to give this opportunity of helping to establish this memorial as a final tribute to a genuine old-timer, and in so doing forever perpetuate those great characteristics which were unquestionably Johnny's eternal possessions.

All donations, large or small, will be gratefully accepted and should be mailed to the POTATO CREEK JOHNNY MEMORIAL FUND, care Deadwood Chamber of Commerce, Deadwood, South Dakota, together with your name and address, which will be recorded with the Potato Creek Johnny display at the Adams Memorial Museum in Deadwood.

H. E. ERICKSON, Chairman
Potato Creek Johnny Memorial Fund.

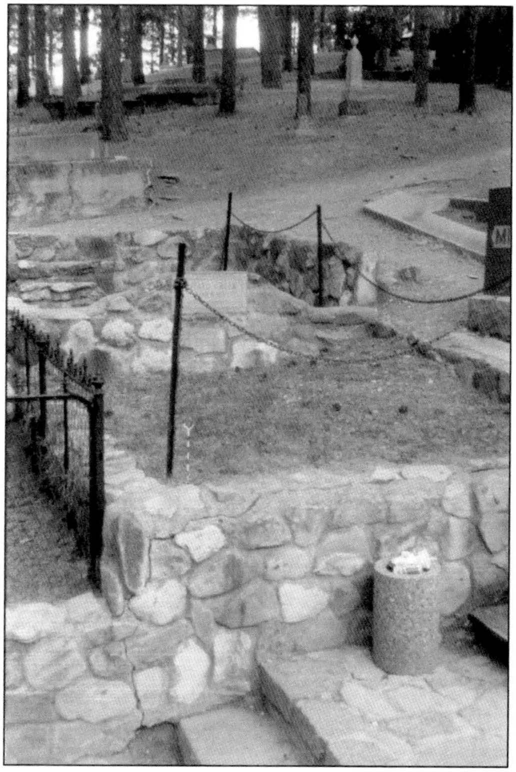

After the death of John Perrett, the Deadwood Chamber of Commerce established the Potato Creek Johnny Memorial Fund, a capital campaign to raise money for a suitable memorial. The chamber received hundreds of handwritten letters from people all across the United States donating money to Perrett's marker. Within 10 years, the chamber received enough funds for the project. In July 1953, chamber representative Norman Hendrickson began refacing the celebrity retaining walls using fieldstones embedded in concrete. Paul Akrop, of the Deadwood Granite and Marble Works, designed and installed three rectangular Rock of Ages granite markers for the celebrity graves. One month later, the Hickok, Canary, and Perrett plots were connected together with new granite memorials. (All, courtesy of CODA.)

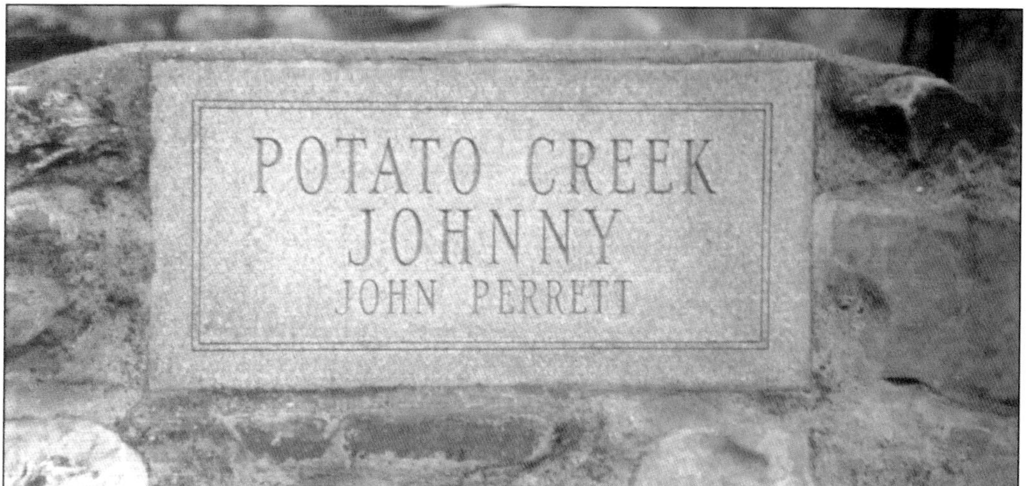

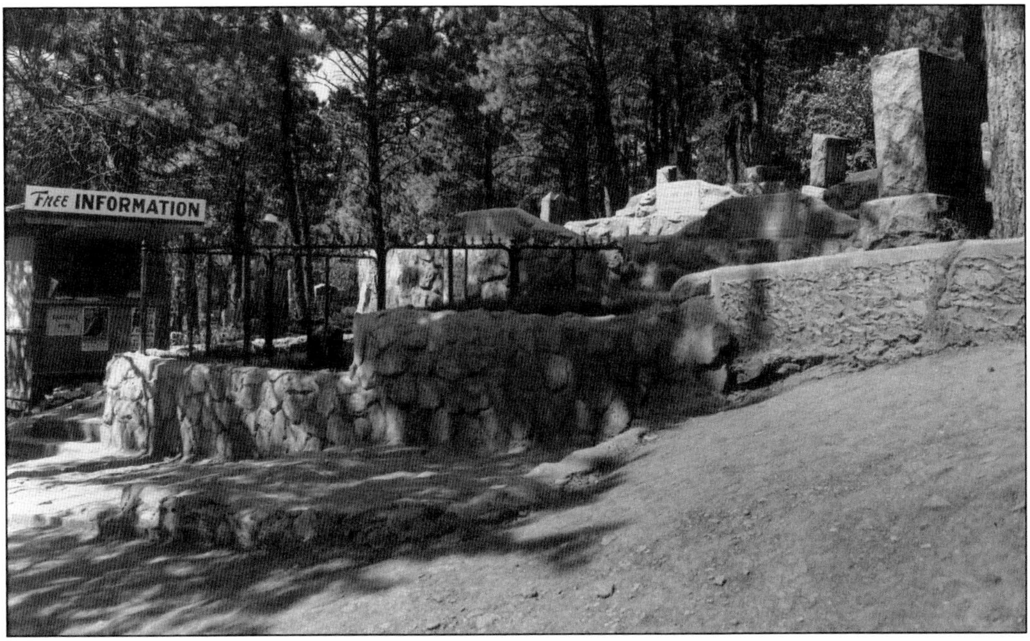

In the 1960s, a movement to beautify Mount Moriah was initiated by three local women's organizations—the Thursday Club, the Round Table Club, and the Twentieth Century Club. Known as the Tri-Club, this organization became instrumental in hiring the landscape architectural firm Theodore J. Wirth & Associates of Billings, Montana, to develop a master plan for the cemetery. Recommendations outlined in the plan included the elimination of vehicular traffic in the cemetery, the development of a parking area outside the cemetery, the installation of a lockable gateway, and the removal of the information hut located beside the celebrity graves. One of the more radical recommendations that was not implemented was a gondola lift system that would transport visitors from Deadwood's downtown to the overlook area in the cemetery. (Above, courtesy of Deadwood Public Library; below, courtesy of CODA.)

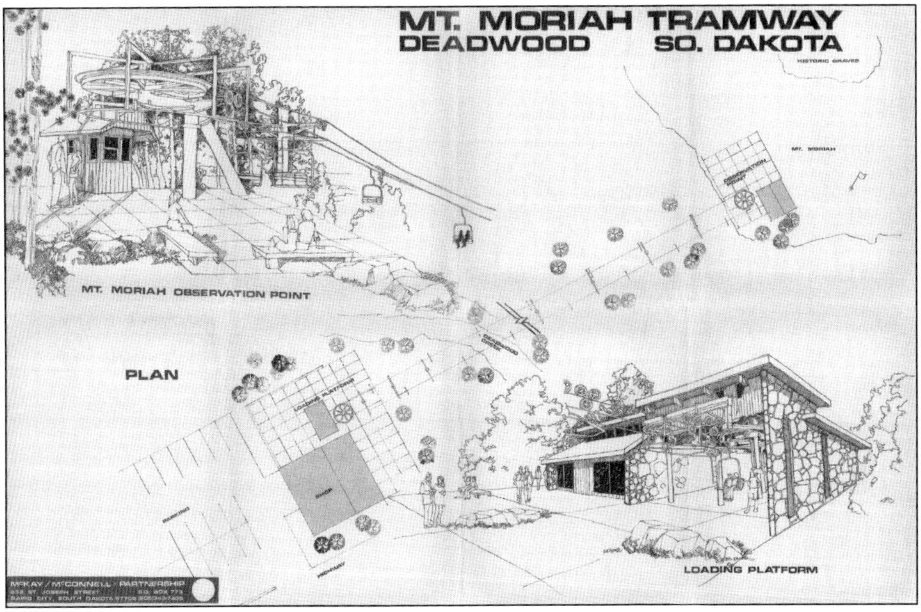

In 1968, as part of the proposed cemetery master plan, a new gateway was erected on the eastern end of Third Addition Sections 1 and 2. The City of Deadwood, in conjunction with the Tri-Club, hired local stone mason Howard Thoresen to build two stone pillars for the gateway. The photograph at right shows Hannah Elward, the Tri-Club chairwoman, inspecting the right pillar. The new Mount Moriah gateway used a combination of native Black Hills minerals and rock, including Deadwood Formation conglomerate, micotta limestone, Deadwood Formation quartzite, phonolite with aegirine crystals, and monazite. Upon completion, the new gateway had a wooden entry sign and a lockable gate, preventing vehicular traffic into the cemetery. (Both, courtesy of CODA.)

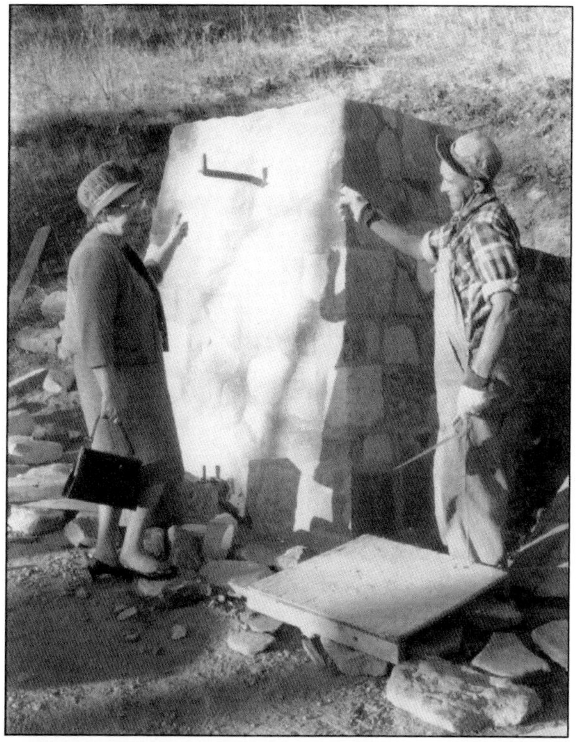

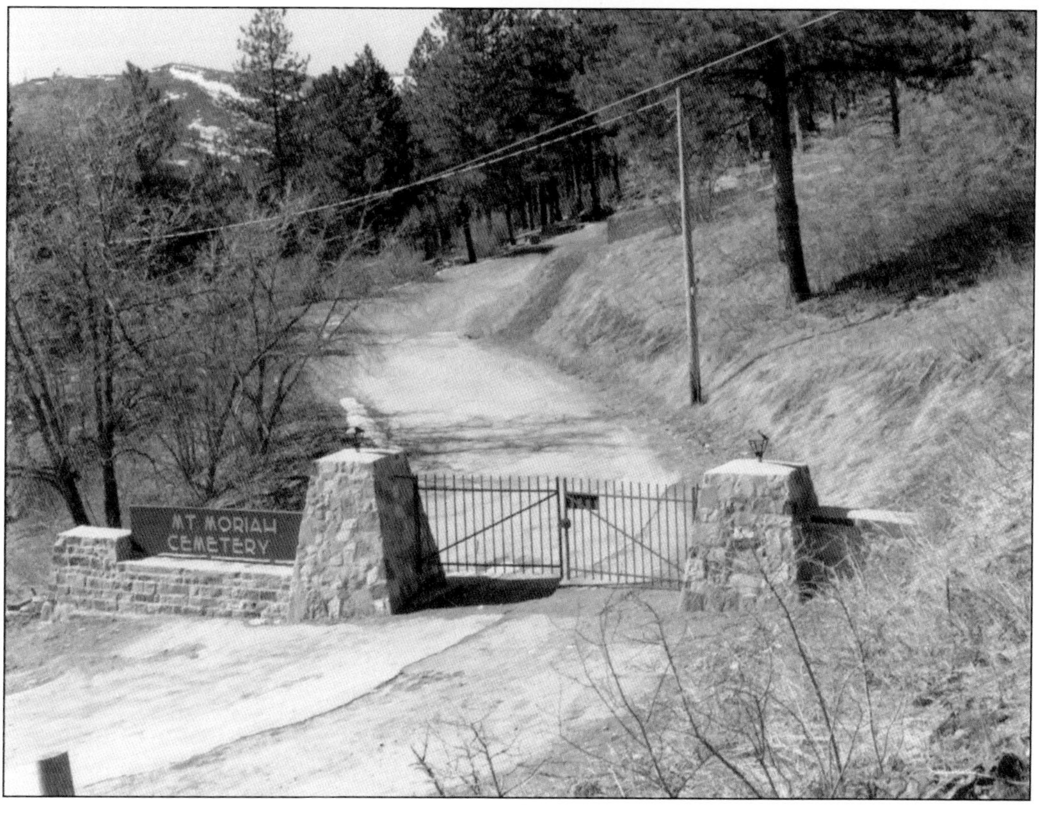

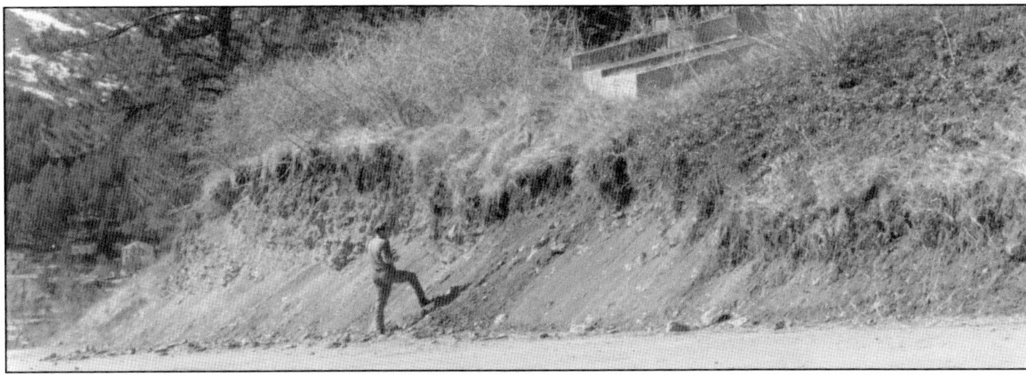

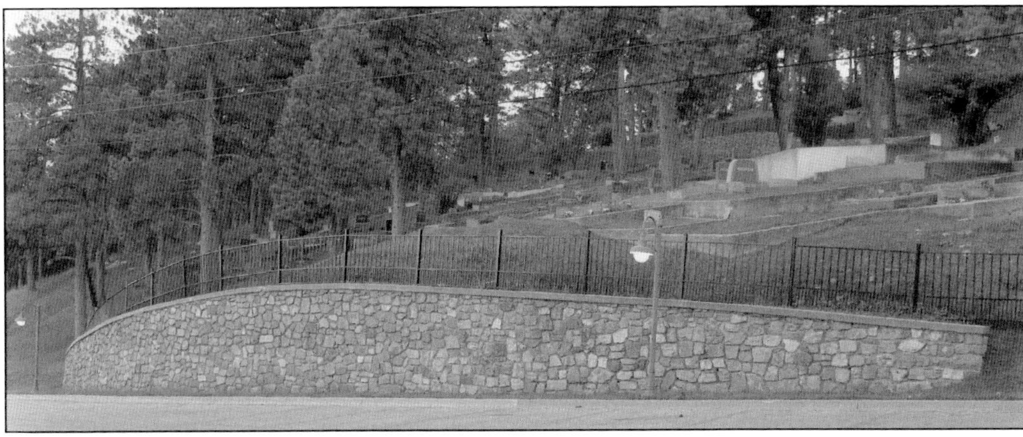

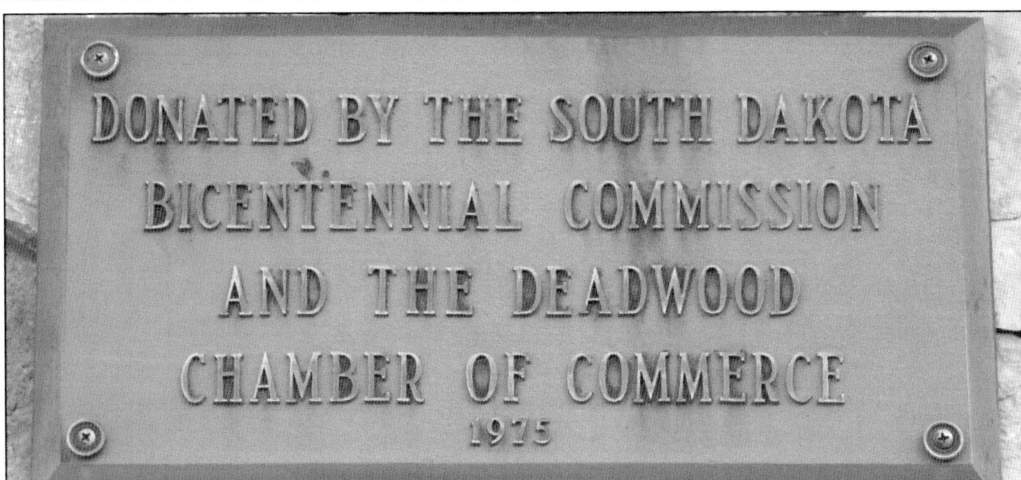

Another recommendation proposed in the master plan was the development of a parking lot adjacent to the cemetery. Since the arrival of the first automobile in the cemetery in 1909, vehicular traffic had become an ever-growing problem. To combat this issue, part of the hillslope below Third Addition Section 1 was removed and leveled for a parking lot. Over time, the exposed 10-foot cut began to erode. In November 1974, the Deadwood Chamber of Commerce and the South Dakota Bicentennial Commission received funding for the construction of a retaining wall. Upon completion of the project one year later, a bronze plaque was placed in the center of the wall. Today, over 80,000 tourists use this parking lot. (All, courtesy of CODA.)

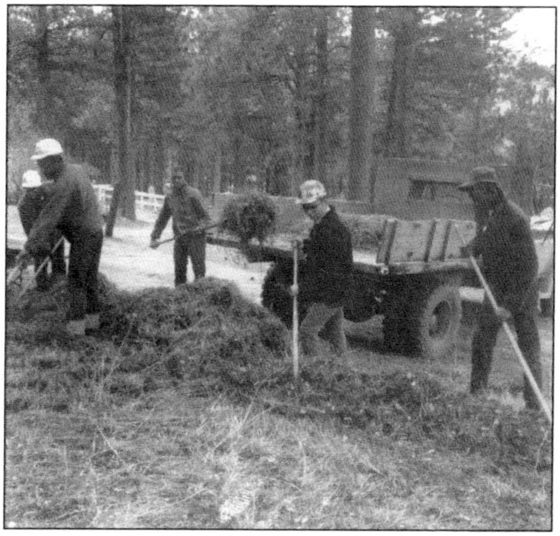

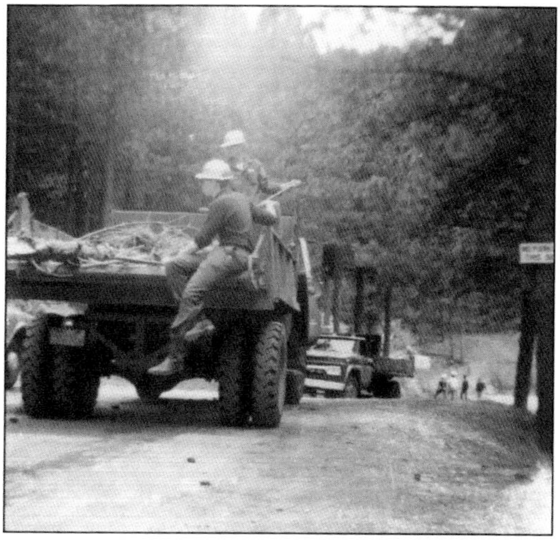

In addition to the development of the master plan, the Tri-Club also sponsored several community-wide cleanups of Mount Moriah Cemetery. These photographs, taken in 1968, 1969, and 1971, record students from the Boxelder Civil Conservation Corps (Job Corps) in Nemo, South Dakota, participating in a cleanup. The women from the Tri-Club provided the workers with an ample supply of baked goods for their diligent work. (All, courtesy of CODA.)

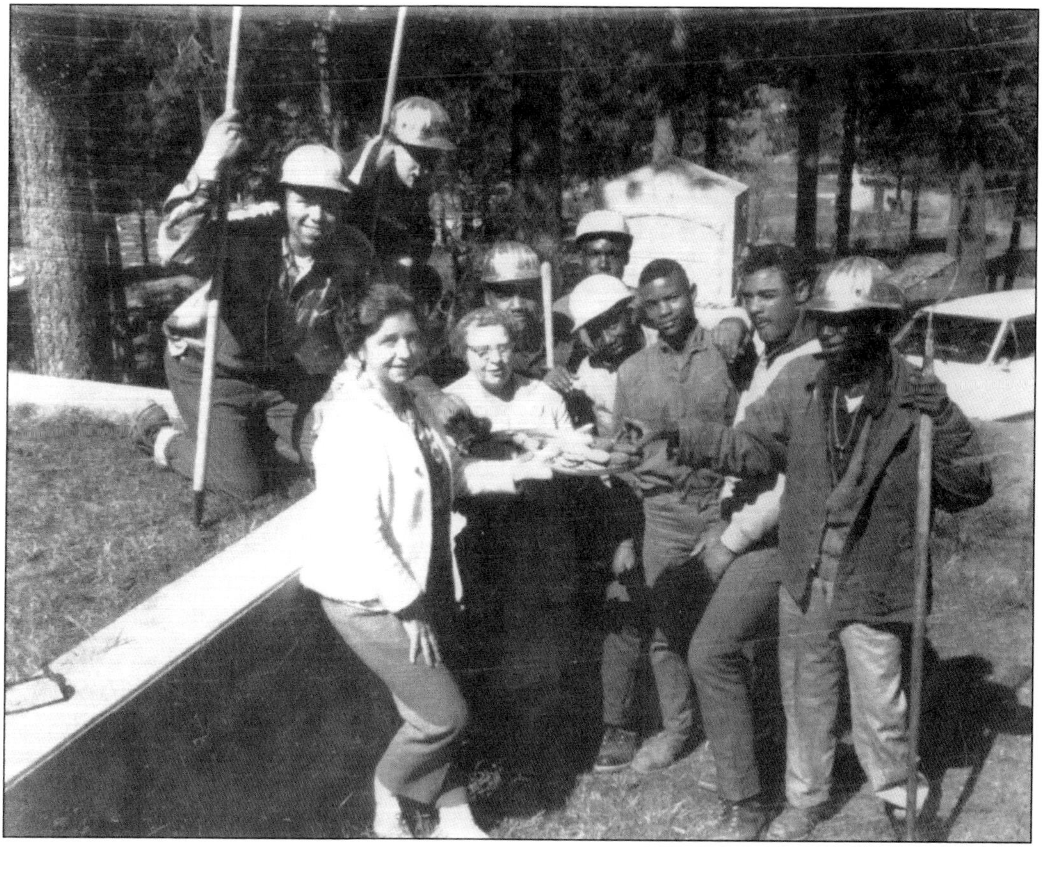

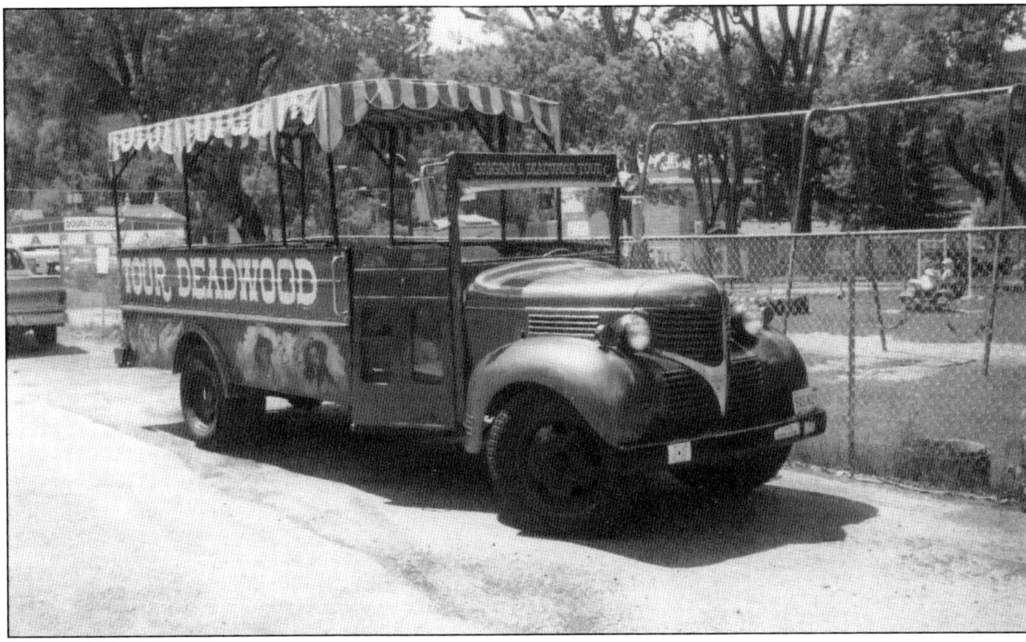

As an offshoot of the 1968 master plan, a motor coach industry was soon developed to transport tourists to and from the cemetery. One of the first tour bus businesses in Deadwood was Original Deadwood Tours, established in 1974. Tour bus operator Jan Van Tassel, posing below in front of the 22-passenger 1939 Dodge tour bus, has been with Original Deadwood Tours for over 36 years. Today, three tour bus companies provide guided tours of downtown Deadwood and Mount Moriah Cemetery. (Both, courtesy of Jan Van Tassel, Original Deadwood Tours.)

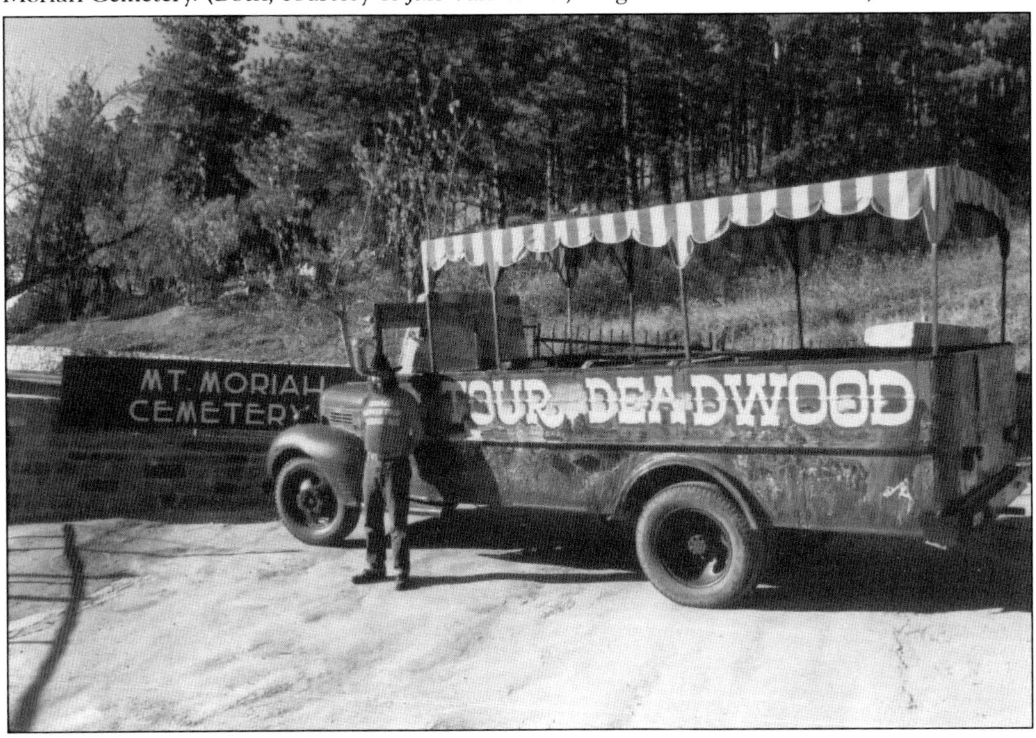

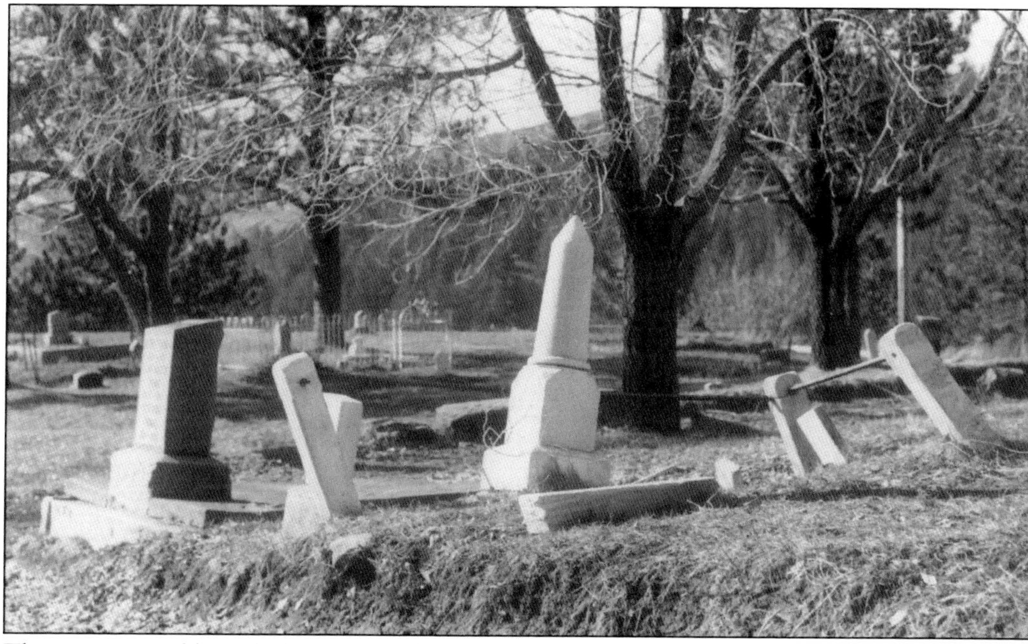

Thirty years would pass before Mount Moriah would undergo another restoration and rejuvenation project. In 1997, eight years after the legalization of limited stakes gaming, the newly formed Deadwood Historic Preservation Commission hired the landscape architectural firm Wyss Associates of Rapid City to develop a master plan for the cemetery. The primary objectives of this project were to inventory and assess the preexisting condition of the monuments, vegetation, and retaining walls within the cemetery and develop a priority list of cemetery plots that needed work. The plan also provided recommendations on drainage and erosion caused by the severe slope of the cemetery and continual pedestrian foot traffic. (Both, courtesy of CODA.)

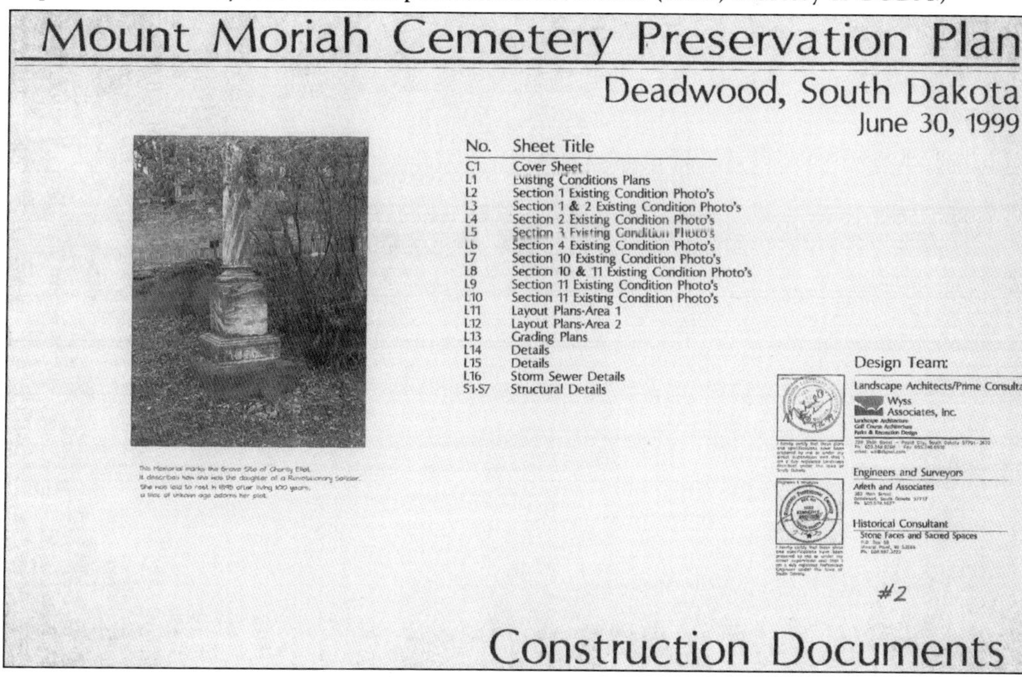

Mount Moriah Cemetery Preservation Plan

Deadwood, South Dakota
June 30, 1999

This Memorial marks the Grave Site of Charity Eliot.
It describes how she was the daughter of a Revolutionary Soldier.
She was laid to rest in 1895 after living 100 years,
a lilac of unkown age adorns her plot.

No.	Sheet Title
C1	Cover Sheet
L1	Existing Conditions Plans
L2	Section 1 Existing Condition Photo's
L3	Section 1 & 2 Existing Condition Photo's
L4	Section 2 Existing Condition Photo's
L5	Section 3 Existing Condition Photo's
L6	Section 4 Existing Condition Photo's
L7	Section 10 Existing Condition Photo's
L8	Section 10 & 11 Existing Condition Photo's
L9	Section 11 Existing Condition Photo's
L10	Section 11 Existing Condition Photo's
L11	Layout Plans-Area 1
L12	Layout Plans-Area 2
L13	Grading Plans
L14	Details
L15	Details
L16	Storm Sewer Details
S1-S7	Structural Details

Design Team:

Landscape Architects/Prime Consultant
Wyss Associates, Inc.

Engineers and Surveyors
Arleth and Associates

Historical Consultant
Stone Faces and Sacred Spaces

#2

Construction Documents

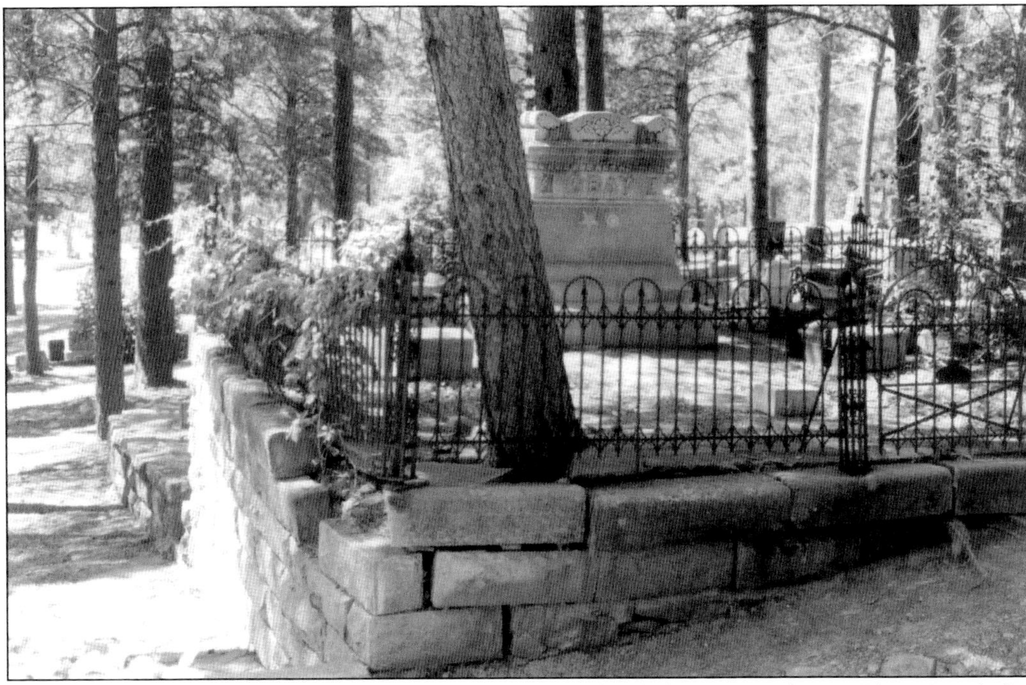

Construction work began in 1998, and the project was divided into two phases. Phase I included the installation of drainage pipe and the development of material standards to be incorporated on all restorations within the cemetery. The John Gray plot, located in Section 10, Lot 2, was selected as a standards plot for the restoration. This was in part due to the diversity of restoration needs that included ironwork, a cut stone wall reconstruction, tuckpointing/mortar joints, monument cleaning, and the rehabilitation of two metal urns. Once completed, the Gray plot was used to demonstrate the number of restoration techniques that could be applied throughout the project and provide quality control for the entire cemetery. (Both, courtesy of CODA.)

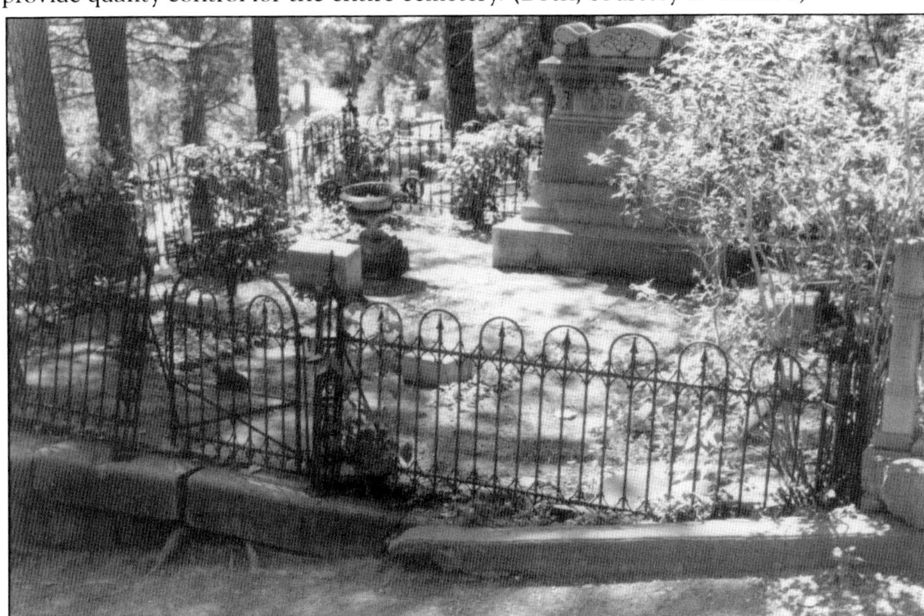

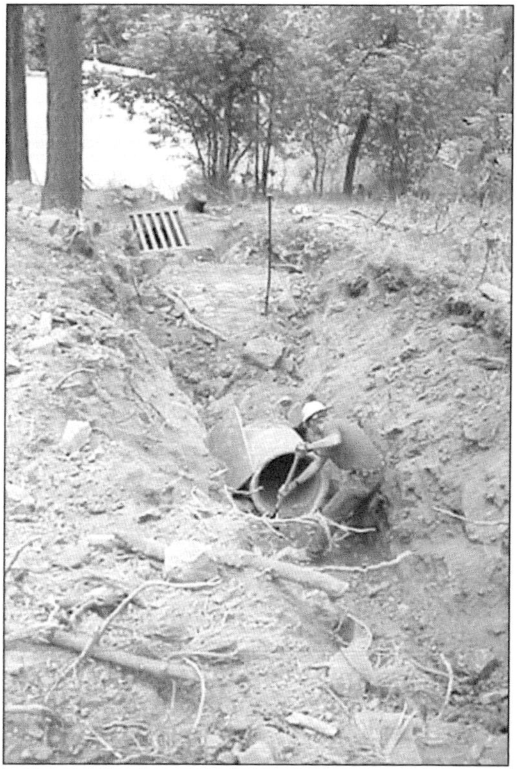

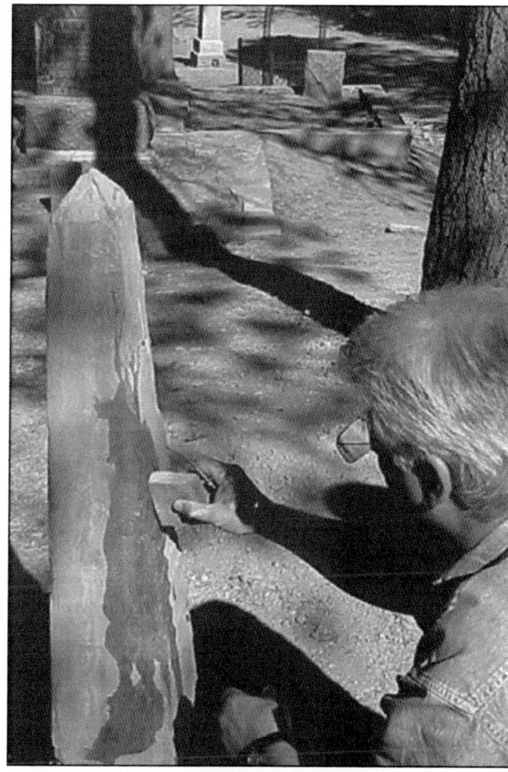

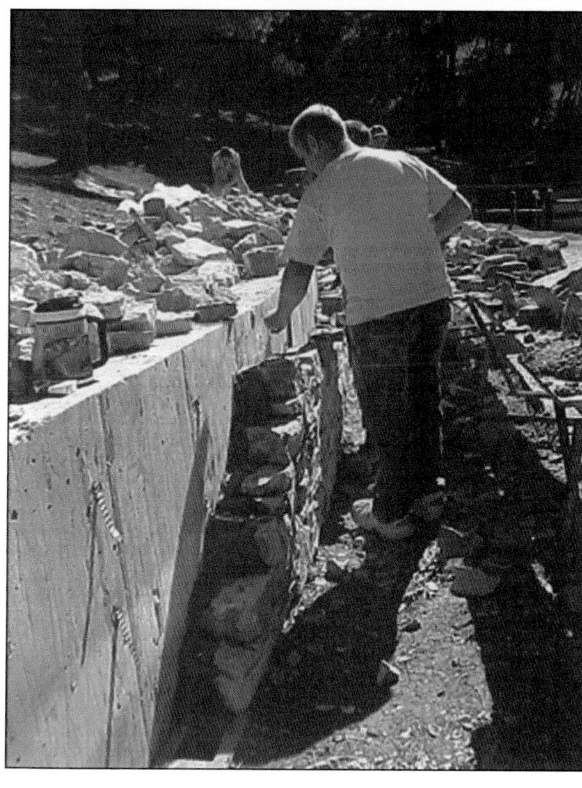

MAC Construction of Rapid City was selected for the project, and Deadwood Granite and Marble Works received the subcontract for setting and cleaning the monuments. Phase II of the project began in 2000 and consisted of the rehabilitation of approximately 450 cemetery plots. Construction crews also worked on stabilizing the retaining wall along David Street and installing paving, curbing, and storm sewer piping along the bus route. (All, courtesy of Wyss Associates.)

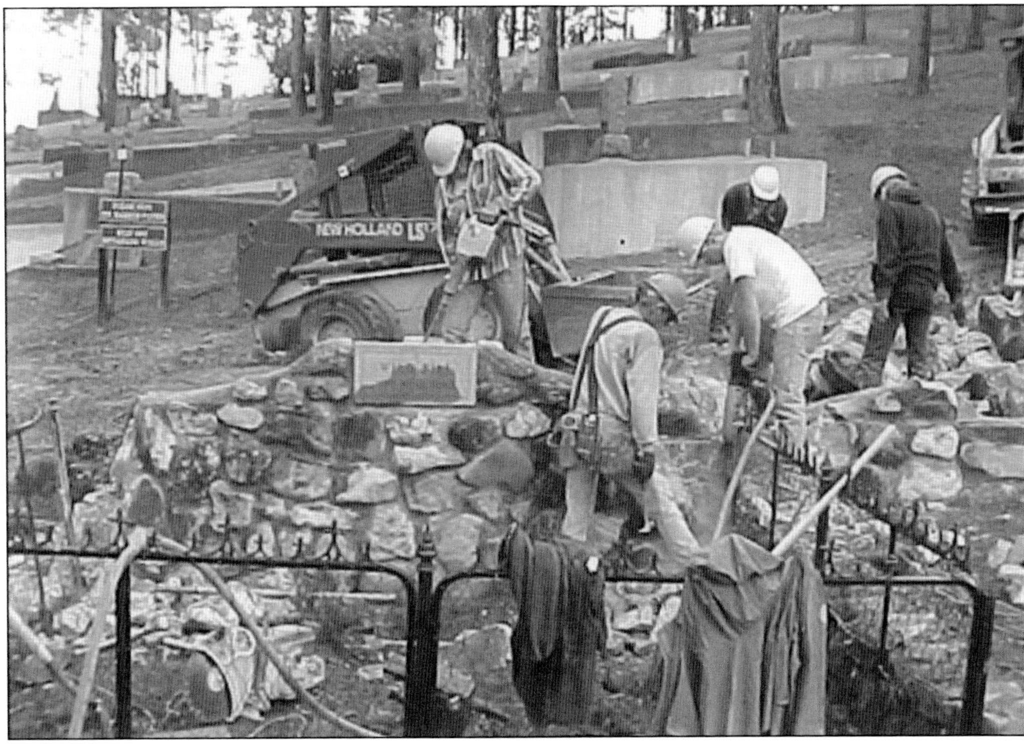

During Phase II of the project, the celebrity graves received a complete overhaul. Before work could proceed, Maxim Technologies Inc. of Rapid City conducted ground-penetrating radar surveys on the Hickok and Canary plots. This data helped determine grave position, burial orientation, and metal anomalies within the Hickok and Canary coffins. Once this was established, MAC Construction began work on disassembling the 1953 retaining wall, pouring new footings, and facing the new retaining walls with a rock veneer. (Above, courtesy of Wyss Associates; below, courtesy of CODA.)

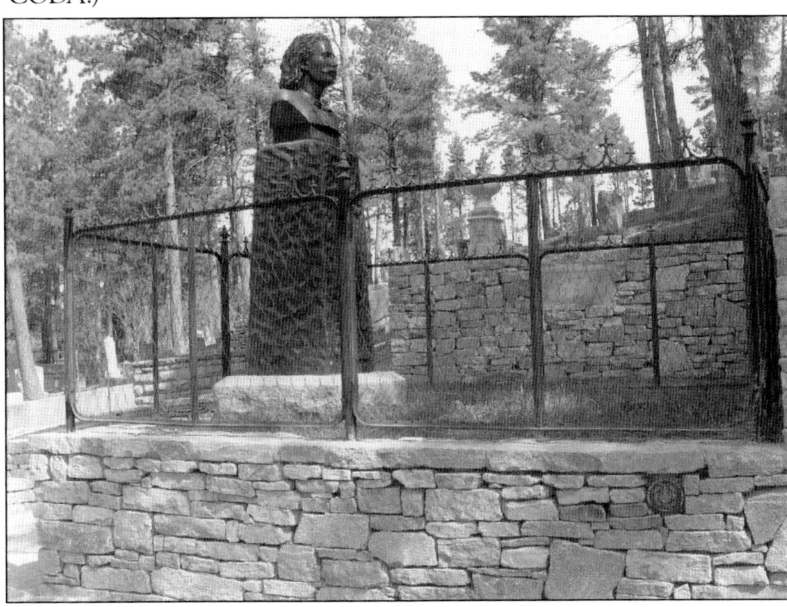

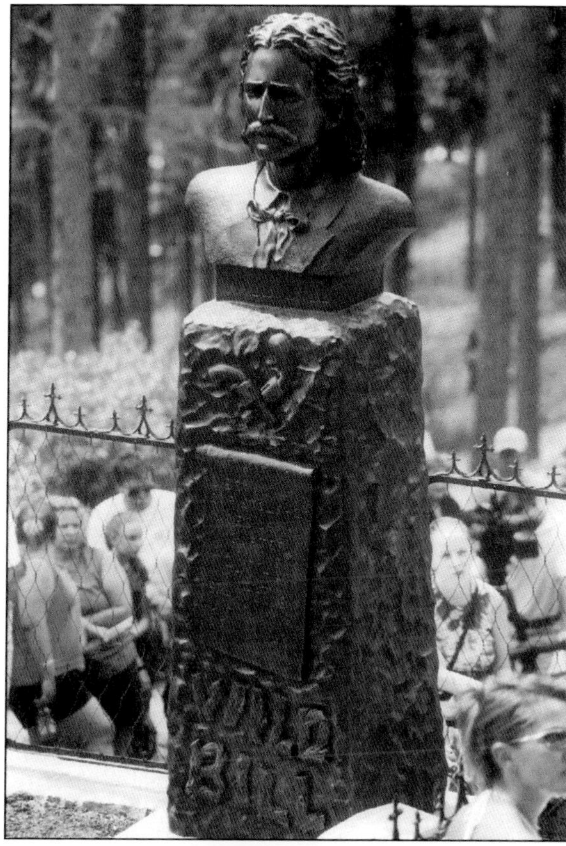

In unison with Phase II of the restoration, the Deadwood Historic Preservation Commission asked Nebraska sculptor David R. Young to develop a bonze monument in the likeness of the 1891 Hickok monument. Young worked on the monument in Deadwood during the summer of 2001. On August 2, 2002, the bonze monument was unveiled on the 126th anniversary of James Butler Hickok's death. The bronze monument also celebrated the completion of the Mount Moriah Cemetery restoration project. Reenactors from Deadwood Alive helped dedicate the statue in front of a large crowd. (Both, courtesy of Dick Termes and Termesphere Gallery.)

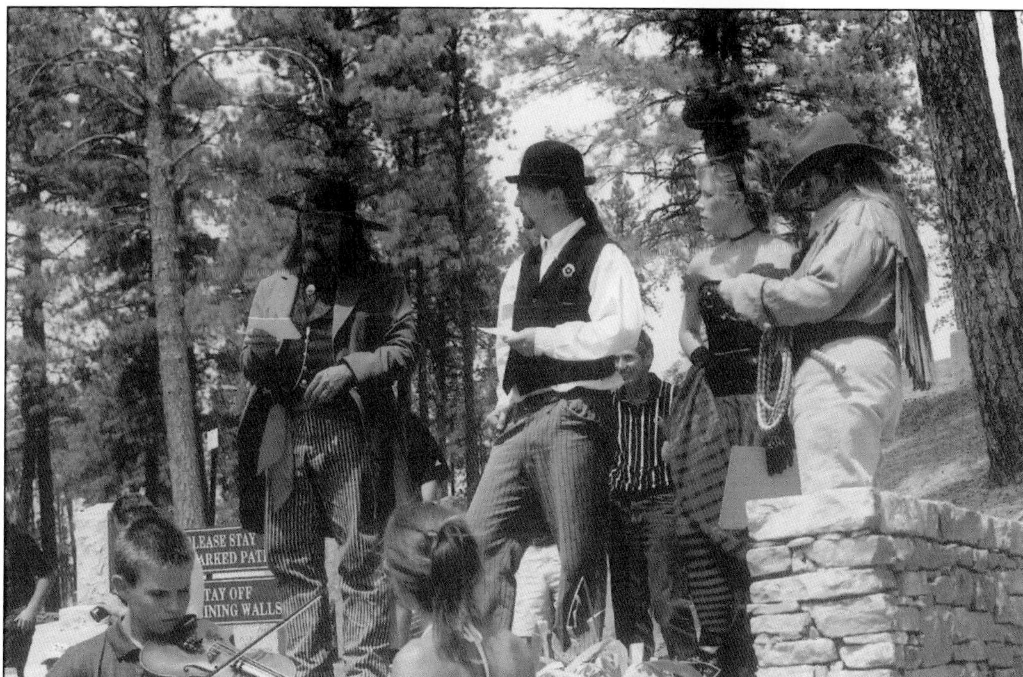

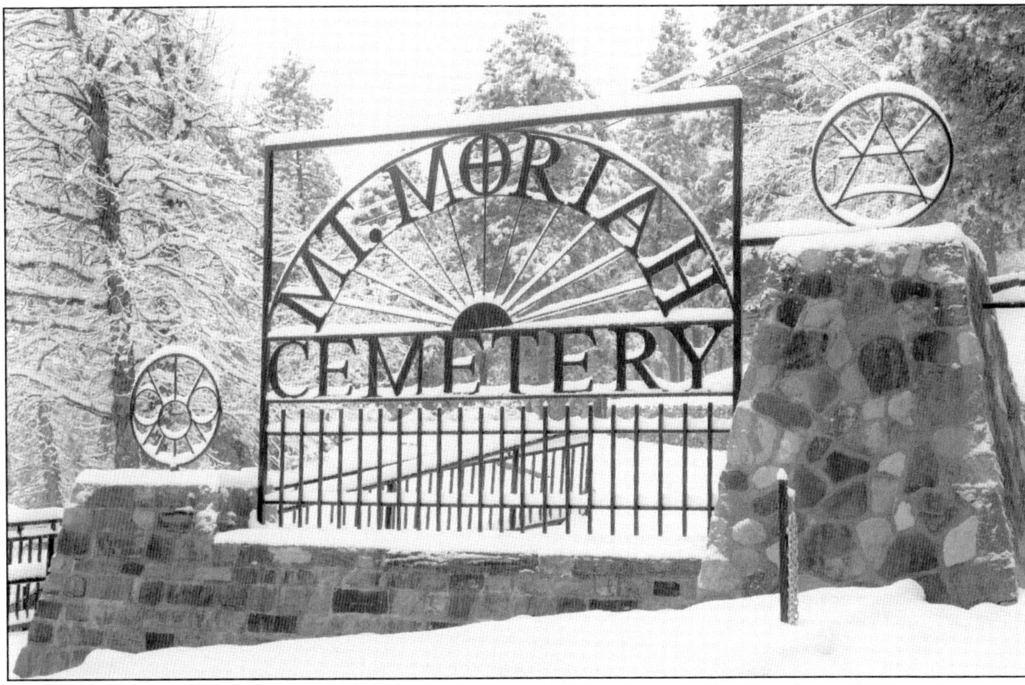

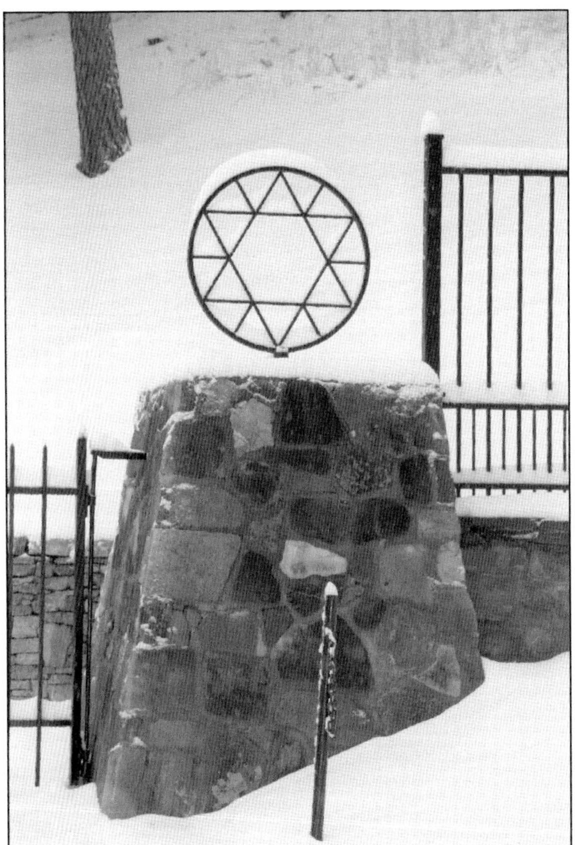

In 2003, the Deadwood Historic Preservation Commission decided to replace the wooden entry sign at the Mount Moriah gateway. Rapid City artist Darrel Nelson was commissioned to design a new wrought iron sign. Upon completion, the new sign mimicked the original wrought iron gateway created by the E.T. Bormans Company of Detroit, Michigan. Nelson incorporated three symbols into the design. Two prominent fraternal organizations, the Independent Order of Odd Fellows (three connected circles) and Freemasonry (square and compass), appear on the left side of the gate. The right side contains the Star of David, signifying the Jewish section of Mount Moriah Cemetery. (Both, courtesy of CODA.)

Three

Sections 1–4 and Sections 10 and 11

Of all the sections in Mount Moriah Cemetery, Sections 1 through 4 are the most significant. These sections together make up the original oval configuration that was platted in 1878. Jerusalem Street running on a north/south axis and Solomon Street running on an east/west axis divide the cemetery into the four sections and contain approximately 1,121 recorded burials. Many of the oldest burials in the cemetery are located in Sections 2 and 3. These sections also contain some of the more elaborate Late Victorian–era funerary art and symbolism in the cemetery. Since the 1890s, numerous local fraternal groups have purchased segments of Sections 1 through 4 for the burial of their dead. Fourteen fraternal organizations are represented in Mount Moriah Cemetery, including Freemasonry, Independent Order of Odd Fellows, Ancient Order of United Workmen, Modern Woodmen of America, Grand Army of the Republic, Benevolent and Protective Order of Elks, Knights of Pythias, Society of Black Hills Pioneers, and the Deadwood Fire Department.

Sections 10 and 11 were added with the redrawing of the 1895 Mount Moriah Cemetery plat map. These two sections are located in the centermost part of the oval and were reserved for members of Deadwood Masonic Lodge No. 7 and Deadwood Eureka Lodge No. 13 of the Independent Order of Odd Fellows. Several times during the early development of the cemetery, the Deadwood Masons requested and received permission to beautify Section 10. The most recognizable improvement occurred in 1914 when the Masons replatted this section and transformed it into a celestial lodge. As part of the 1998–2003 restoration of the cemetery, these six sections were restored to their former grandeur. Today, Sections 1 through 4 and 10 and 11 are a must-see when visiting Mount Moriah Cemetery.

Much of the history surrounding the celebrity graves was discussed in the previous chapter. The focal point of this and the subsequent chapters in this book is not to relate the stories of every person buried in Mount Moriah Cemetery, but to discuss several of the noted individuals and some of the unique monuments and features within these sections.

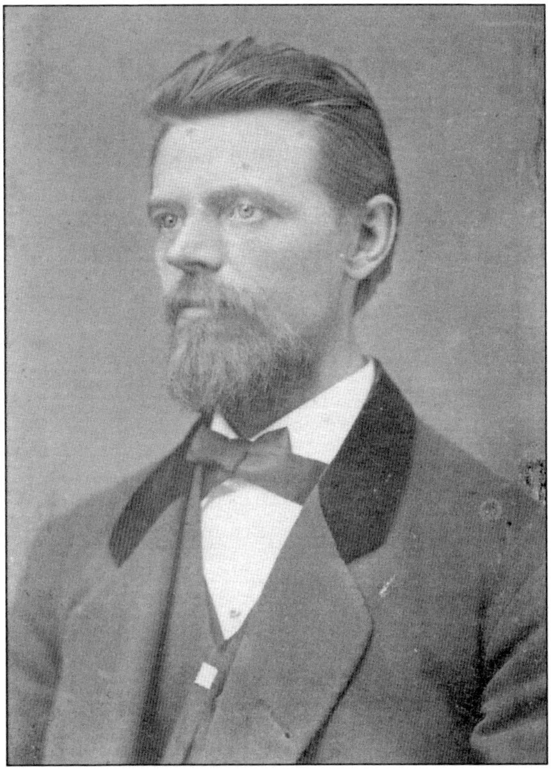

John Lawrence was the namesake of Lawrence County in western South Dakota. He was born in Reading, Berkshire, England, in 1839. At an early age, Lawrence's family emigrated to Canada and later to Antrim County, Michigan. In 1858, Lawrence was one of the first settlers in Sioux Falls, Dakota Territory. He became involved in the governmental affairs of the territory, serving as territorial legislator for Sioux Falls, a member of the Dakota Territorial Council, sergeant-at-arms of the US House of Representatives, and deputy US marshal of Dakota. Dakota governor Andrew J. Faulk bestowed Lawrence with the honorary title "colonel." In March 1877, Lawrence was appointed county treasurer in Lawrence County but was voted out of office in October. In 1986, the Lawrence County Historical Society placed this granite monument on his grave. (Left, courtesy of Deadwood Public Library; below, courtesy of CODA.)

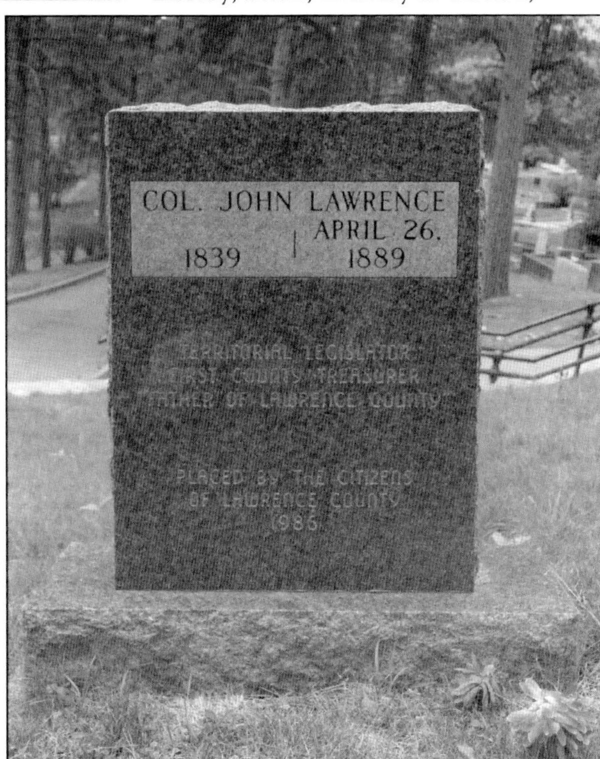

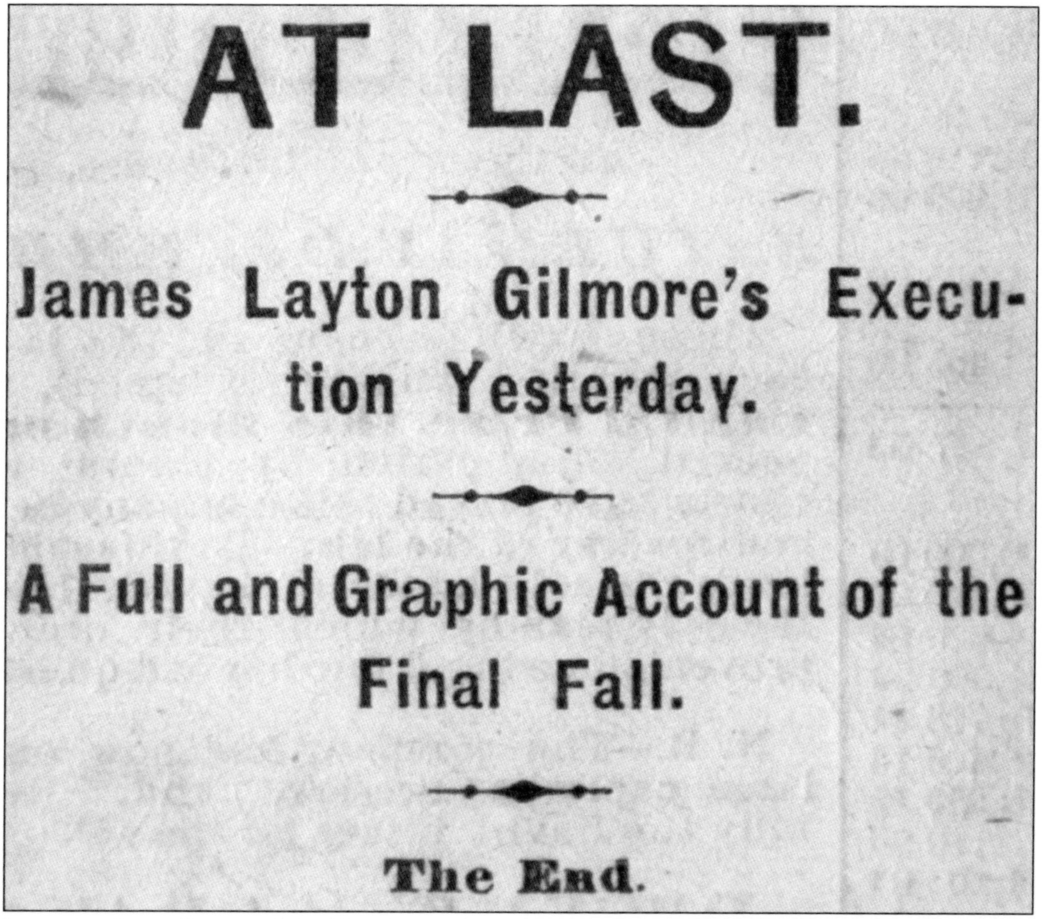
AT LAST.

James Layton Gilmore's Execution Yesterday.

A Full and Graphic Account of the Final Fall.

The End.

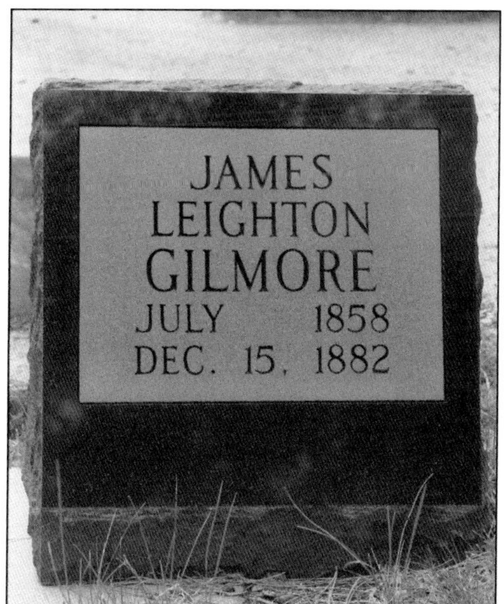

James Leighton Gilmore (July 1858–December 15, 1882) was the first public execution in Deadwood and the second legal execution in Dakota Territory. In 1879, Gilmore killed Bicente Ortez along the Ft. Pierre to Deadwood Trail. After the shooting, Gilmore fled to Nebraska and opened a dance hall. In 1881, he was accused of being an accomplice in a homicide at the dance hall. He fled but was captured in Pierre, Dakota Territory, before being transported to Deadwood where he awaited trial. Gilmore was found guilty and was sentenced to death by hanging. On December 15, 1882, he was publicly executed in the courtyard of Deadwood's first county jail. In 2006, the Deadwood Historic Preservation Commission, through the Cemetery Headstone Grant program, placed a granite monument on Gilmore's previously unmarked grave. (Above, courtesy of Deadwood Public Library; right, courtesy of CODA.)

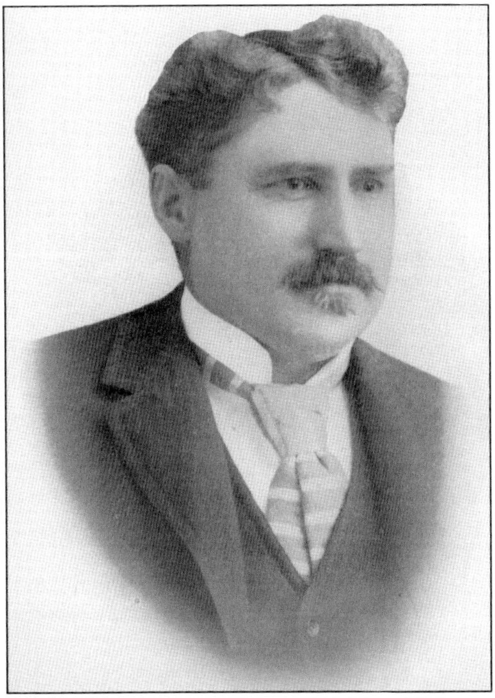

Julius Deetken (October 27, 1844–April 19, 1915) was a Deadwood pharmacist and a highly regarded citizen of the community. Born in Baden, Germany, Deetken, at the age of 17, enrolled in a pharmaceutical apprenticeship—a decision that helped build a successful career throughout his life. In 1867, Deetken immigrated to the United States, first settling in Council Bluffs, Iowa. In 1876, he opened a pharmaceutical business on Deadwood's Main Street. In 1909, he was elected president of the Pharmaceutical Association of South Dakota. He was an active member of the Society of Black Hills Pioneers, serving as the secretary. Deetken was instrumental in organizing and collecting public subscriptions for a monument honoring Henry Weston "Preacher" Smith, located along US Highway 85 near the top of Deadwood Hill. (All, courtesy of CODA.)

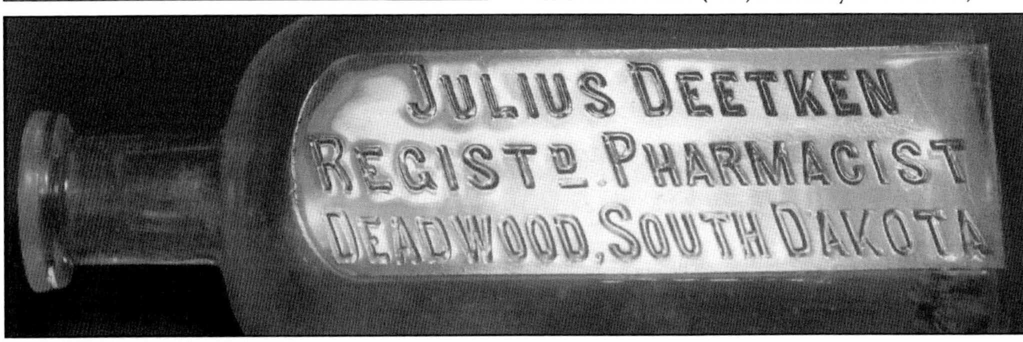

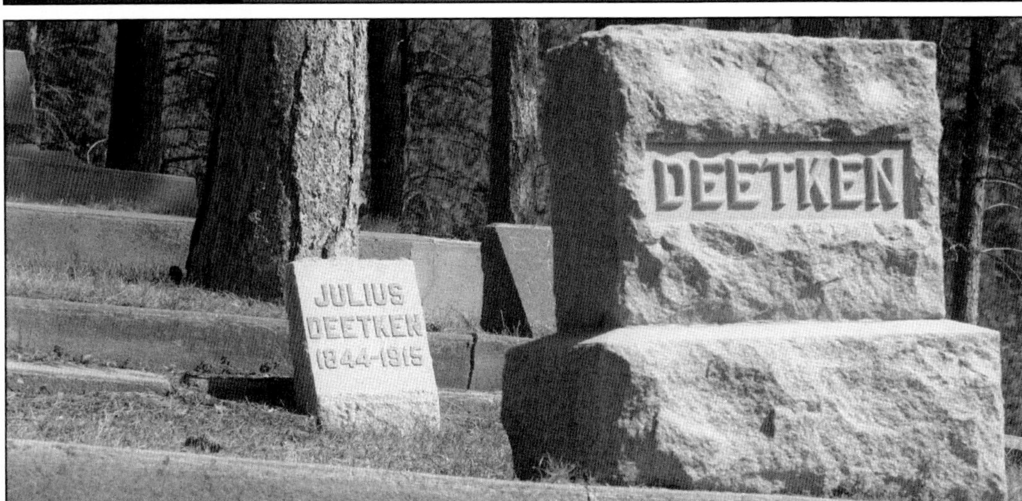

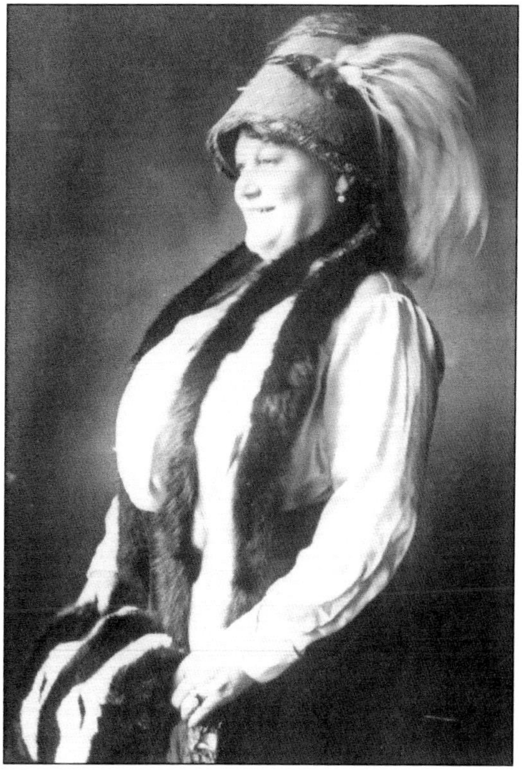

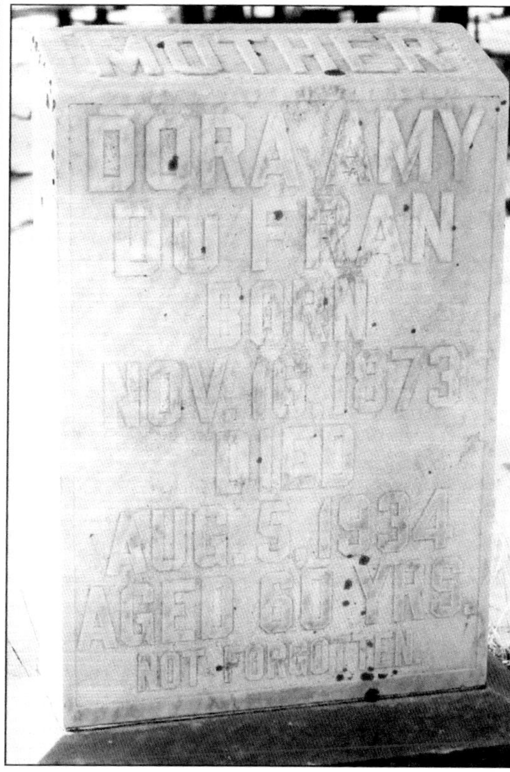

The infamous Dora Dufran was born Amie Helen Dorothea Bolshow in England in 1873 and immigrated to the United States with her parents, who settled in Nebraska. By 1889, she was married to Joseph Dufran and opened a brothel in Deadwood devoted to gambling, dancing, drinking, and "fancy entertainment" for its guests. Dufran operated two similar establishments in Belle Fourche and Rapid City, South Dakota, prior to 1917. After the closing of the houses in Rapid City, Dufran took up nursing and played an active role in helping the destitute and poor during the 1918 influenza epidemic. Several days after her death in 1934, the *Rapid City Daily Journal* wrote a half-page eulogy commemorating the life of Dufran. Today, Dufran is buried in Mount Moriah Cemetery beside her husband and pet parrot, Fred. (Above left, courtesy of Deadwood Public Library; above right and below, courtesy of CODA.)

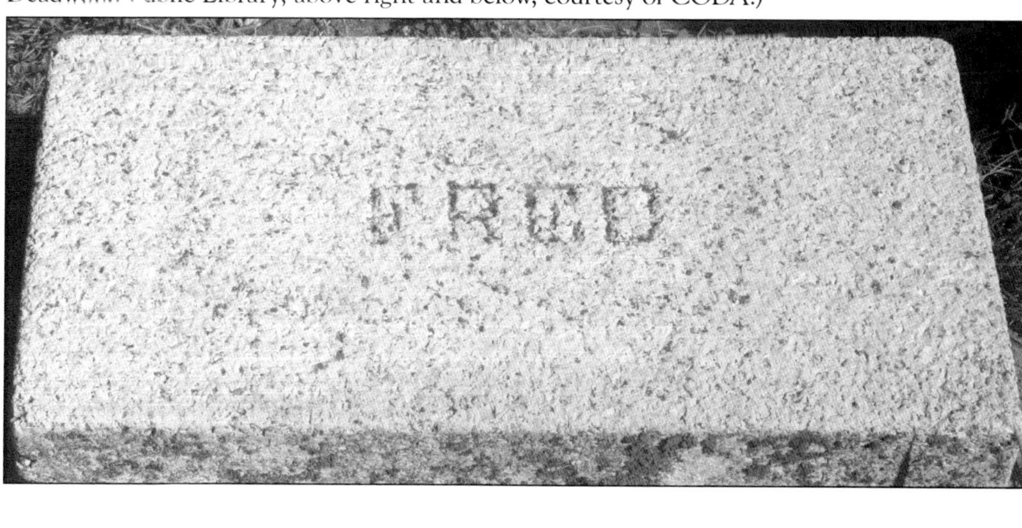

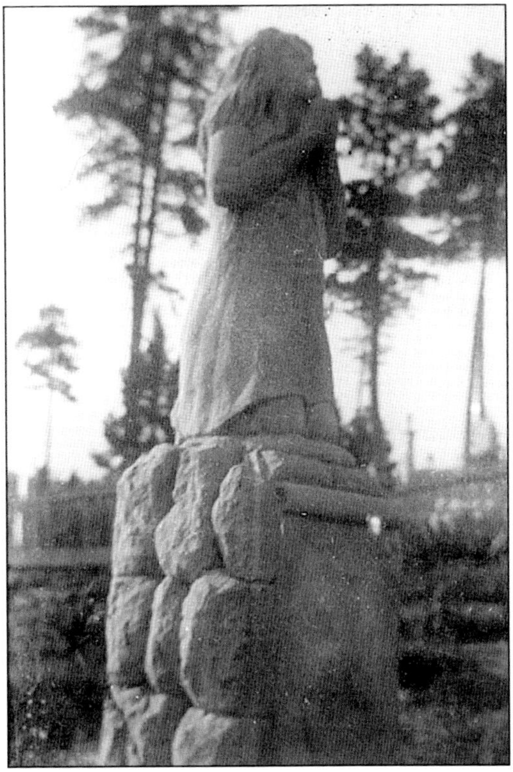

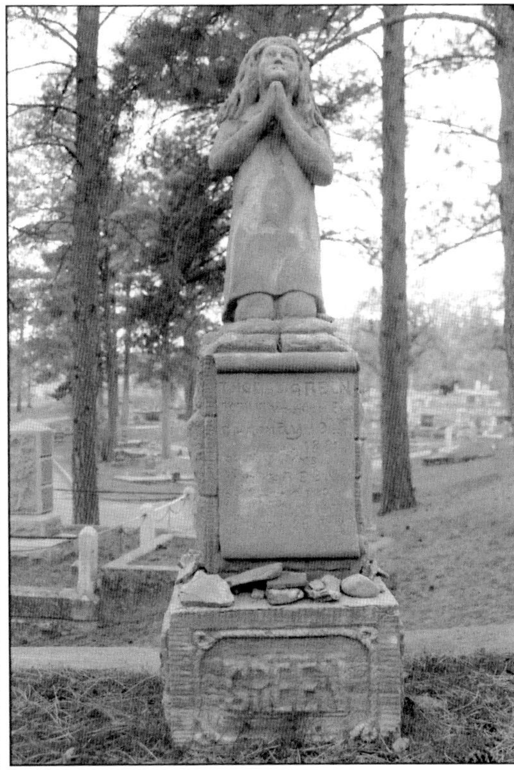

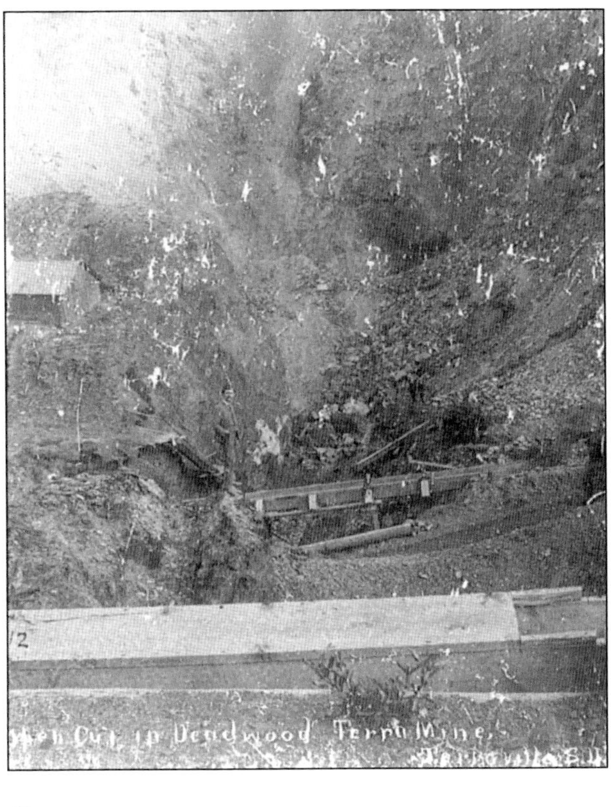

The Green plot features one of the more interesting monuments. It is the only full-body statue in the cemetery and depicts a young girl kneeling in prayer with her face tilted up towards the sky. Mable Gertrude Green and her father, Thomas, died approximately two months apart. On March 9, 1881, Mable, who was just an infant, died from inflammation of the lungs after being sick for 24 hours. Two months later, on May 19, 1881, the connecting tunnel between the Golden Terra Mine and the Highland Mine partially collapsed, killing Thomas Green and two other men and trapping nine miners in the tunnel. Local newspapers ran lengthy articles covering this mining accident and the recovery efforts that ultimately saved the lives of some of the trapped miners. (Above left and below, courtesy of Deadwood History Inc., Adams Museum Collection; above right, courtesy of CODA.)

Lucien W. Stilwell (March 24, 1844–November 26, 1932) was a national and international dealer in anthropological, geological, and natural specimens. Born in Manlius, New York, Stilwell graduated from Ripon College in Wisconsin and settled in Elgin, Illinois, before moving to Deadwood in 1879. He started a successful mail order business selling natural, geological, and anthropological objects from his home on Lincoln Avenue. Two of his many clients included the Milwaukee Public Museum and the Chicago Field Museum. In 1891, Stilwell successfully raised funds for the creation of a life-size statue of martyred Methodist minister Henry Weston Smith. Stilwell was a founding member of the Deadwood Cemetery Association and served as the secretary for many years. He helped organize the Deadwood Methodist Church and served on the church council as secretary. (Both, courtesy of CODA.)

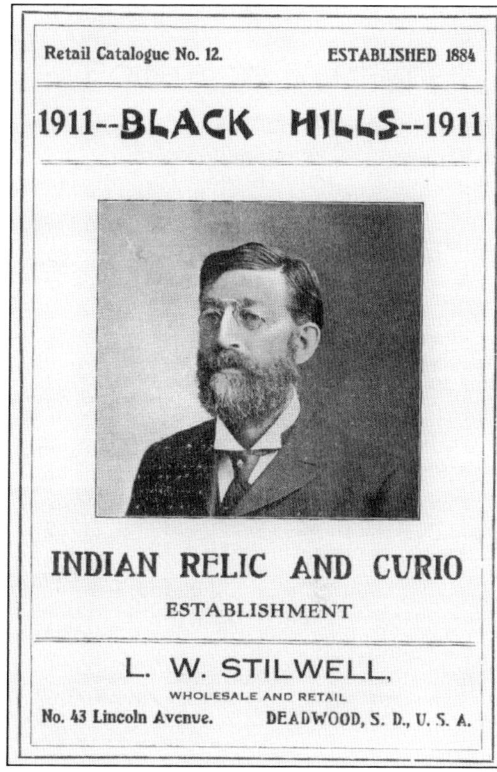

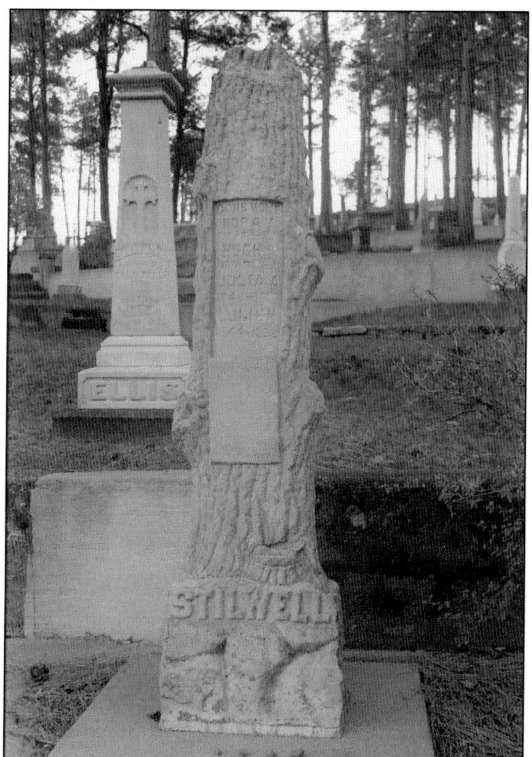

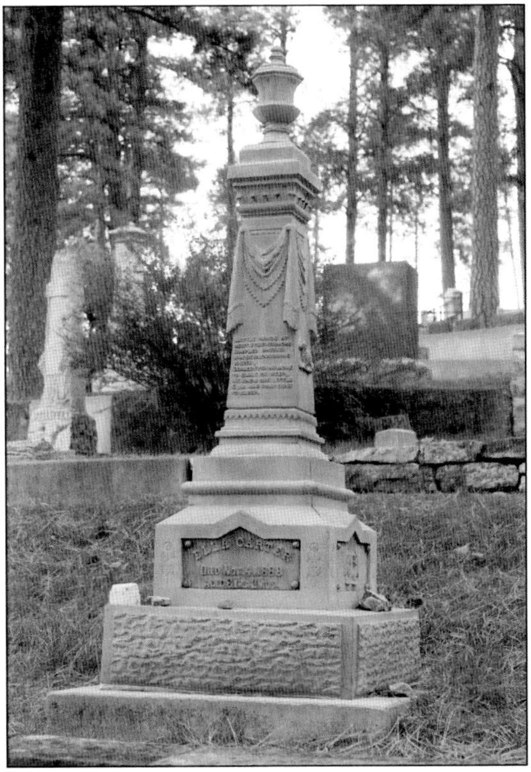

In 1888, Thomas and Ella Carter died and were interred in Section 2, Lot 74. After their deaths, the family placed a white bronze monument on their graves. White bronze memorials were cast zinc panels joined together to form a monument. From the 1870s until the first quarter of the 20th century, the Monumental Bronze Company of Bridgeport, Connecticut, offered an alternative to the traditional stone monuments. White bronze monuments provided buyers with greater flexibility for designing a custom-looking memorial. Sales agents armed with catalogs traveled to communities rather than having a showroom. Potential buyers could then select the size, design, and iconography to personalize their monument. The Carter monument is one of two white bronzes in the cemetery. (Left, courtesy of CODA; below, courtesy of Pennsylvania US GenWeb Archives.)

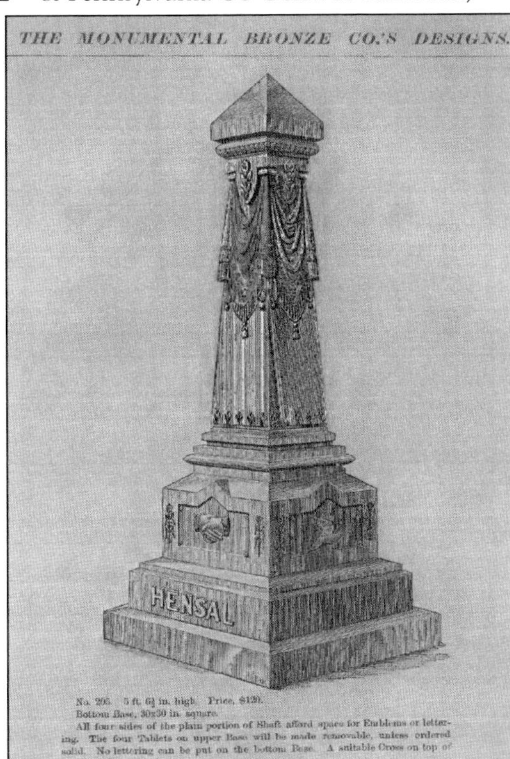

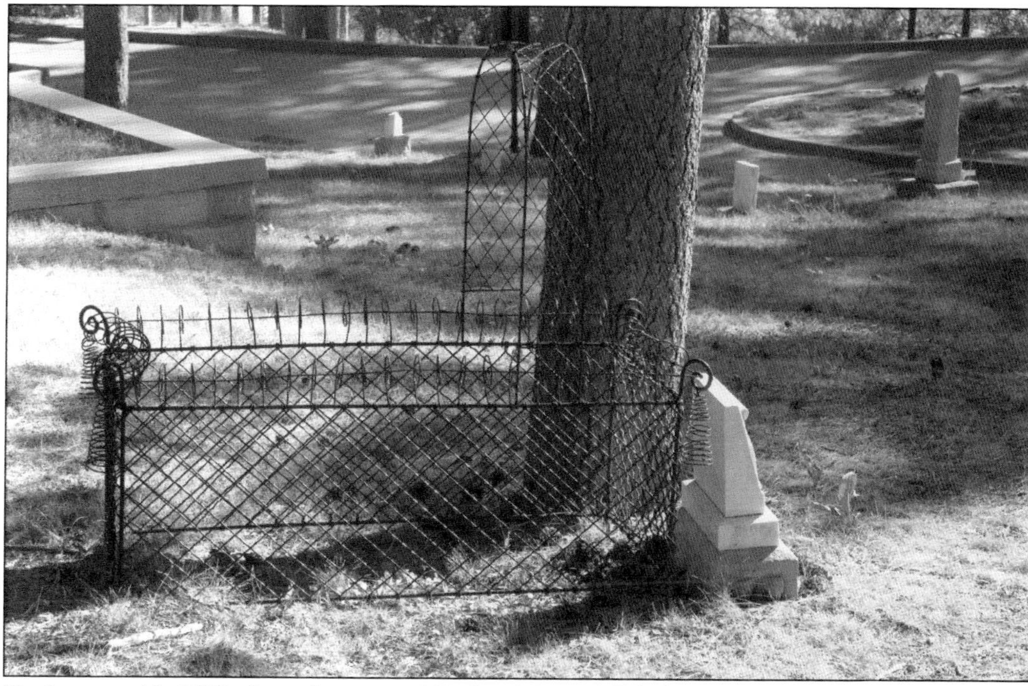

On January 15, 1893, the infant son of Richard C. and Ethel Barnard died at their home after being sick for more than a week. The father, Richard C. Barnard, was the former proprietor of the Bodega and Club Restaurants and manager of the Keystone and Wentworth Hotels on Deadwood's upper Main Street. The Barnards buried their son in Section 2, Lot 93 and placed a marble stone with a partially rolled scroll carved in relief that reads, "Baby Richard." The gravesite is decorated with a wrought iron and wire enclosure called a grave guard. Grave guards served two purposes: to protect the burial and ornament the grave. An advertisement for a grave guard appeared in the 1902 Sears, Roebuck and Co. catalogue. There are two grave guards in the cemetery; the other is located in Section 4. (Both, courtesy of CODA.)

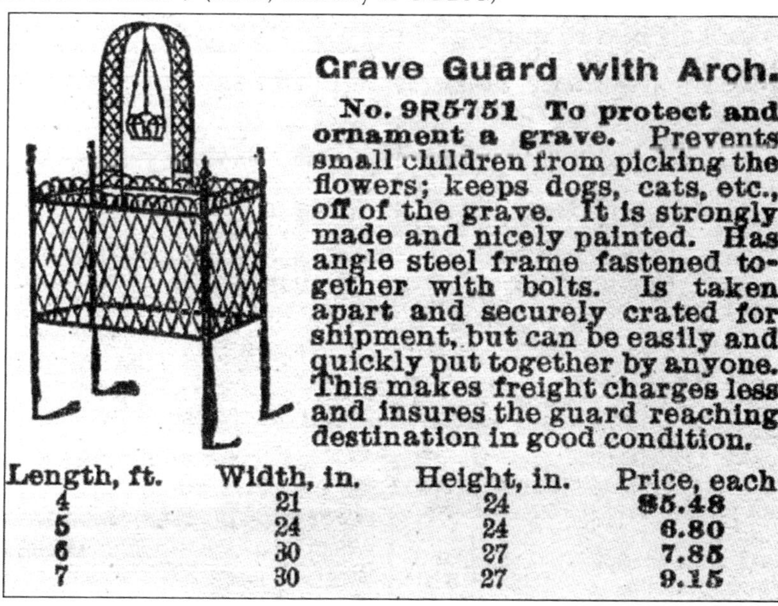

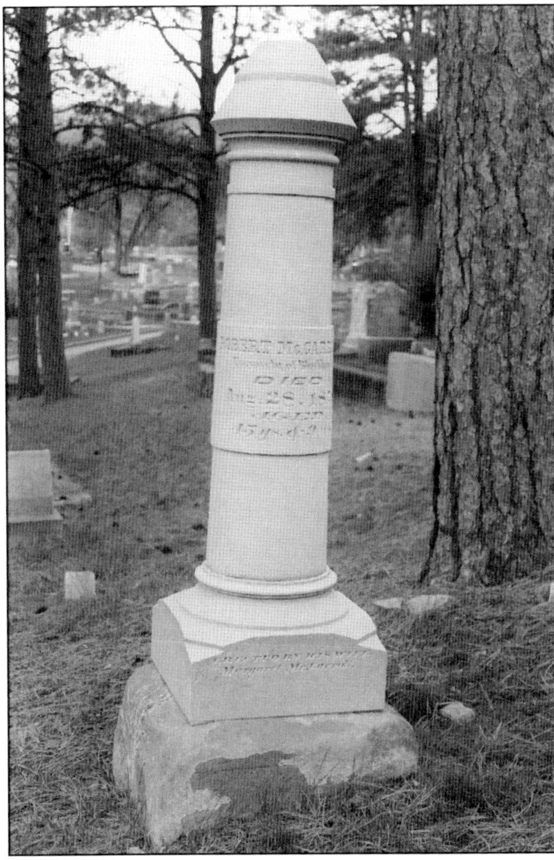

In 1878, the Father DeSmet Mining Company began work on a new 80-stamp amalgamation mill near the mining camp of Central City. Robert McCarroll was hired by the company as a carpenter to help build the new mill. On August 26, 1878, McCarroll was accidently thrown from the framework of the mill and fell approximately 20 feet. One of the timbers from the framework detached and severely crushed McCarroll. Two days after the accident, McCarroll died and was buried in a small cemetery along Poorman Gulch near Lead City. In 1881, McCarroll's relatives hired Louis Schofield to exhume and reinter McCarroll's remains in Mount Moriah Cemetery. The engraving on the base reads, "Erected by his wife Margaret McCarroll." (Both, courtesy of CODA.)

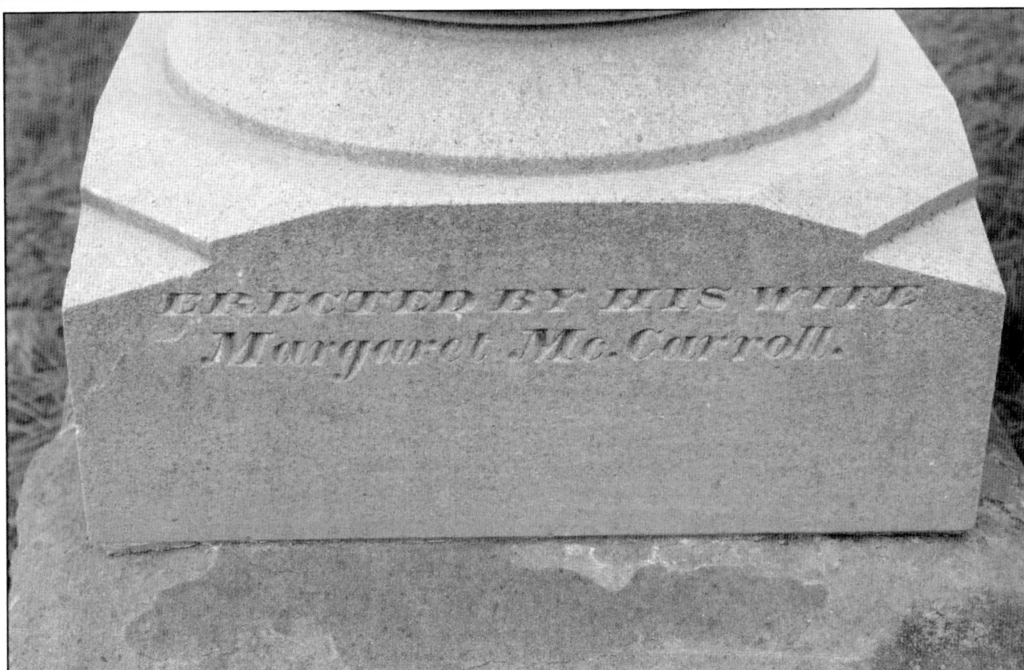

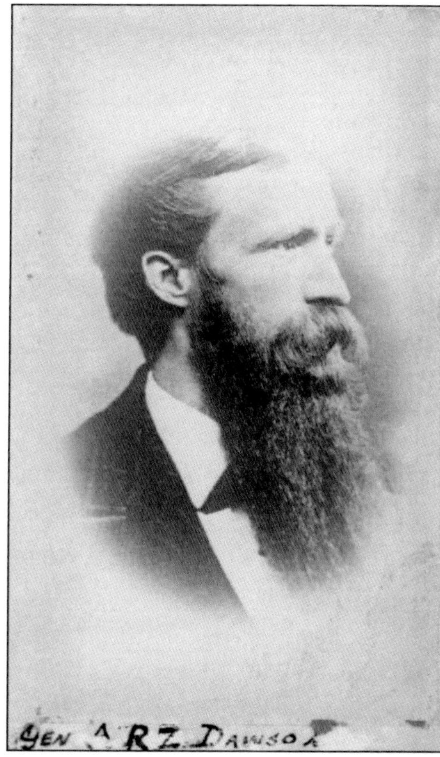

Andrew R.Z. Dawson (May 10, 1835–July 19, 1896) was one of Deadwood's highest-ranking Civil War veterans. Dawson was born in Hagerville, Ohio, and enlisted in the Union army as second lieutenant of the 15th Ohio Volunteers on April 19, 1861. In four years, Dawson was appointed colonel of the newly formed 187th Regiment of the Ohio Infantry and was honorably discharged from the service on January 20, 1866. Ten years later, he arrived in Deadwood Gulch and worked as the collector of internal revenue before being appointed clerk of the US Court for the Black Hills District. In 1884, Dawson founded the Deadwood Keogh Post 64, Grand Army of the Republic (GAR). In addition to the GAR, Dawson was involved with the Society of Black Hills Pioneers. (Right, courtesy of Deadwood History Inc., Adams Museum Collection; below, courtesy of CODA.)

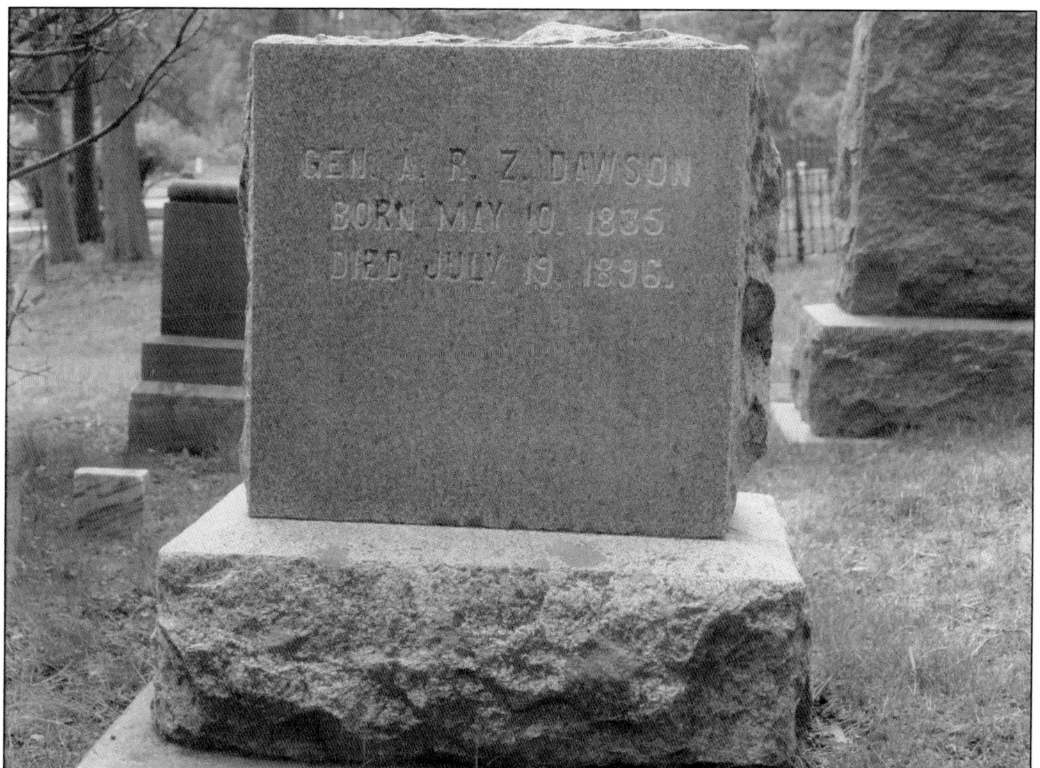

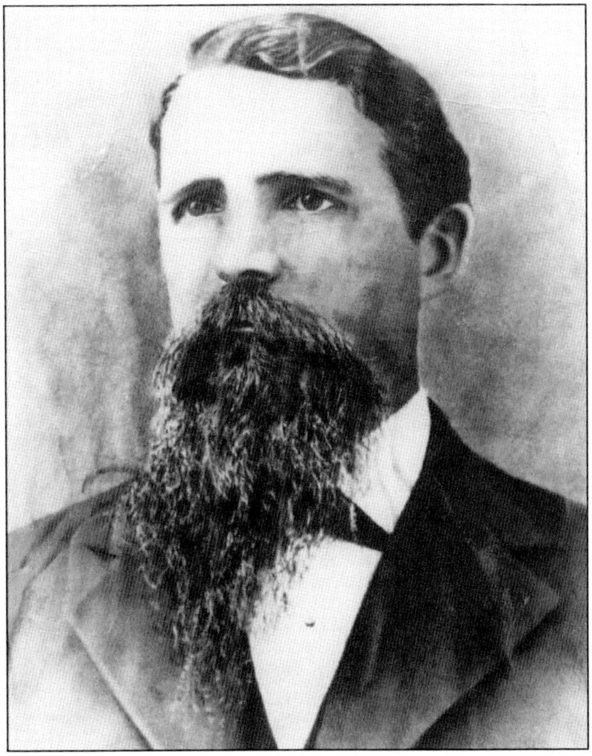

John P. Belding (July 12, 1837–February 19, 1917) was a city official and lawman in Lawrence County. Born in Madison County, New York, Belding moved to Missouri at age 20 and worked for the railroad. In 1861, he enlisted in the Union army and served with the 9th Missouri Volunteer Cavalry. He was discharged with the rank of captain. Belding went west to prospect for gold in Montana, Wyoming, and Utah. In 1868, he found work with the Union Pacific Railroad and was present for the driving of the golden spike at Promontory Summit, Utah Territory, on May 10, 1869. Six years later, Belding arrived in Deadwood and took on numerous civic duties, including county sheriff, Deadwood alderman, and fire chief. In 1898, Belding was appointed deputy US marshal, serving for eight years. (Left, courtesy of Beverly Wells; below, courtesy of CODA.)

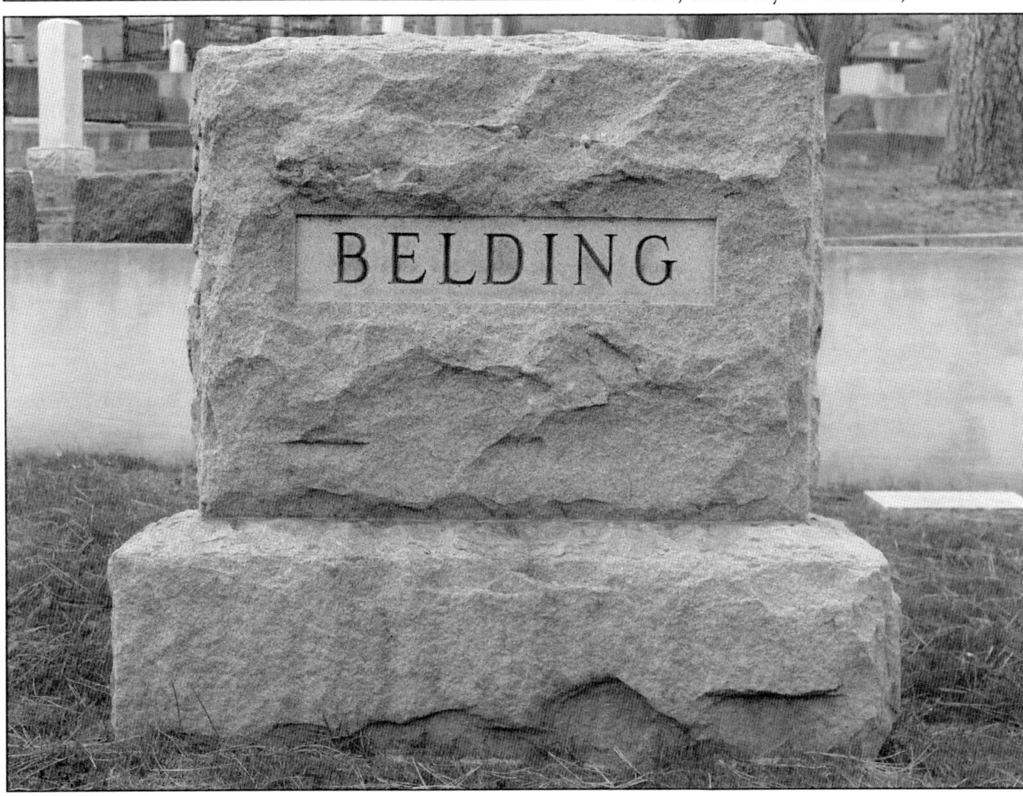

Charles Henry Robinson was a mortician and the sexton of Mount Moriah Cemetery for many years. Robinson was born on August 4, 1869, in Clarksburg, West Virginia. Seven years later, Robinson's family moved to Deadwood. Robinson's father, Henry, partnered with mortician Barclay P. Smith, who operated a funeral home in Deadwood. For 16 years, Henry Robinson and Smith were business partners. In 1892, Henry purchased Smith's interest in the business. In 1893, the Deadwood Cemetery Association selected Henry as the sexton of Mount Moriah Cemetery. Six years later, Charles received a certificate of embalming and a funeral director diploma from the Chicago College of Embalming and took over the business. One of the more interesting individuals the Robinsons prepared for burial was Martha "Calamity Jane" Canary, who died on August 1, 1903. (Right, courtesy of Denver Public Library; below, courtesy of CODA.)

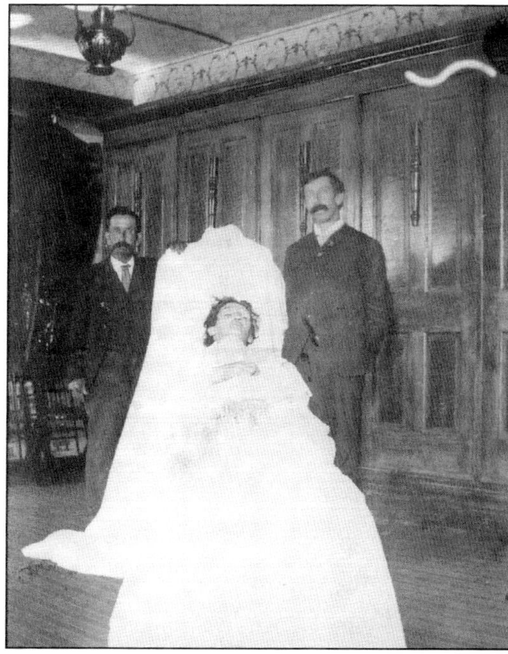

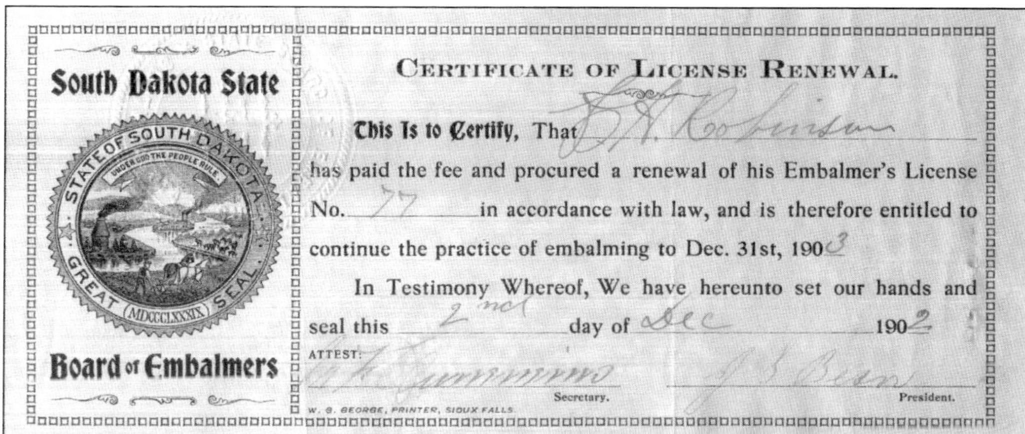

South Dakota State

State of South Dakota · Under God the People Rule · Great Seal · MDCCCLXXXIX

Board of Embalmers

CERTIFICATE OF LICENSE RENEWAL.

This Is to Certify, That [illegible] Robinson

has paid the fee and procured a renewal of his Embalmer's License No. 77 in accordance with law, and is therefore entitled to continue the practice of embalming to Dec. 31st, 1903

In Testimony Whereof, We have hereunto set our hands and seal this 2nd day of Dec 1902

ATTEST: [illegible] Secretary. [illegible] President.

W. B. GEORGE, PRINTER, SIOUX FALLS.

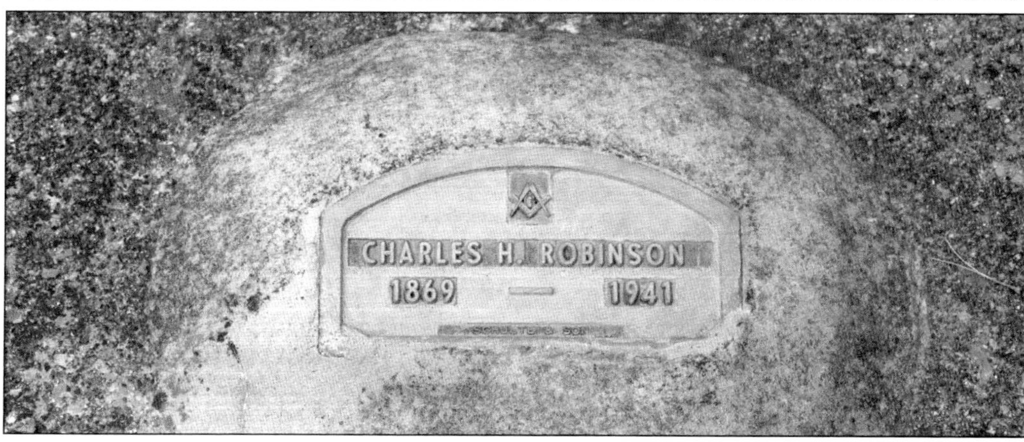

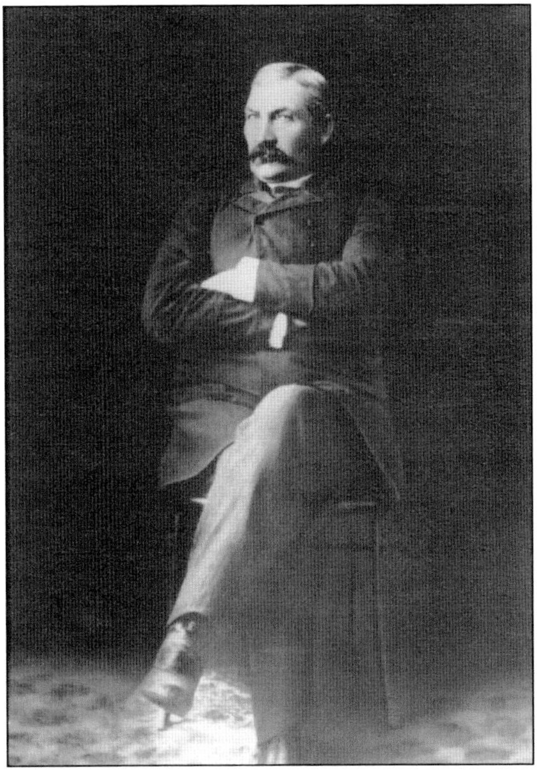

Judge Granville G. Bennett was one of Lawrence County's most decorated attorneys. Bennett was born near Middletown, Ohio, on October 9, 1833. He studied law at Washington College in Iowa and was admitted to the Iowa Bar in 1859. Two years later, Bennett enlisted with the 7th Iowa Infantry as a commissioned officer and served under Gen. Thomas J. McKean. In 1875, Bennett was appointed justice of the Supreme Court of Dakota Territory and held this position for two years. In 1877, Bennett was reassigned as judge of the First Judicial District and helped organize the court system in the Black Hills. In 1902, he was elected Lawrence County probate judge and served three terms before his death in 1910. (Left, courtesy of Deadwood History Inc., Adams Museum Collection; below, courtesy of CODA.)

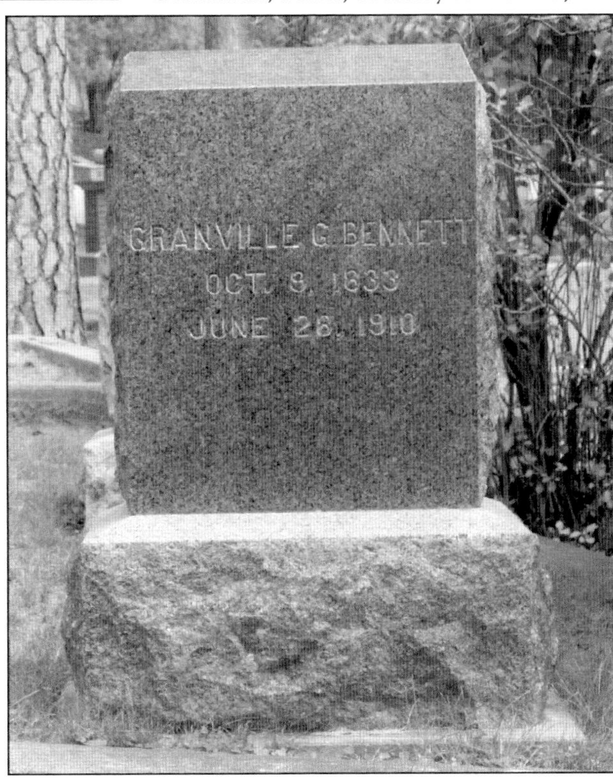

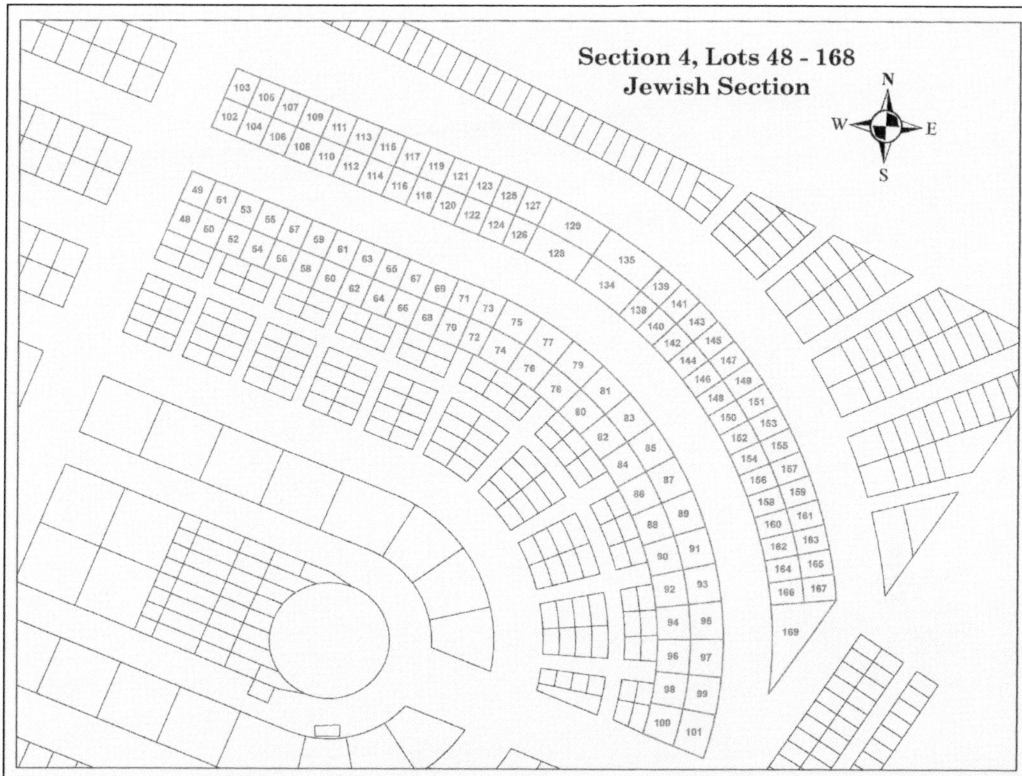

Within the first six months after establishing Mount Moriah, three Jewish burials were interred in Section 4. They were Ben Holstein's child (Lot 107); Bertha Colman, child of Amalia and Nathan Colman (Lot 109); and H. Hutter, who was relocated from Deadwood's first cemetery (Lot 113). Though isolated at first, these burials would eventually become part of the Jewish section in the cemetery. In 1893, the Deadwood Cemetery Association records indicate that the Hebrew Society purchased 119 lots for $200 in Section 4 exclusively for Deadwood's Jewish community. A total of 84 individuals, including some of Deadwood's most noted Jewish families, were buried within these confines. (Both, courtesy of CODA.)

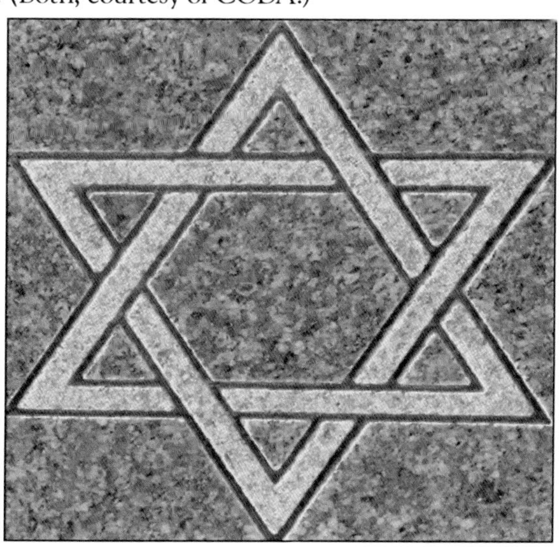

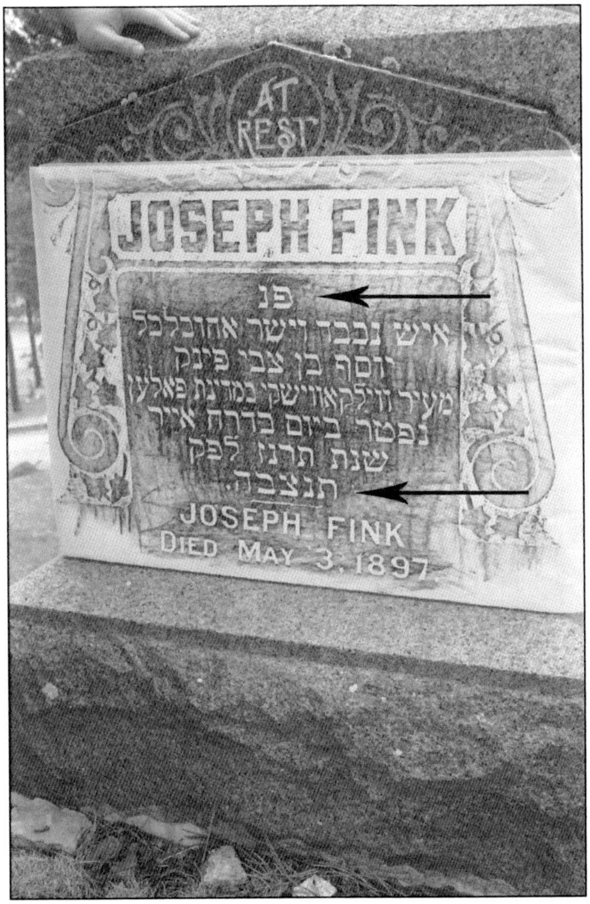

Seven monuments in Section 4 are engraved in Hebrew. In 2010, staff from the Deadwood Historic Preservation Office collected gravestone rubbings for the purpose of transcribing the text. Six monuments contain the Hebrew words *po nikbar* or *po nitman*, which translates to "here lies." These words are located at the top center of the gravestones. The last line of Hebrew text at left contains the phrase, "May he/she be bound up in the bond of everlasting life," which is derived from the book of I Samuel 25:29 and paraphrases the words that Abigail told King David. The epitaph on the Jacob Wertheimer monument (below, Lot 135) contains a paraphrased verse from the book of Lamentations 1:16 that reads "For these things I weep; My eyes run with water on the passing of my husband Jacob the son of Zev Wertheimer." (Both, courtesy of CODA.)

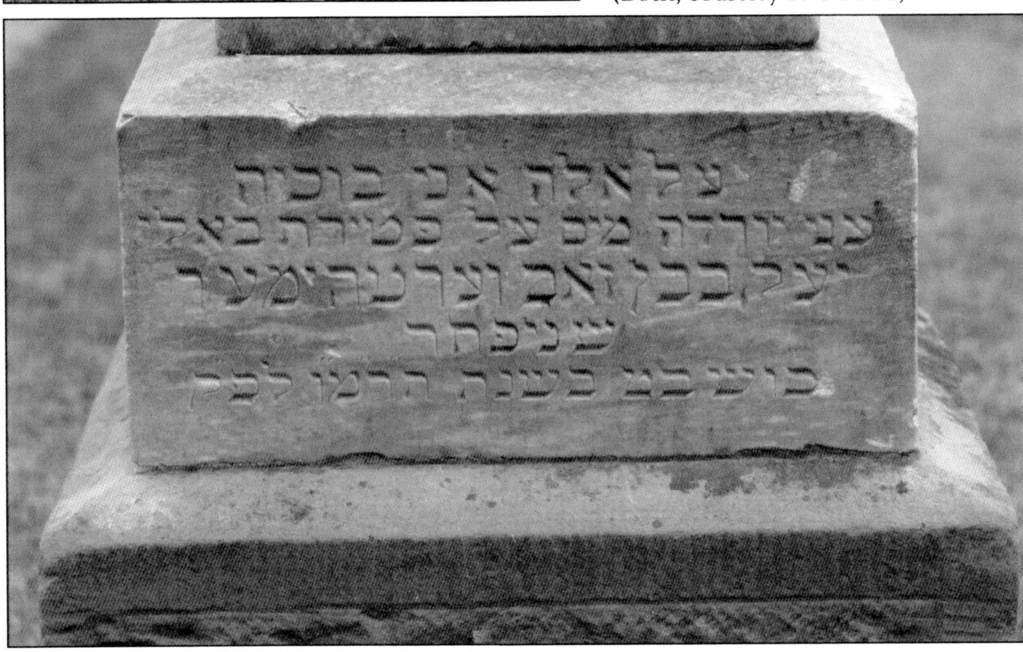

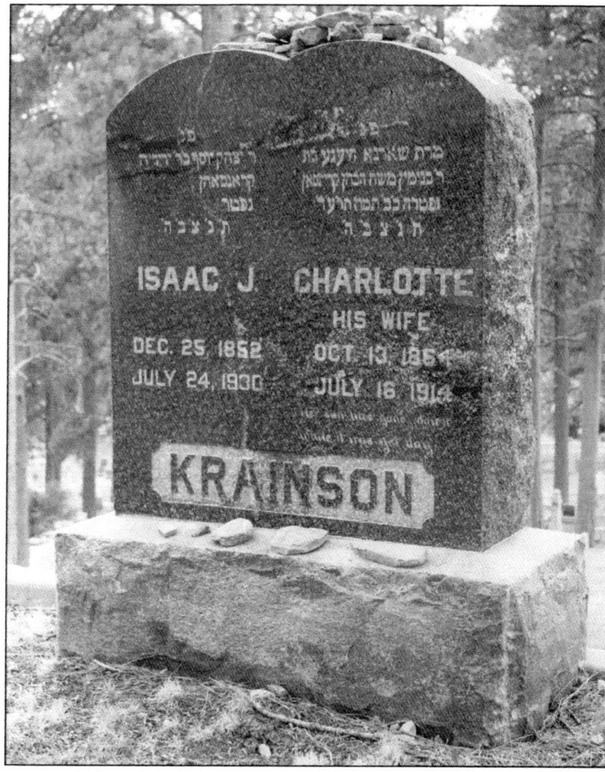

Isaac J. Krainson (December 25, 1852–July 24, 1930) was a soldier and tailor from Lead, South Dakota. Born in Lithuania, Krainson immigrated to the United States and enlisted in the US Army on July 20, 1880. For nine years, Krainson served in the 3rd Infantry at Fort Ellis, Montana Territory, where he worked as a tailor and participated in the Crow Rebellion in 1887. Two years later on March 3, 1889, Krainson was honorably discharged at Fort Meade, Dakota Territory, and settled in Lead, South Dakota, were he operated a tailor shop until his death. The Krainson and Goldbloom monuments in Section 4 contain stylistic elements that resemble the Mosaic Decalogue, or Ten Commandments, brought down from Mount Sinai by Moses as recorded in Exodus 20:1–17. (Both, courtesy of CODA.)

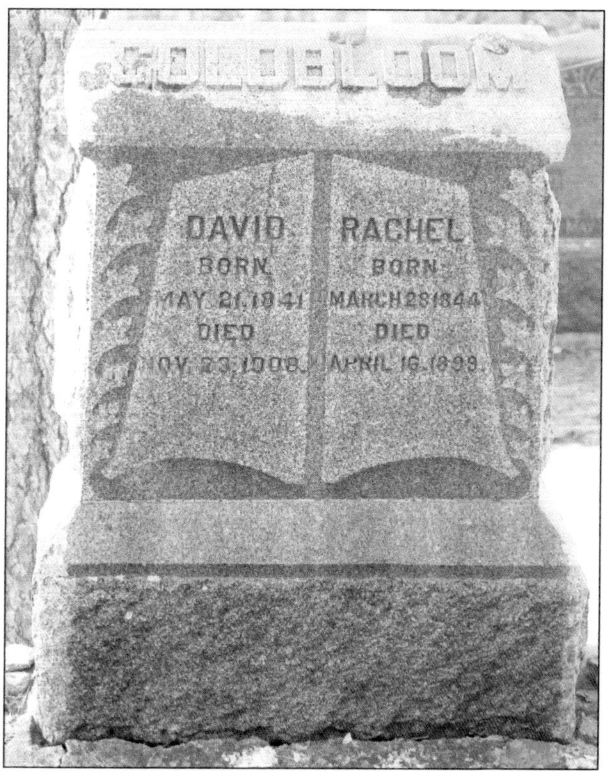

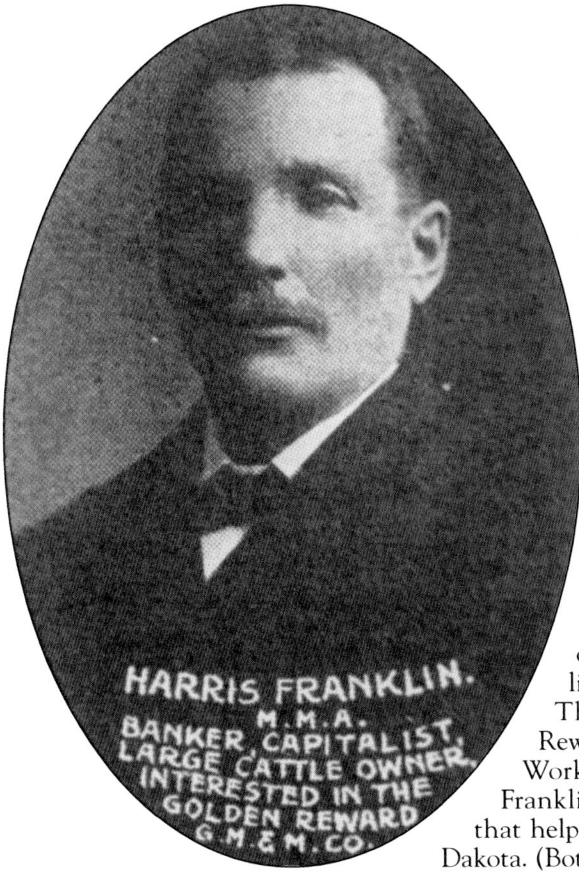

Harris Franklin (March 18, 1849–April 11, 1923) became one of western South Dakota's wealthiest businessmen. Born Harris Finkelstein in either Germany or Poland, in 1864, he immigrated to the United States, changed his last name to Franklin, and settled in Syracuse, New York. Eleven years later, Franklin operated a wholesale liquor business in Wyoming Territory before relocating to Deadwood Gulch in 1878. In 1884, he partnered with Benjamin Baer, one of his competitors, and their business flourished. By 1900, Franklin had a diverse portfolio of business ventures that included mining, livestock, banking, and hotel management. The Franklin Cattle Company, Golden Reward Mining Company and Chlorination Works, American National Bank, and the Franklin Hotel are a few of Franklin's ventures that helped shape Deadwood and western South Dakota. (Both, courtesy of CODA.)

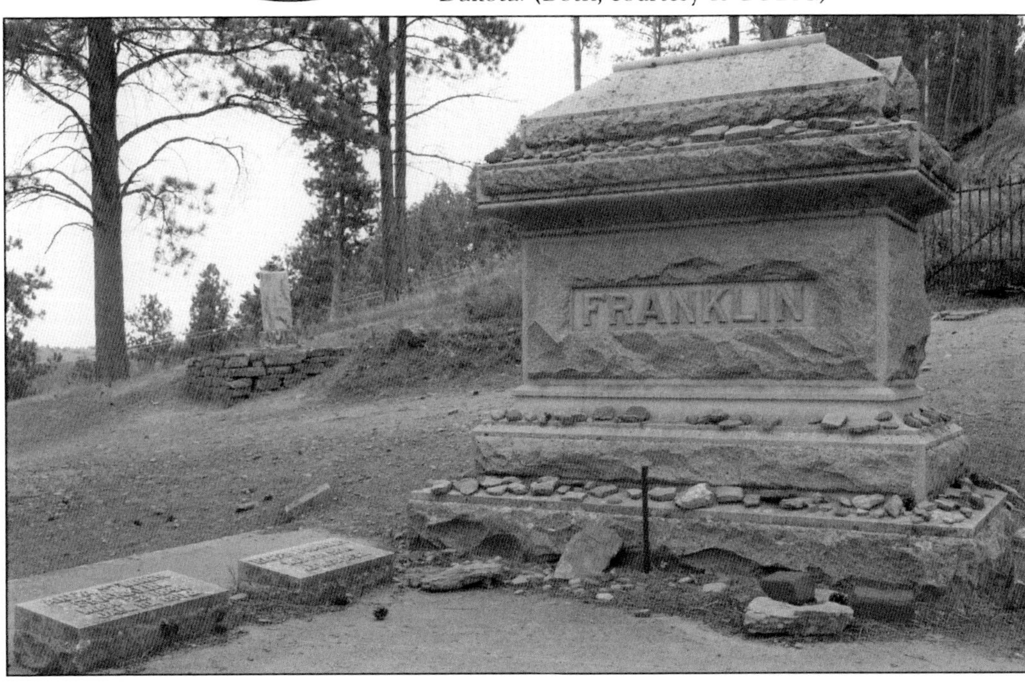

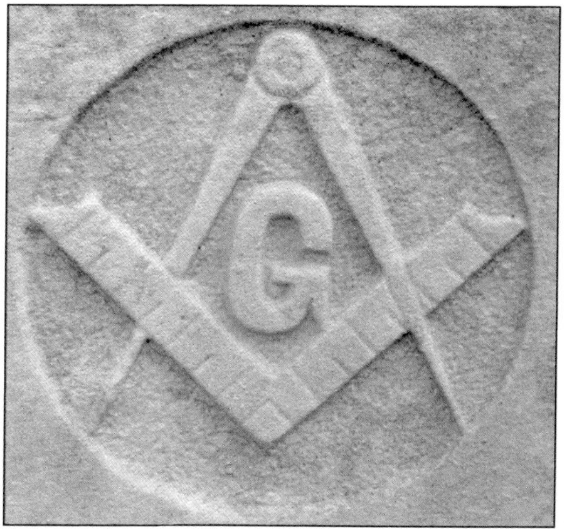

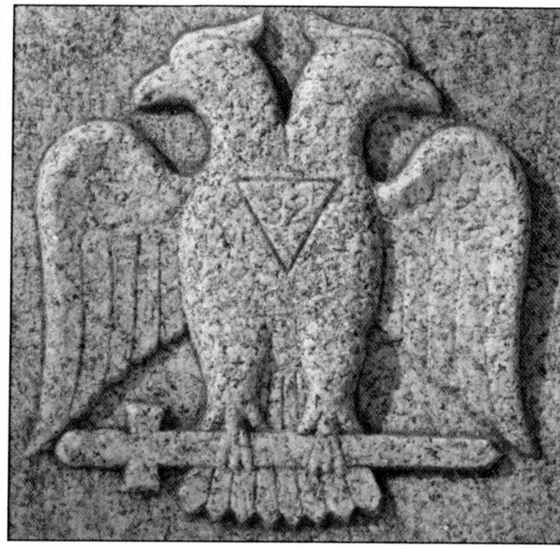

On June 13, 1877, Lodge No. 7 of the Ancient Free and Accepted Masons was incorporated in Deadwood Gulch. By 1900, several concordant bodies of Masonry, including the Scottish Rite, York Rite, Order of the Eastern Star, and the Naja Shriners, were organized in the Deadwood Lodge. Many of the crests from these fraternal organizations adorn the monuments in Mount Moriah Cemetery. Examples include the square and compass (Pollock plot, Section 2, Lot 10), double-headed eagle of the Scottish Rite (Phillips plot, Section 10, Lot 4), inverted five-point star of Order of the Eastern Star (Allen plot, Section 1, Lot 118), and the crescent and scimitar of the Naja Shriners (Williams plot, Section 10, Lot 51). (All, courtesy of CODA.)

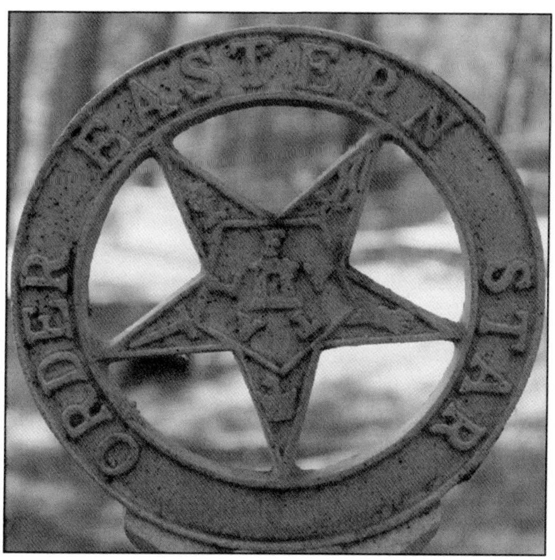

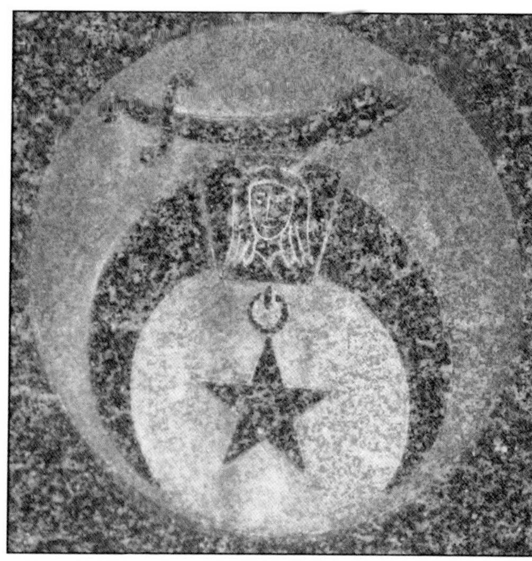

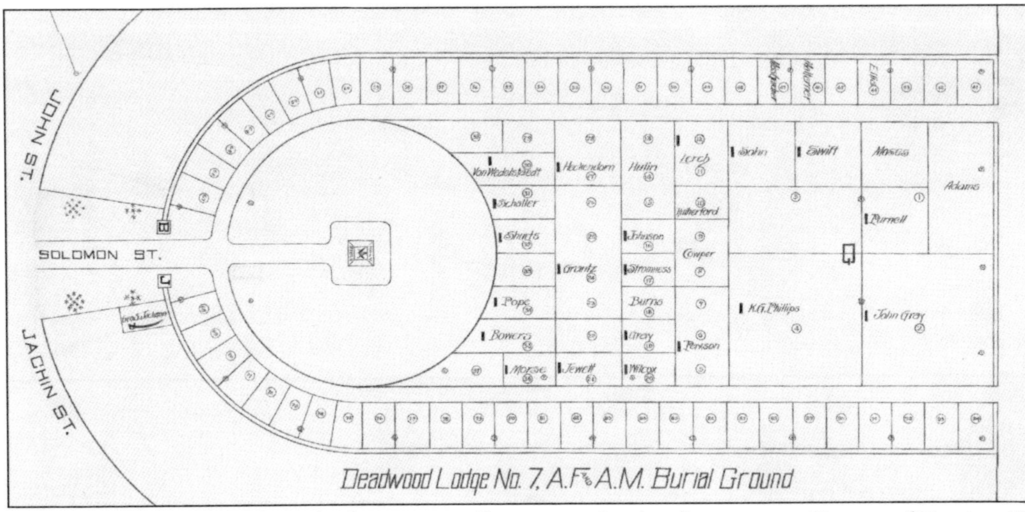

The Deadwood Masons have had a strong influence on the development and layout of Section 10. In 1887, Lodge No. 7 purchased 1.5 acres, including Lots 1 through 7 and A through E, according to the 1879 cemetery map. After 1894, Section 10 became recognized as the Masonic Section. Ten years later, Lodge No. 7 began a beautification project that included concrete sidewalks, a low wall, and an altar made from St. Cloud granite. The altar base contains the names of 18 individuals buried within 25 feet of this monument. Section 10 embodies a physical representation of a Masonic celestial lodge complete with a tiler, pillars, altar, and worshipful master. (Above, courtesy of Deadwood Historic Lodge No. 7; below, courtesy of CODA.)

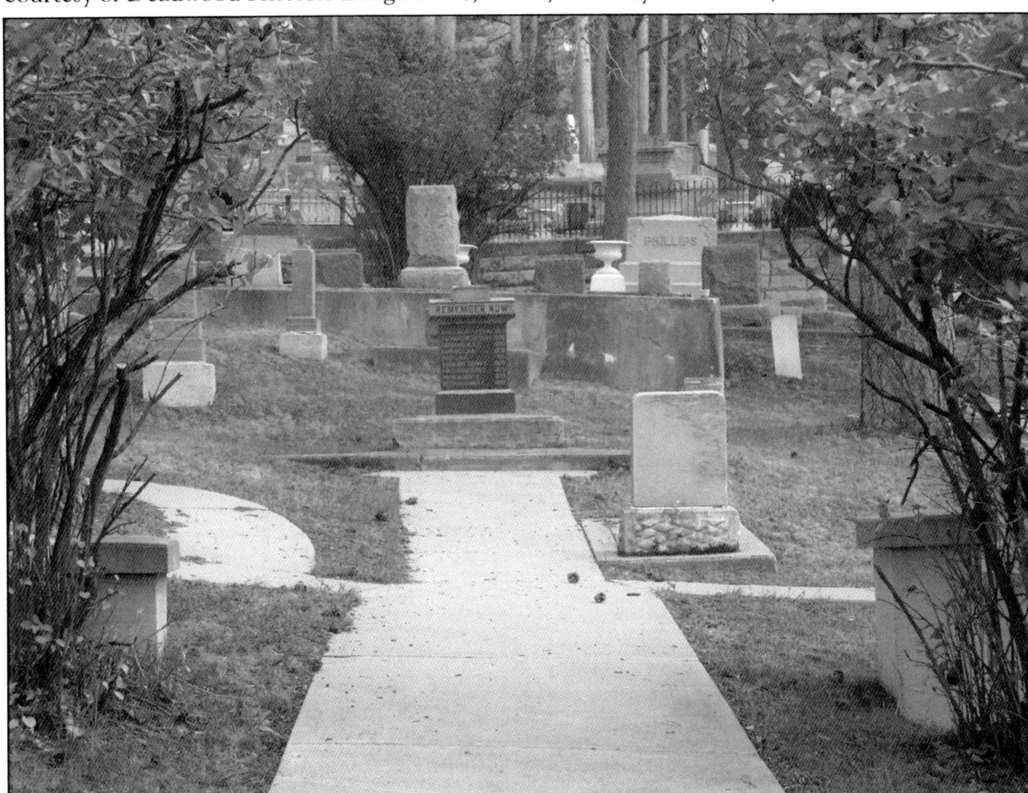

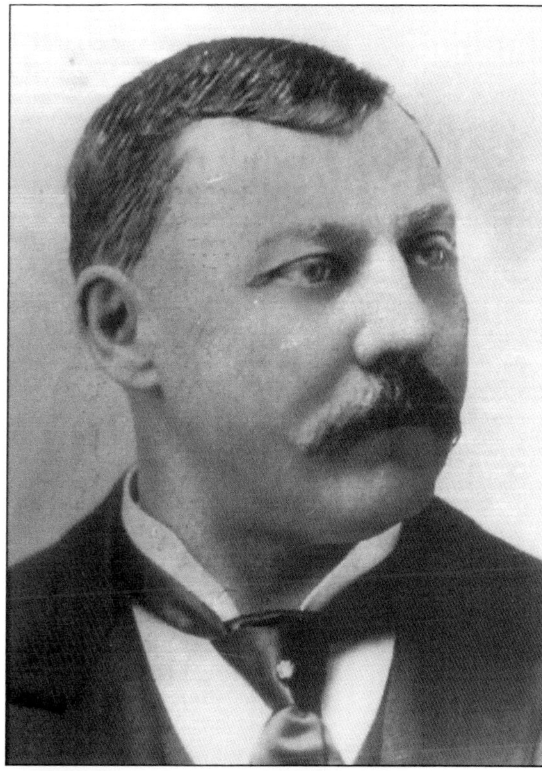

Kirk Gunby Phillips (November 25, 1851–August 7, 1913) was a prominent Deadwood Mason and well-known civil servant. In 1876, Phillips came to Deadwood Gulch and opened a pharmaceutical business on Main Street and soon became involved in local, county, and state government. In 1882, Phillips was elected Deadwood mayor. Three years later, he was elected Lawrence County treasurer and served for six years. From 1894 to 1896, Phillips served two terms as the South Dakota state treasurer before running for governor and losing by a very narrow margin. Phillips was a member of Deadwood's Masonic lodge and obtained the 32nd degree in the Scottish Rite. (Both, courtesy of CODA.)

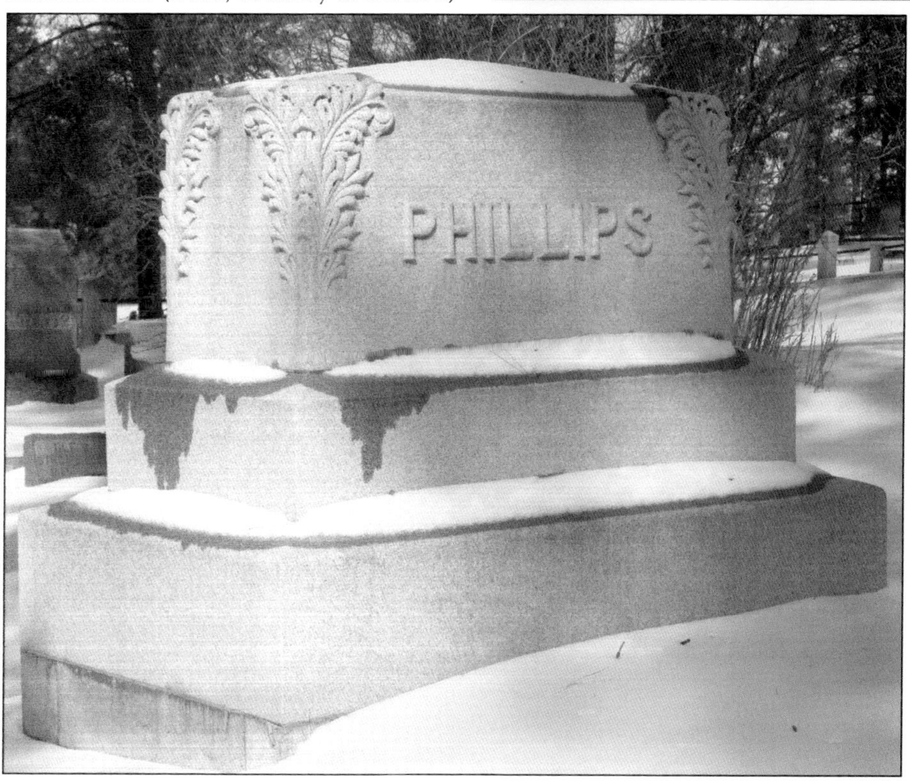

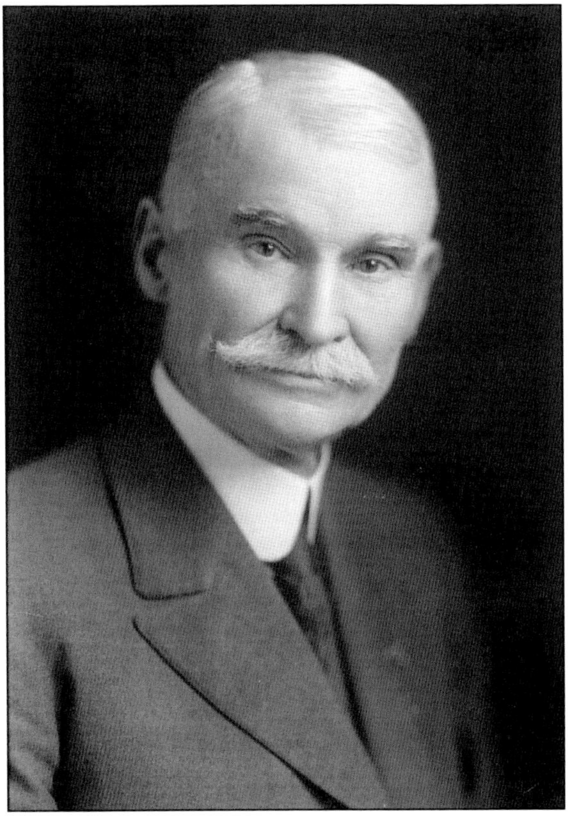

William Emery Adams was one of Deadwood's most successful businessmen. Born in Bertrand, Michigan, he grew up on a farm near Faribault, Minnesota. In March 1877, Adams and his brother opened a wholesale and retail grocery store near the corner of Main and Wall Streets in Deadwood. The Adams Bros. Company became one of the largest businesses in western South Dakota. The Adams Block, on Sherman Street, supplied businesses in Wyoming, Montana, and western South Dakota. Adams served five terms as mayor of Deadwood. His greatest accomplishment was the Adams Memorial Museum, built in 1930 at a cost of $75,000. The museum was then presented to the City of Deadwood. Although Adams and his family are buried in California, they still have a marked plot in Mount Moriah. (Left, courtesy of Deadwood Public Library; below, courtesy of CODA.)

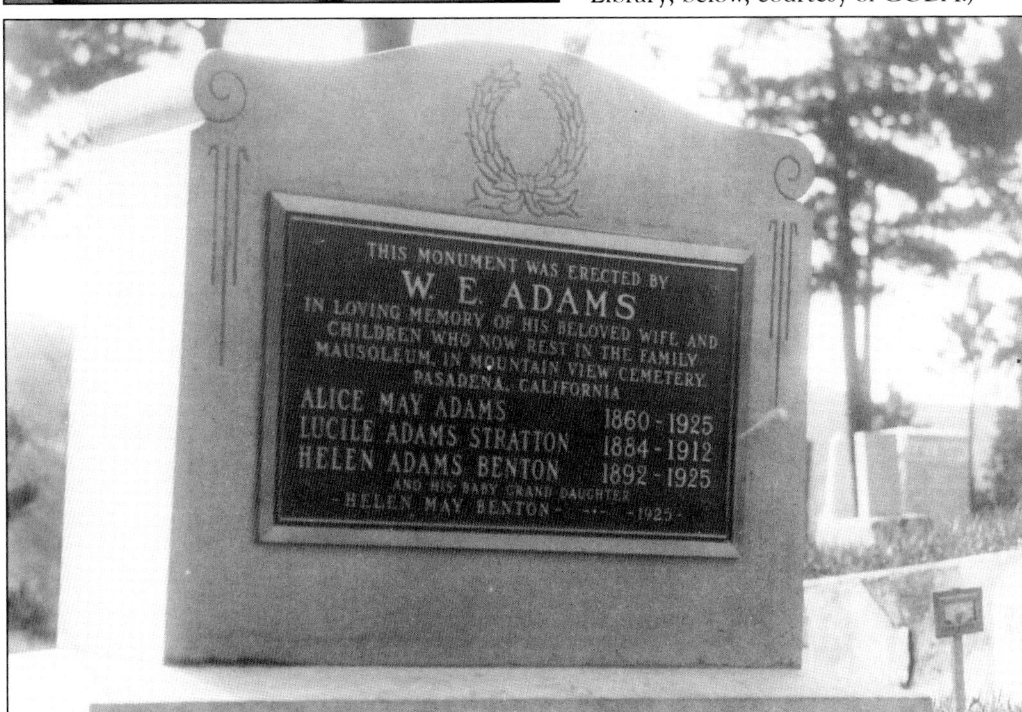

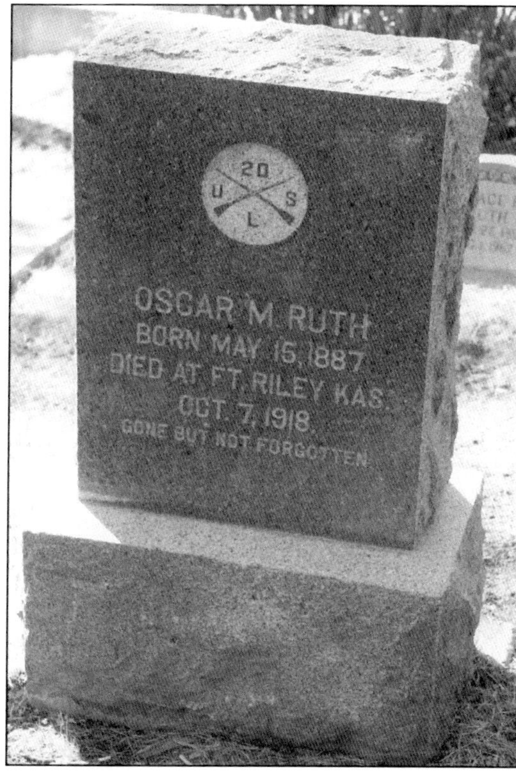

Oscar Ruth (May 15, 1887–October 7, 1918) was one of Lawrence County's World War I military casualties. In 1918, Ruth was called for the draft as part of the Lawrence County contingent. That fall, the United States suffered a nationwide epidemic of Spanish influenza. The symptoms began as a common cold that escalated into a deadly strain of pneumonia. Areas hardest hit by this epidemic were large urban centers and Army training camps, including Camp Funston located at Fort Riley, near Manhattan, Kansas. On October 7, 1918, Ruth died at Camp Funston after contracting the flu. His remains were sent to Deadwood for burial in Mount Moriah. Though Ruth never made it overseas, his name was included on a memorial in front of the Lawrence County Courthouse commemorating those who lost their lives during World War I. (Both, courtesy of CODA.)

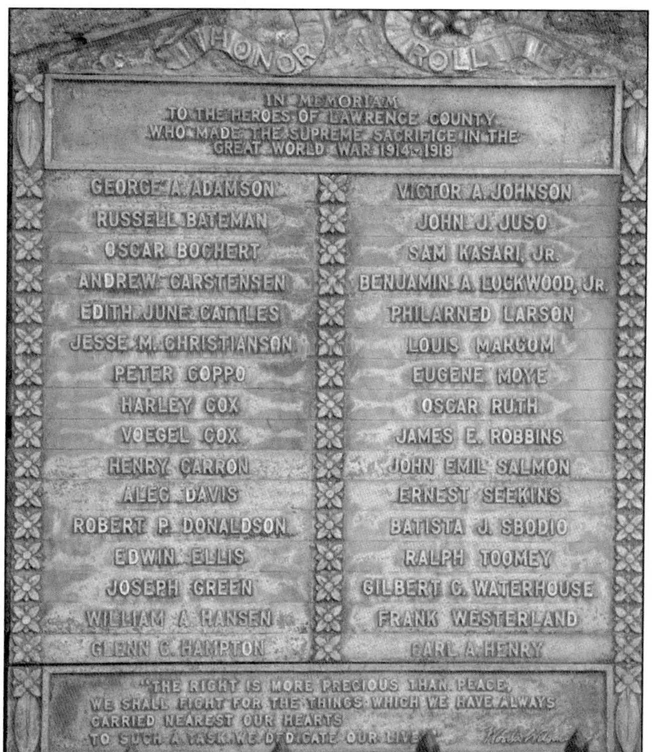

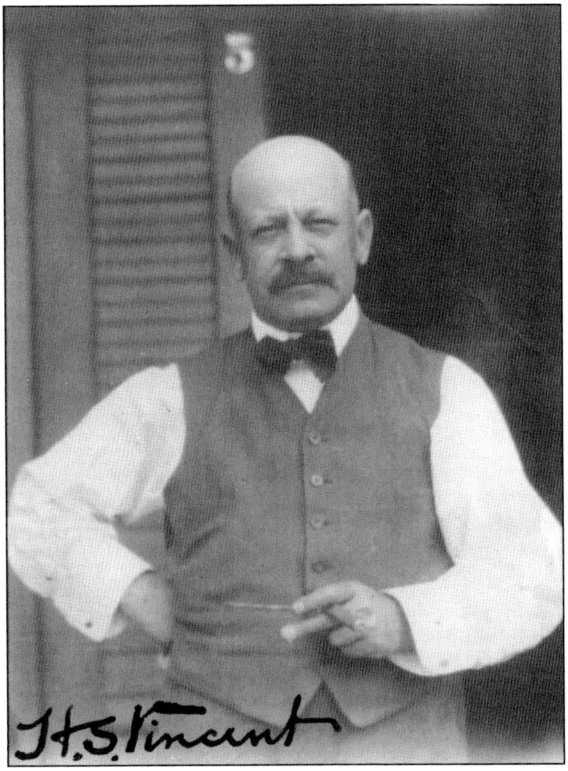

Hobart S. Vincent was a civil engineer, mine manager, and mayor of Deadwood. He was born on January 22, 1867, in Pennsylvania and spent most of his childhood in Onawa, Iowa. Vincent received his formal education from Shattuck Military Academy in Faribault, Minnesota, where he learned civil engineering. In 1889, he found employment as a civil engineer working for several railroad companies in western South Dakota before opening a private practice in Deadwood in 1897. Fourteen years later, Vincent became the site superintendent and manager of the Trojan Mining Company based out of Deadwood. He also served as Deadwood mayor from 1918 to 1920 during the Spanish influenza outbreak and coal strike. (Left, courtesy of Colburn family collection; below, courtesy of CODA.)

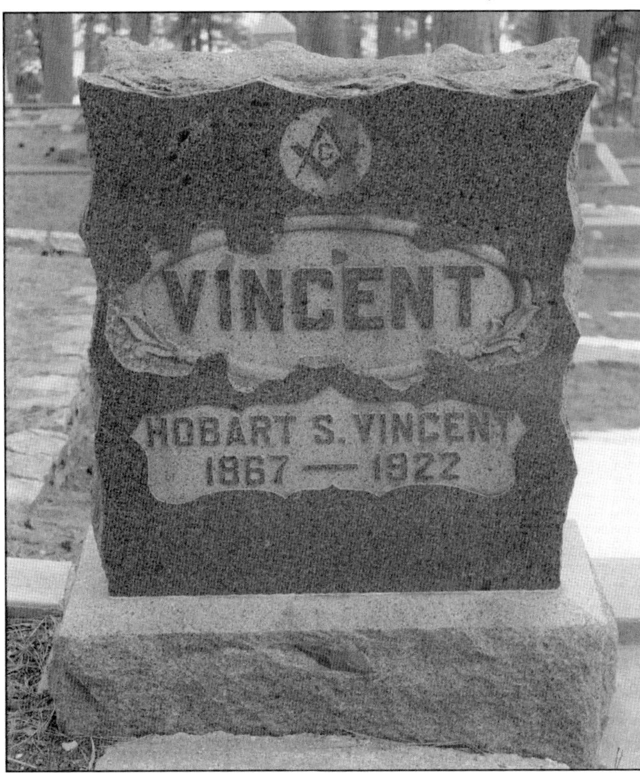

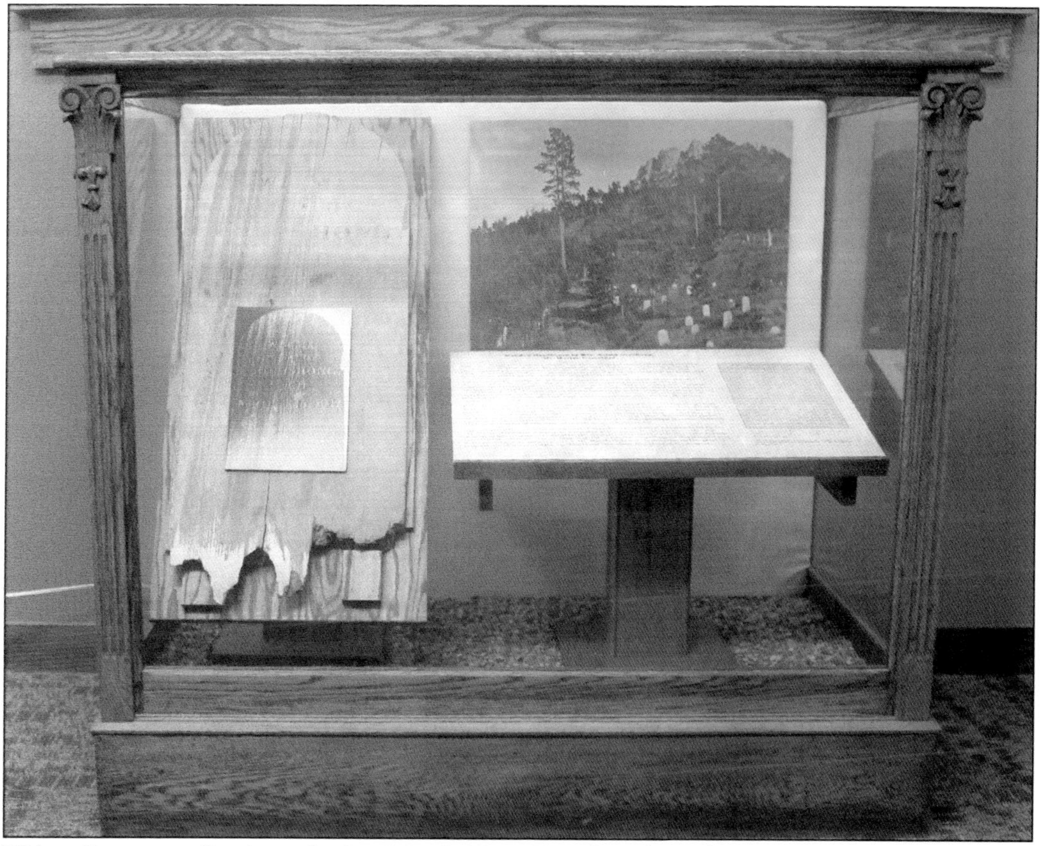

Wilma Crampton Groshong died on March 27, 1917, and was buried in Section 11, Lot 3. Her grave was originally marked with this painted wooden headboard. Wooden headboards were common throughout the 19th century and were manufactured from rot-resistant wood such as cypress, cedar, or heart pine and coated with white paint. The life expectancy was determined by several factors, including weather, maintenance, vandalism, theft, and fire. One or more of these factors are the reason why all of the wooden headboards have vanished from Mount Moriah Cemetery. In 2008, the Groshong headboard was returned to the Deadwood Historic Preservation Office and was placed on exhibit in the Mount Moriah Cemetery Visitor Center. Although it is illegal to remove cemetery monuments, this act of vandalism ultimately preserved Groshong's marker. (Both, courtesy of CODA.)

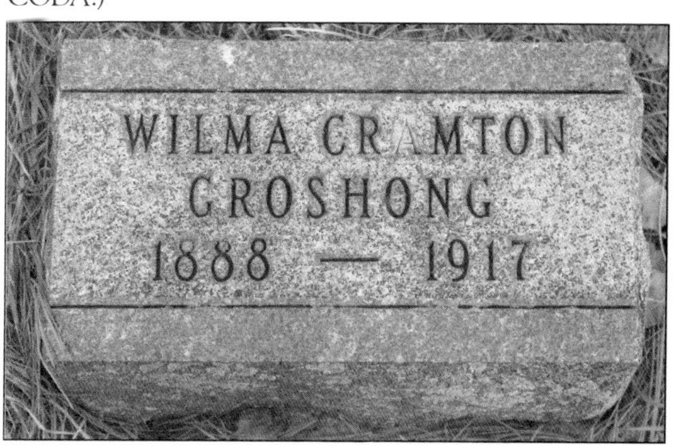

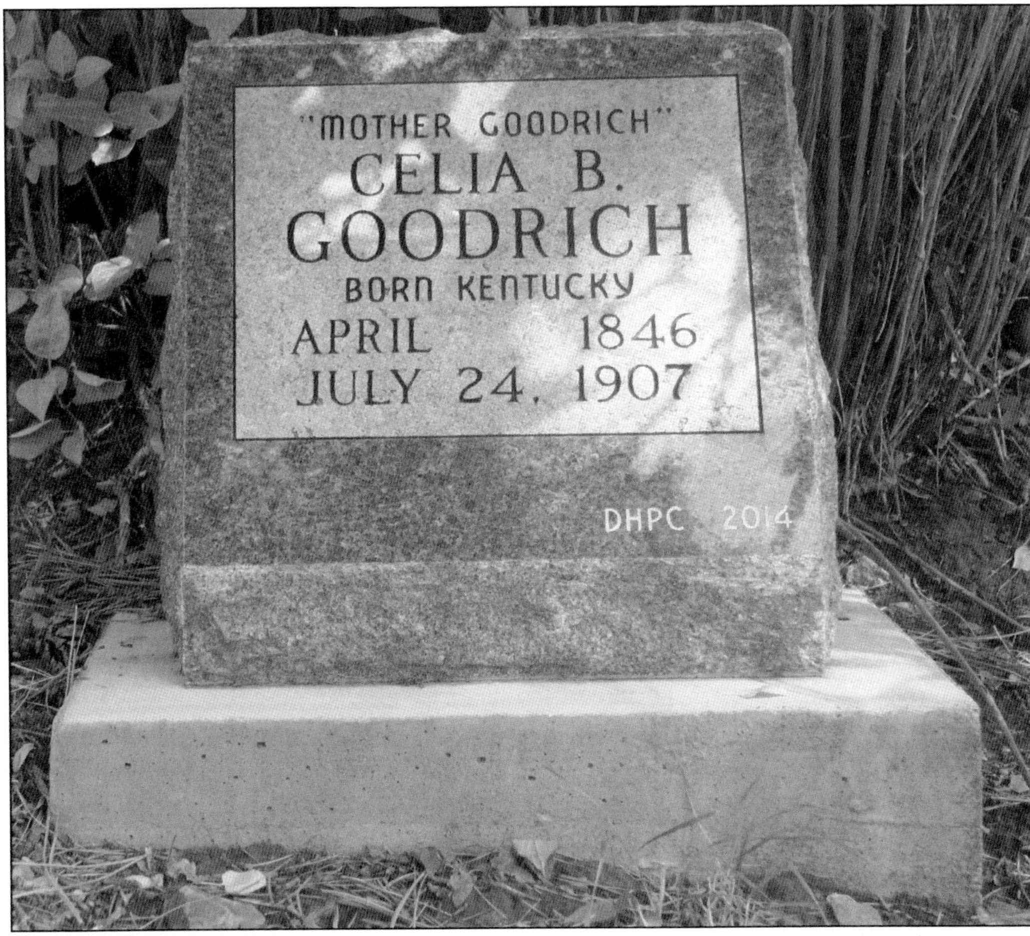

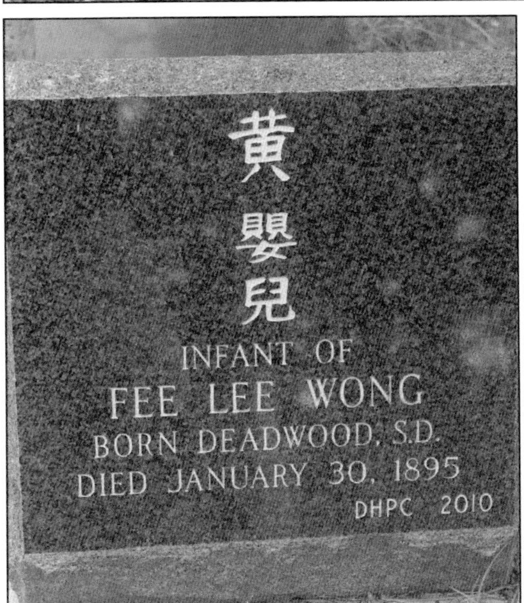

Beginning in 2005, the Deadwood Historic Preservation Commission allocated funds for the creation and installation of permanent cemetery markers for unmarked graves in Mount Moriah Cemetery. It is known as the Cemetery Headstone Grant Program, and family members are encouraged to complete an application and assemble genealogical information on individuals and families interred in Mount Moriah Cemetery. If awarded the grant, the recipient will receive a wedge-shaped granite headstone that contains the basic vital information. The markers will also have the letters DHPC, or Deadwood Historic Preservation Commission, and the year the monument was installed. Burials that predate 1950 are eligible for the program. These two photographs provide a representation of monuments that have been placed as a result of this program. (Both, courtesy of CODA.)

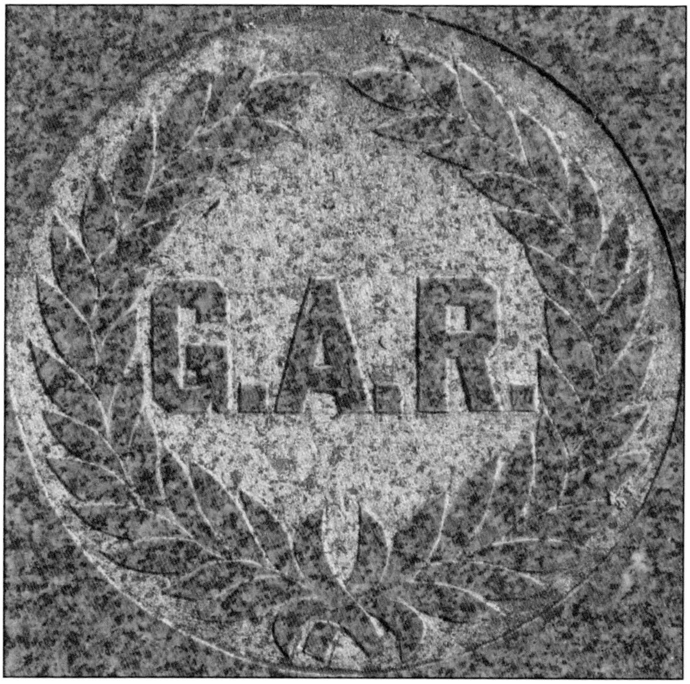

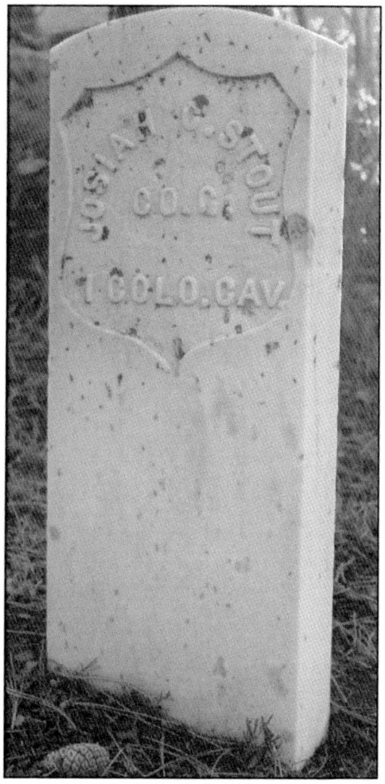

On May 29, 1884, Keogh Post No. 64 of the Grand Army of the Republic (GAR) was formed in Deadwood. The GAR was an organization for honorably discharged Union Civil War veterans. The GAR provided camaraderie for veterans, established soldier's homes, lobbied for soldier's pensions, and established Memorial Day, May 30, as a national day of remembrance. There are 26 burials in Sections 1 and 2 associated with the Deadwood GAR (below). Several of these monuments contain a laurel wreath surrounding the letters "G.A.R." (Rudy plot, Section 1, Lot 1). Other GAR burials contain a government-issued marble grave marker with a recessed shield design (Stout plot, Section 1, Lot 1). This monument design also denotes veterans of the Indian Wars era and the 1898 Spanish-American War. (Above, both courtesy of CODA; below, courtesy of Deadwood Public Library.)

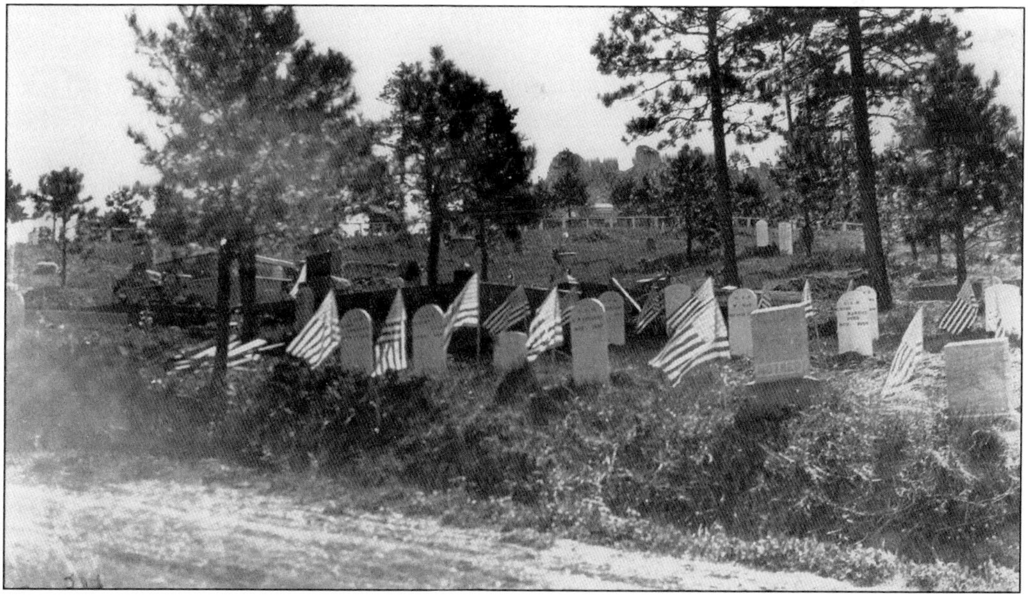

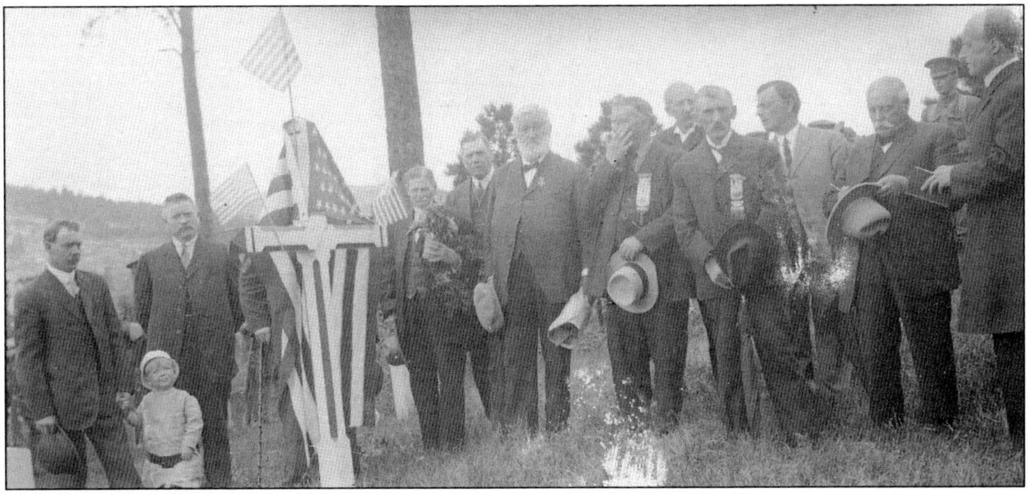

Memorial Day, or Decoration Day, was originally created to honor the men and women who fought and died during the Civil War. Gen. John A. Logan, Union officer, founder of the Grand Army of the Republic, and longtime politician, has been credited with initiating this holiday. Communities such as Deadwood were encouraged to close their businesses and decorate the graves of veterans and loved ones. The first observed Memorial Day in Deadwood occurred on May 29, 1884, and coincided with the organization of the Deadwood GAR Keogh Post No. 64. Early Memorial Day observations were community-wide events that included an assortment of activities, public addresses, and music. Local newspapers ran lengthy articles covering the day's events and published excerpts from the speeches. Visitation to Mount Moriah Cemetery was always part of this annual event. (Both, courtesy of Deadwood Public Library.)

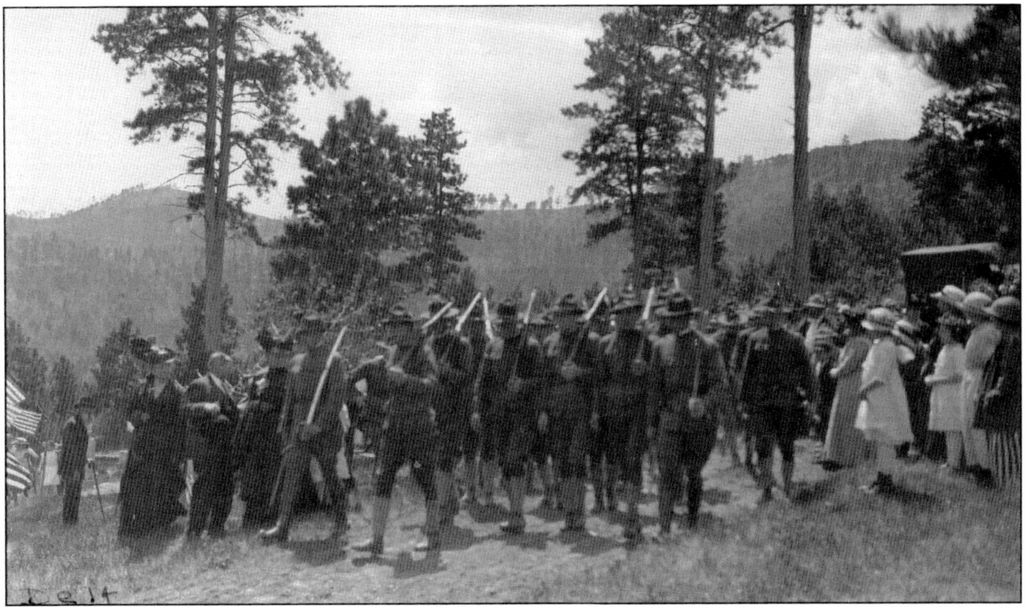

Some fraternal organizations offered benefits to their members. Examples of these organizations represented in Mount Moriah Cemetery are the Ancient Order of United Workmen (AOUW) and the Modern Woodmen of America (MWA). In 1887, Deadwood Lodge No. 51 of the AOUW was chartered and offered life insurance to its members. Members of this organization can be identified by the emblem containing the letters "A.O.U.W." inside a Swiss-style shield in front of an anchor (Conant plot, Section 4, Lot 2). Deadwood Camp No. 1186 of the Modern Woodmen of America was chartered in the 1890s and also offered life insurance to its members. Members of this organization can be recognized by the letters "MWA" inside a log or maple leaf. A crossed ax and maul are sometimes included in the organization's insignia (Landfried plot, Section 1, Lot 24). (Both, courtesy of CODA.)

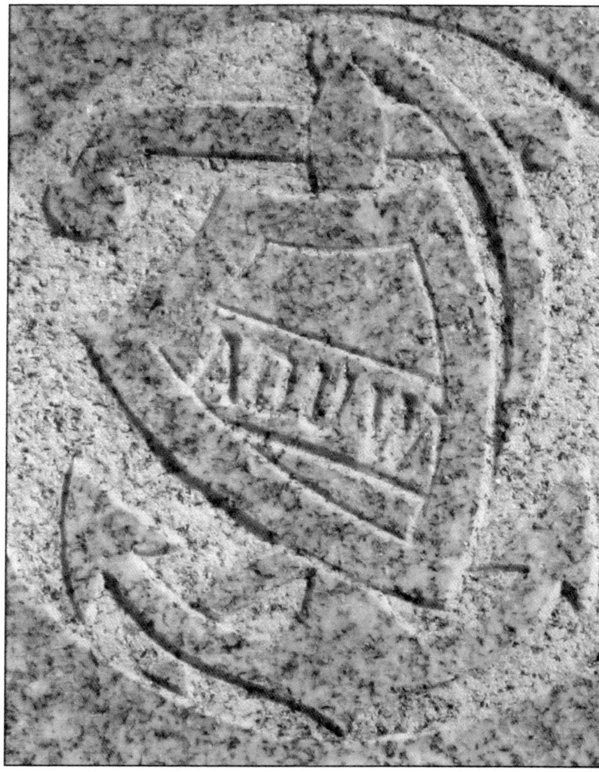

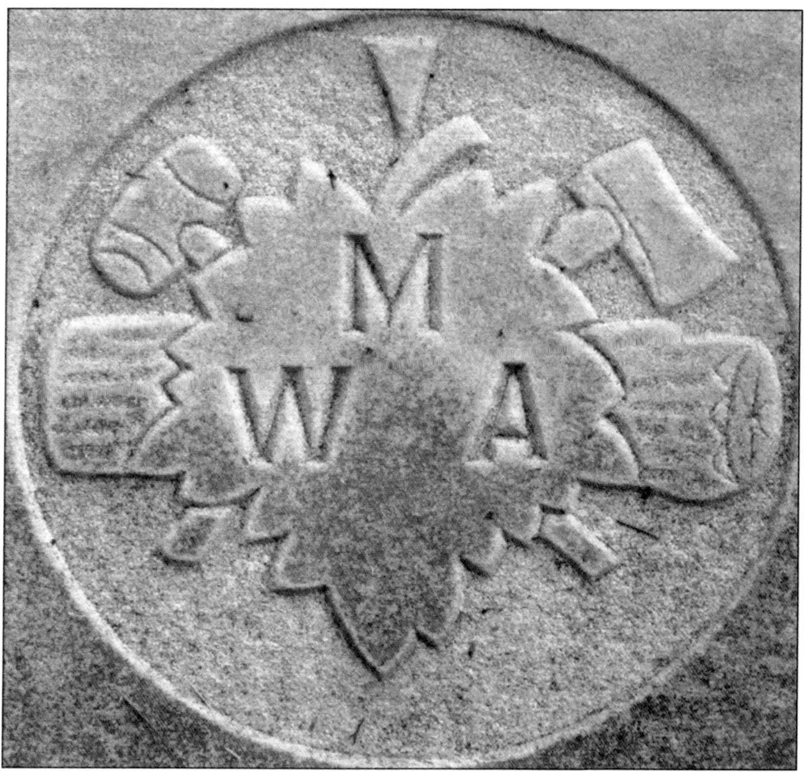

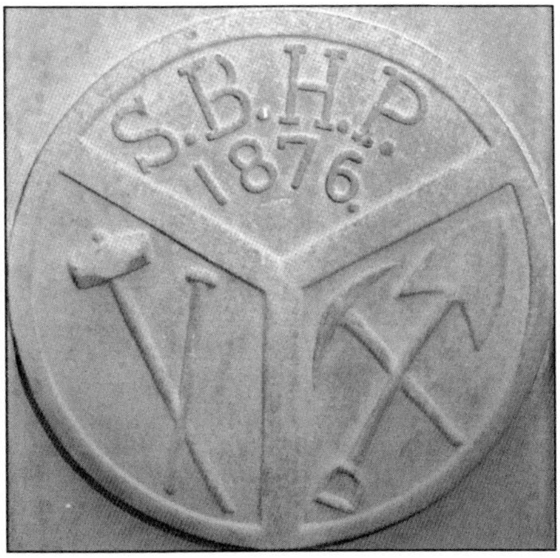

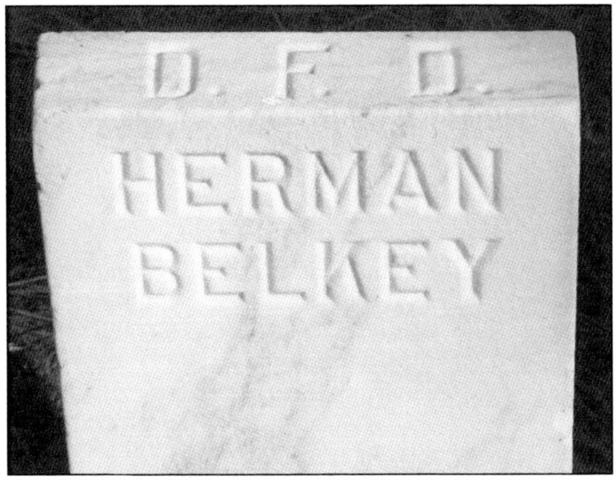

The Society of the Black Hills Pioneers is a local fraternal group that organized on January 8, 1889, to recognize individuals who arrived in the Black Hills before December 31, 1876. The Flynn plot (Section 9, Lot 23) is one of several examples showing the society's crest. After 1877, several fire brigades were organized in Deadwood Gulch, including the Pioneer Hook & Ladder Company, the South Deadwood Hose Company, the Deadwood Hose Company, the Homestake Hose Company, and the Fountain City Hose & Ladder Company. In 1941, the brigades were combined to form the Deadwood Volunteer Fire Department. Numerous plots in the cemetery contain "D.F.D.," denoting the fire department, or contain a fireman's helmet, ladder, pike pole, and nozzle, as on the Rogers monument in Section 3, Lot 82. (All, courtesy of CODA.)

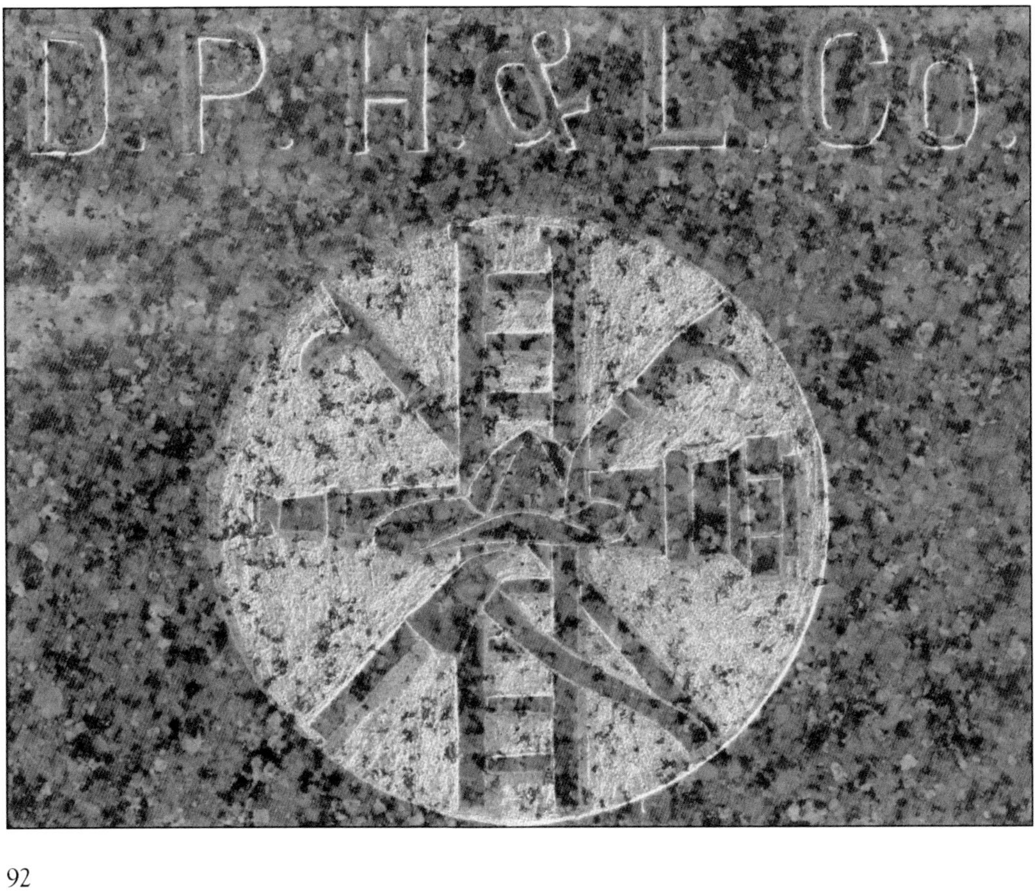

On April 13, 1879, the Knights of Pythias (KOP) No. 3 Lodge, Marco Bozzaris, was organized in Deadwood Gulch with 60 members. The KOP is a fraternal organization with its beliefs originating from the Greek story of Damon and Pythias. The letters "F.C.B." are derived from the Knights motto, "Friendship, Charity, and Benevolence," as seen on the Mills plot (Section 1, Lot 75). The Deadwood lodge was named after Marco Bozzaris, a Greek general of the Greek War of Independence. Deadwood's Benevolent and Protective Order of Elks Lodge No. 508 was chartered on August 11, 1899, with 50 members. The Elks is the largest of the animal-themed fraternal organizations in America. Several monuments in the cemetery contain the letters "B.P.O.E." or an elk head with the same letters (Forest plot, Section 3, Lot 2). (Both, courtesy of CODA.)

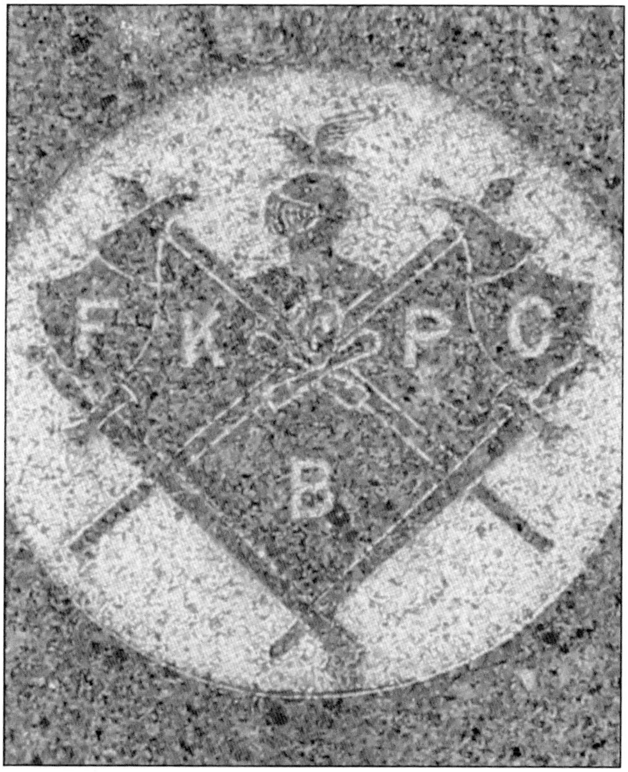

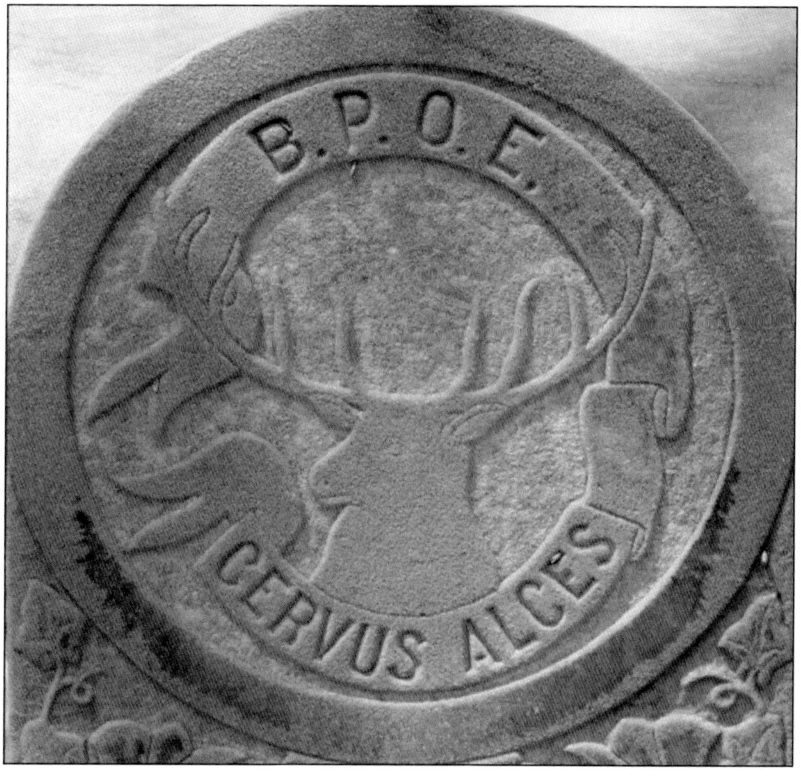

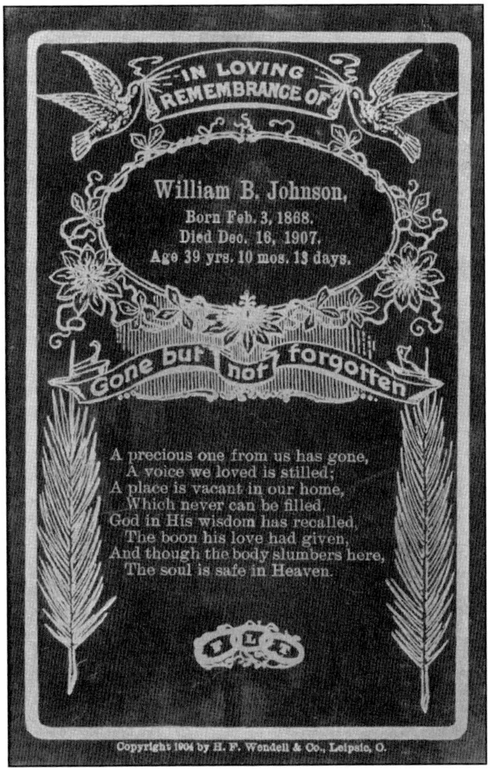

On July 5, 1877, Eureka Lodge No. 13 of the Independent Order of Odd Fellows (IOOF) was incorporated in Deadwood Gulch and became one of Deadwood's more popular fraternal associations. This fraternal group is easily recognized by the three-link chain with the letters F, L, and T (Friendship, Love, and Truth) placed in the center of each link. In addition to providing fellowship and camaraderie, the Odd Fellows offered death benefits, including funeral arrangements, burial, and grave markers, to its members. Section 11 of Mount Moriah Cemetery was devoted to the burial of IOOF members. However, many Odd Fellow cemetery markers are located throughout the cemetery (Roas plot, Third Addition, Section 1, Lot 27). (Both, courtesy of CODA.)

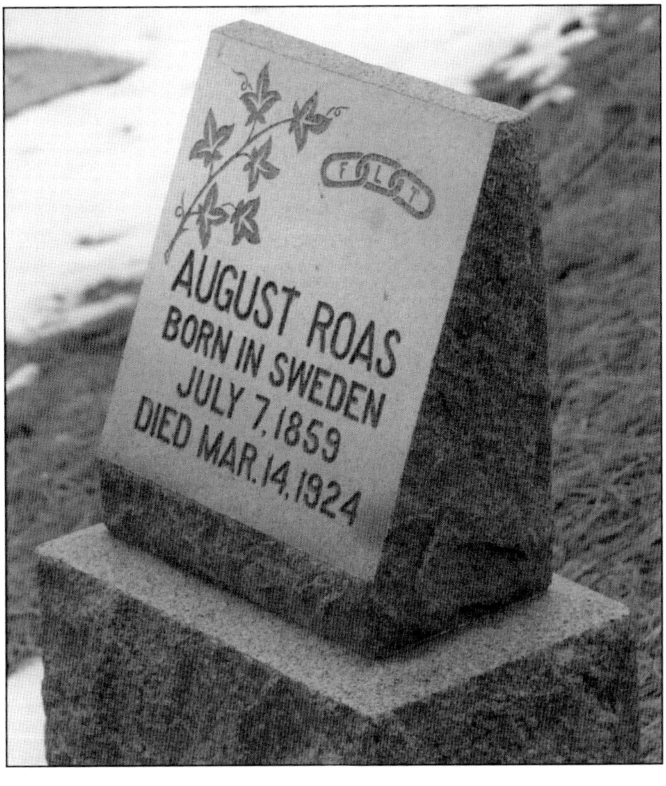

Four

Third Addition, Sections 1 and 2

In 1914, the Deadwood Cemetery Association acquired 9.5 acres of land to the east of the original oval boundary from the Austin Mabbs estate for $450. Of the total acreage, approximately one-third could be readily used for burials. This land acquisition came at a perfect time. According to a newspaper article published on January 16, 1914, "It was calculated that the grounds now in use will last not over 8 or 10 years longer; hence the new ground was secured timely." In 1921, the Deadwood Cemetery Association hired civil engineer Frank S. Peck to plat the new land. Upon completion, David Street would divide the newly acquired land into two sections. Over time, these sections would pose some interesting challenges in the way of hillslope drainage and soil erosion. To combat these issues, concrete retaining walls were installed around some of the plots. Despite best efforts, the continual drainage problem began to compromise the monuments and retaining walls. Many of the monuments in this section postdate 1914 and are carved from an assortment of regional and national granites. This section also has a few homespun monuments that add a unique character to the cemetery.

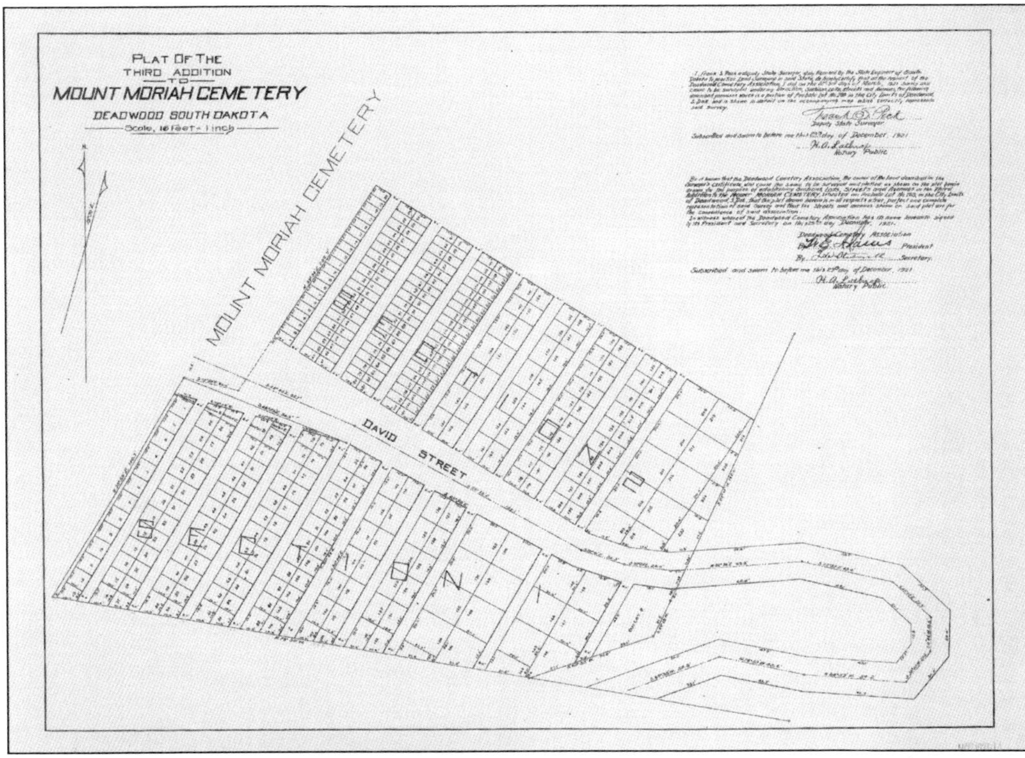

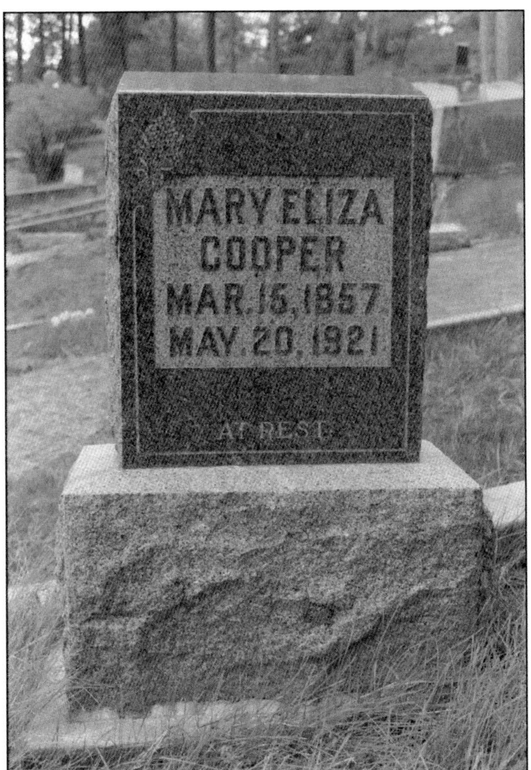

When visitors see Mount Moriah Cemetery for the first time, they are actually looking at the Third Addition, the newer part of the cemetery. Third Addition Sections 1 and 2 were purchased in 1914 by the Deadwood Cemetery Association. Seven years after the land acquisition from the Mabbs Estate, the Third Addition was opened for burials. Mary Eliza Cooper was the first burial in the new sections on May 20, 1921. Over the next 95 years, more than 630 people were interred in the Third Addition. The Frank Peck plat map, drawn in 1921, shows the layout of the Third Addition. (Both, courtesy of CODA.)

George M. Butler was the son of Squire T. Butler, jeweler and designer of Black Hills gold jewelry. George was born in 1851 in Havana, New York, and grew up in St. Joseph, Missouri. In 1877, his parents moved to Deadwood and opened a jewelry store. His father manufactured and repaired jewelry, watches, and optical goods and is credited with introducing the grape and leaf design that became synonymous with Black Hills gold jewelry. In 1881, George Butler moved to Deadwood and worked with his father. He and his nephew F.L. Thorpe continued manufacturing and retail sales of Black Hills gold jewelry after Squire Butler's death. In 1930, John "Potato Creek Johnny" Perrett (left) and George Butler (right) posed for this photograph in front of Butler's store at 678 Main Street. (Right, courtesy of Marjorie Pontius Collection; below, courtesy of CODA.)

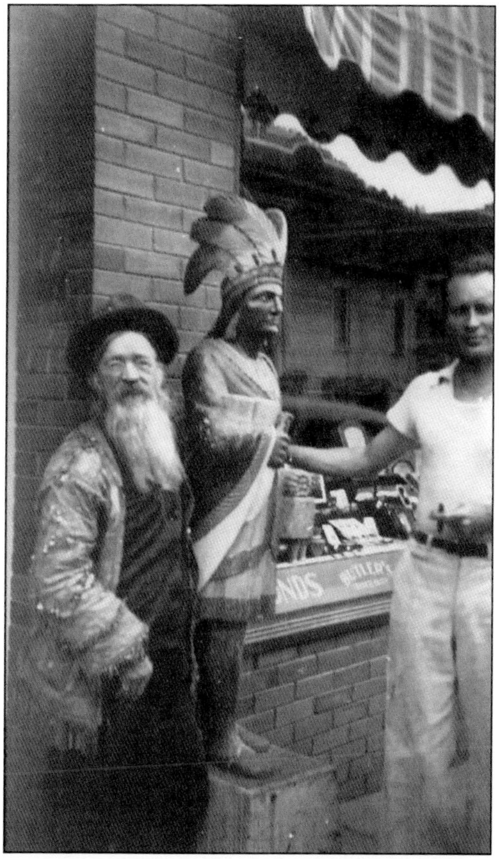

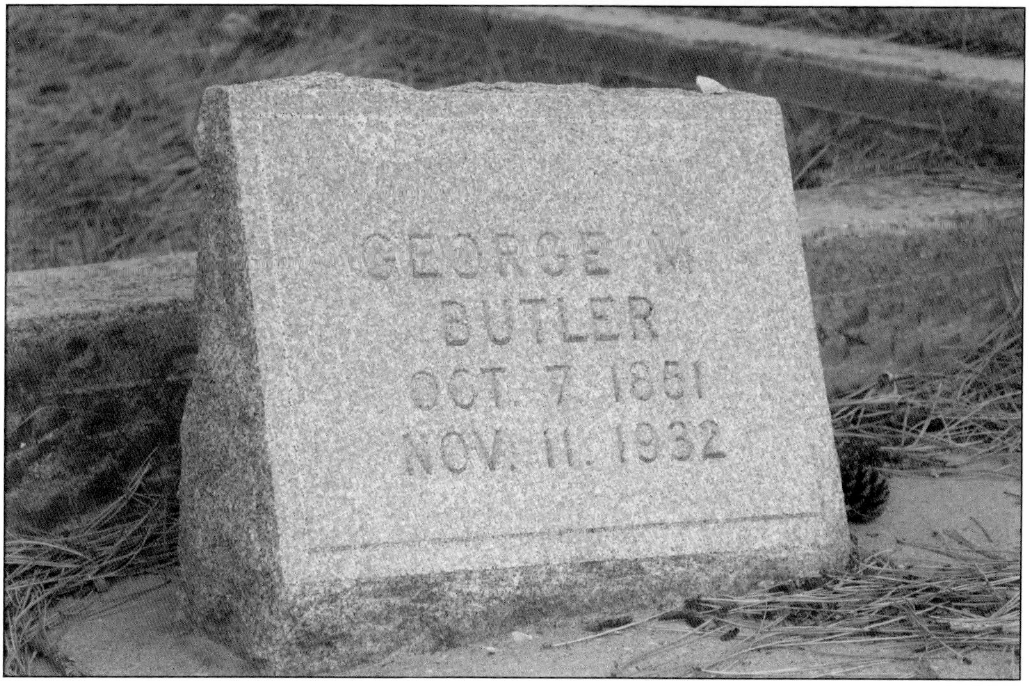

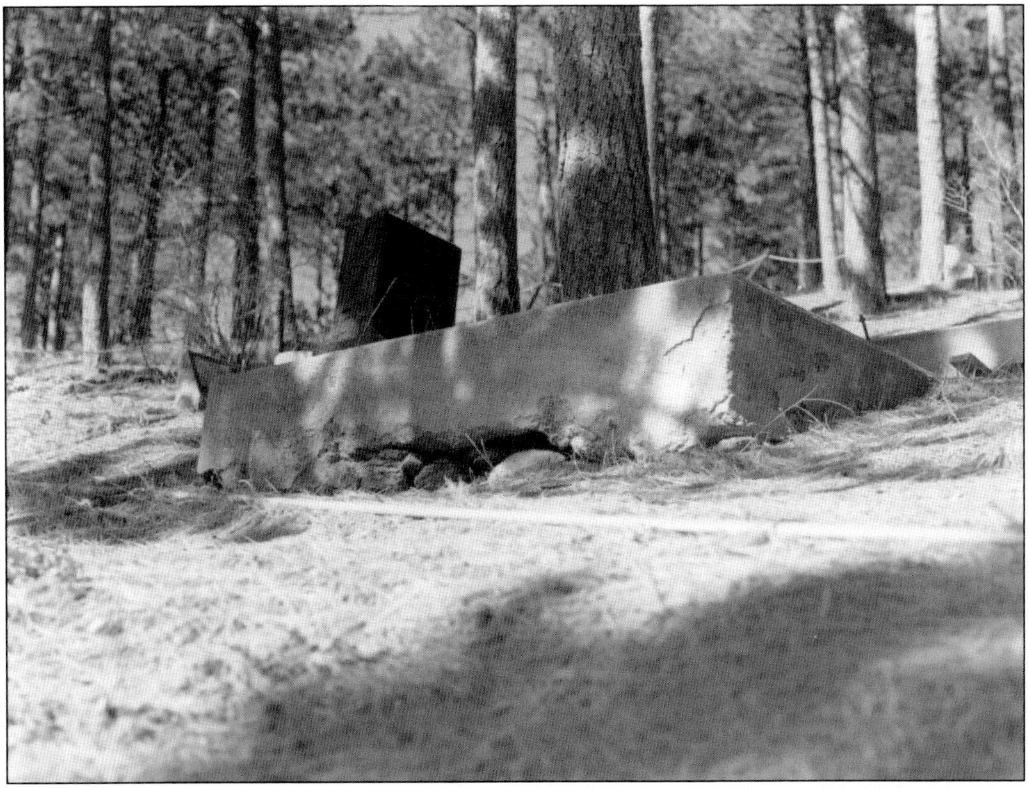

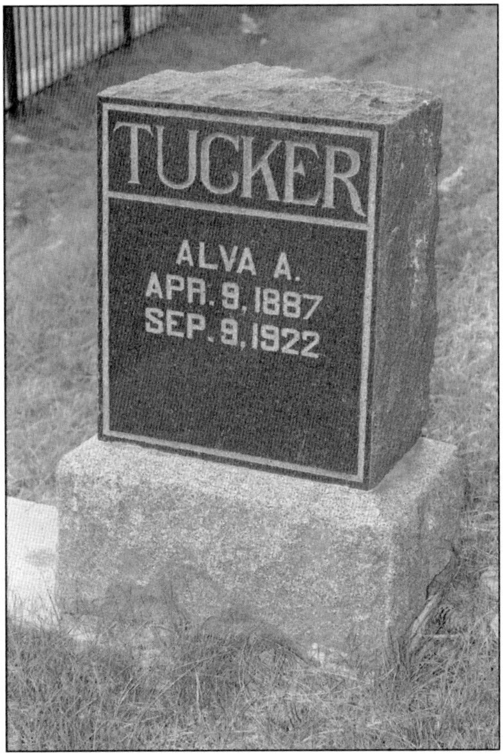

On the evening of August 26, 1922, Alva A. Tucker, a lineman with Consolidated Power & Light Company of the Northern Hills, was working on high tension wires when he was electrocuted. For two weeks, doctors at St. Joseph's Hospital in Deadwood tried to save his life. On September 9, Tucker died from his injuries and was buried in the Third Addition, Section 2, Lot 84. His grave was surrounded by a concrete retaining wall. Over the years, the Tucker plot was damaged by the constant soil erosion around the grave. In 2000, the Tucker grave was one of 450 plots repaired during the Mount Moriah Cemetery restoration. Experts from Deadwood Granite and Marble Works placed a new footing underneath this plot. (Both, courtesy of CODA.)

Matilda Champion Hill has been recognized as one of Deadwood's unsung heroines. Hill was born in Mountsville, Fairfax County, Virginia, on July 29, 1870. At age 30, she had settled at Fort Meade, near Sturgis, South Dakota, where she worked as a cook and child nurse for a commissioned officer and his family. Three years later, Hill settled in Deadwood until her death in 1954. During this time, she became noted for her hardworking and charitable contributions to those who needed help. She raised several orphaned African American children before the day of foster payments from the state. She was instrumental in organizing annual Freedom Day, Fourth of July, and Thanksgiving Day gatherings for the Black Hills African American community. (Right, courtesy of Deadwood Public Library; below, courtesy of CODA.)

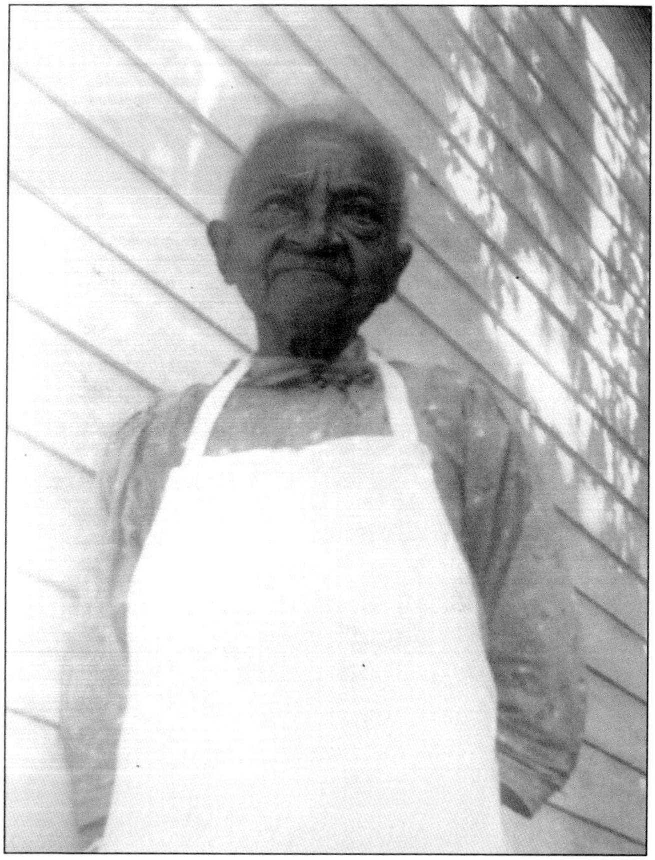

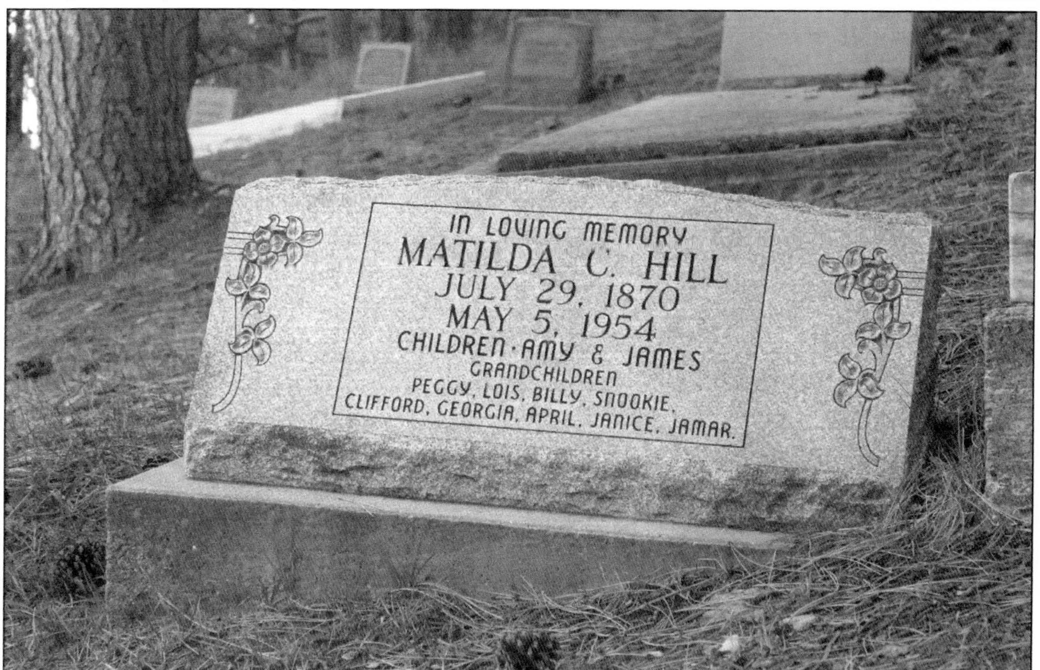

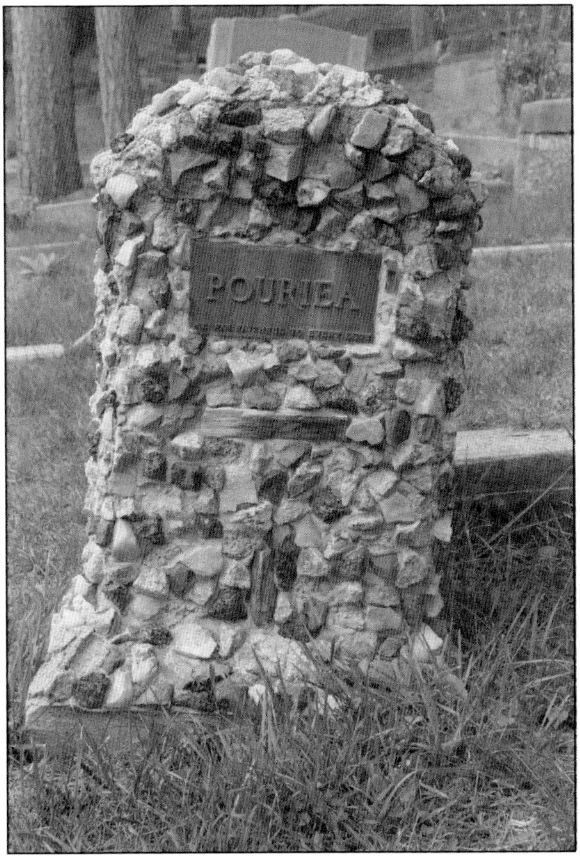

Jesse Joseph Pouriea was born in Montreal, Canada. In the spring of 1879, he came to the Black Hills and settled in Lead City. He was in the freighting business, bringing in supplies from Bismarck, Dakota Territory, and Sidney, Nebraska. Pouriea is credited with bringing the first fruit trees to the northern hills. In his later years, Pouria placer mined near Blacktail and operated the Danish Dairy Depot in Deadwood. The Pouriea plot is a homespun monument constructed from a wooden frame wrapped in chicken wire and coated with concrete. Native Black Hills minerals, including yellow and purple lepidolite, rose quartz, albite with blue tourmaline inclusions, phonolite with aegirine crystals, iron conglomerate, and petrified wood, were pressed into the wet concrete. Similar monuments can be found in many Black Hills cemeteries. (Both, courtesy of CODA.)

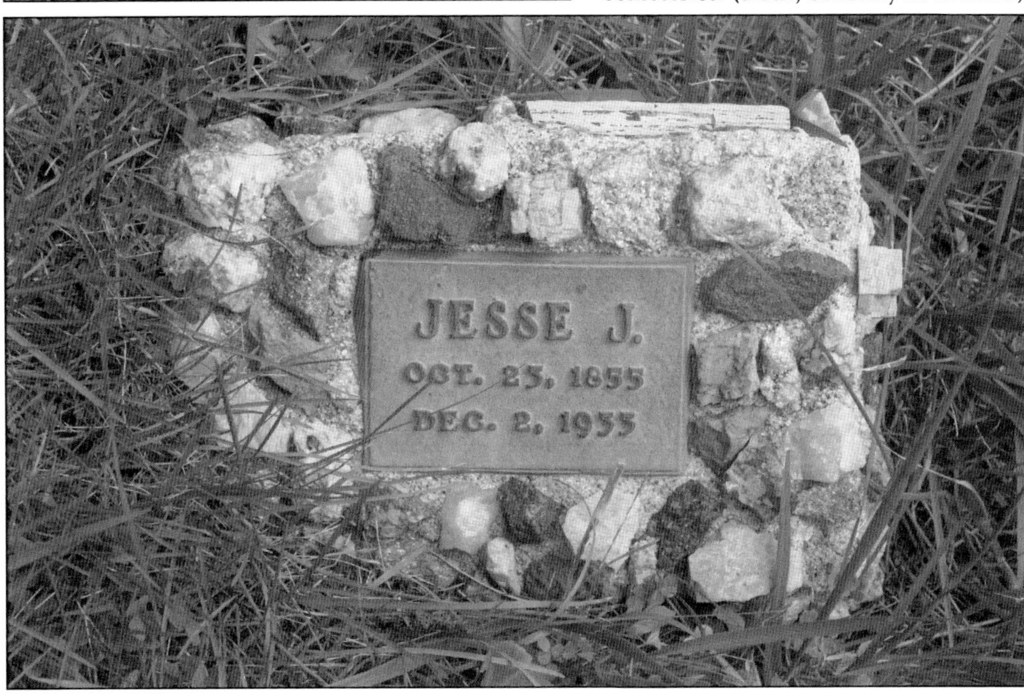

Adoniram J. Plowman was one of Lawrence County's most respected attorneys. Born in Jerseyville, Illinois, he graduated from Union College of Law in Chicago and moved to the Black Hills in 1879 to practice law. In 1881, Plowman helped in the consolidation of the mining camps that became the city of Deadwood. He served as Deadwood's first city attorney and then accepted the position of Lawrence County district attorney. Plowman received national recognition as the attorney for Crow Dog, a member of the Brule band of the Lakota Sioux. On August 5, 1881, Crow Dog killed Spotted Tail on reservation lands. The court's decision in the capital punishment case was appealed before the US Supreme Court, which overturned Crow Dog's death sentence. At right, from left to right, Michael Russell, Crow Dog, and Plowman pose in 1883. (Right, courtesy of Deadwood Public Library; below, courtesy of CODA.)

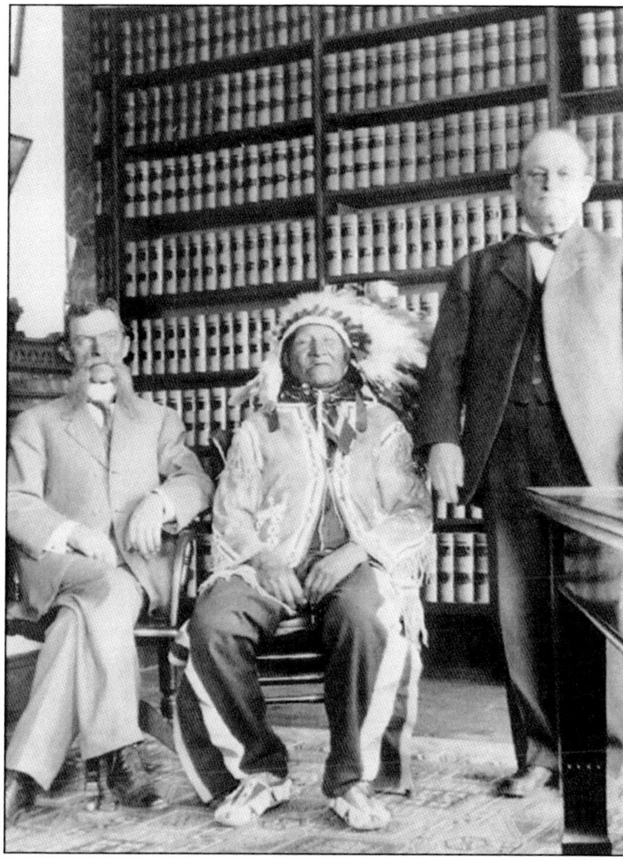

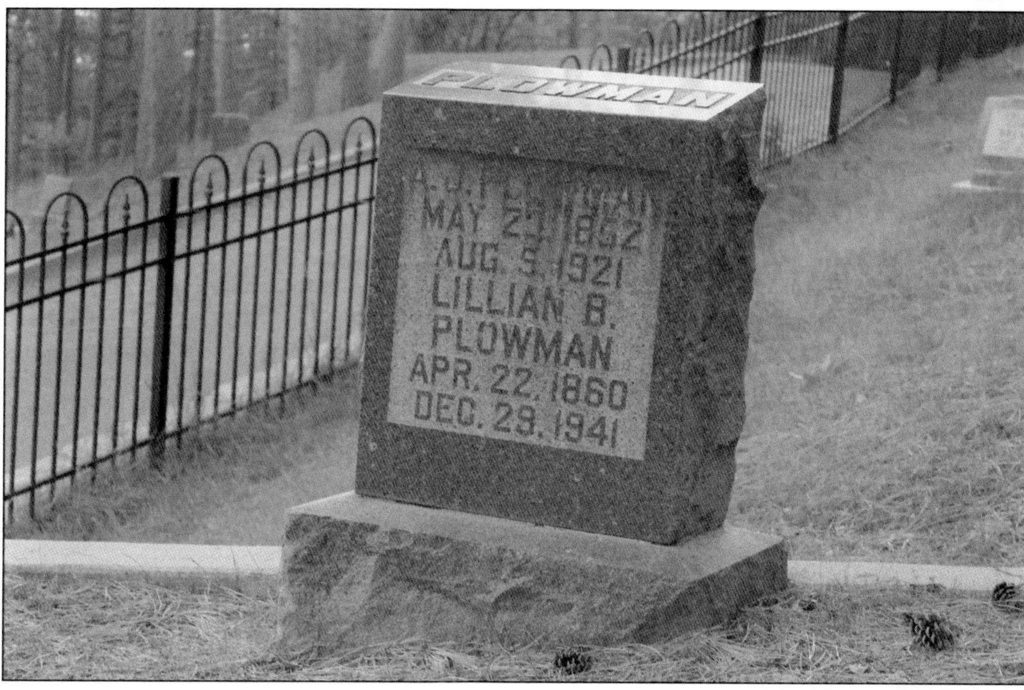

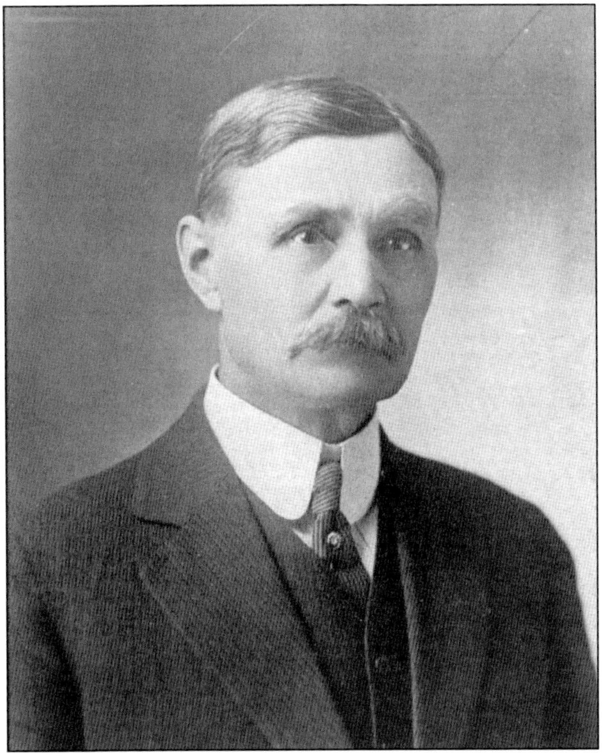

Willis H. Bonham (January 1, 1847–November 30, 1927) was born in Jasper County, Illinois. At age 26, he moved to Colorado and worked as a wallpaper hanger and painter before moving to Deadwood in 1877. Three years later, he worked as a pressman for the *Black Hills Pioneer* newspaper. In 1885, Bonham purchased the *Pioneer* and became publisher and managing editor. In 1897, he purchased the *Black Hills Daily Times* and combined the two as the *Deadwood Pioneer-Times.* The newspaper became a power in the political and social life of Deadwood and Lawrence County, and Bonham was a prominent citizen in the community. He helped organize the South Deadwood Hose Company and served as fire chief, was a charter member of the Deadwood Elks Lodge No. 508, and was an honorary member of the Society of Black Hills Pioneers. (Both, courtesy of CODA.)

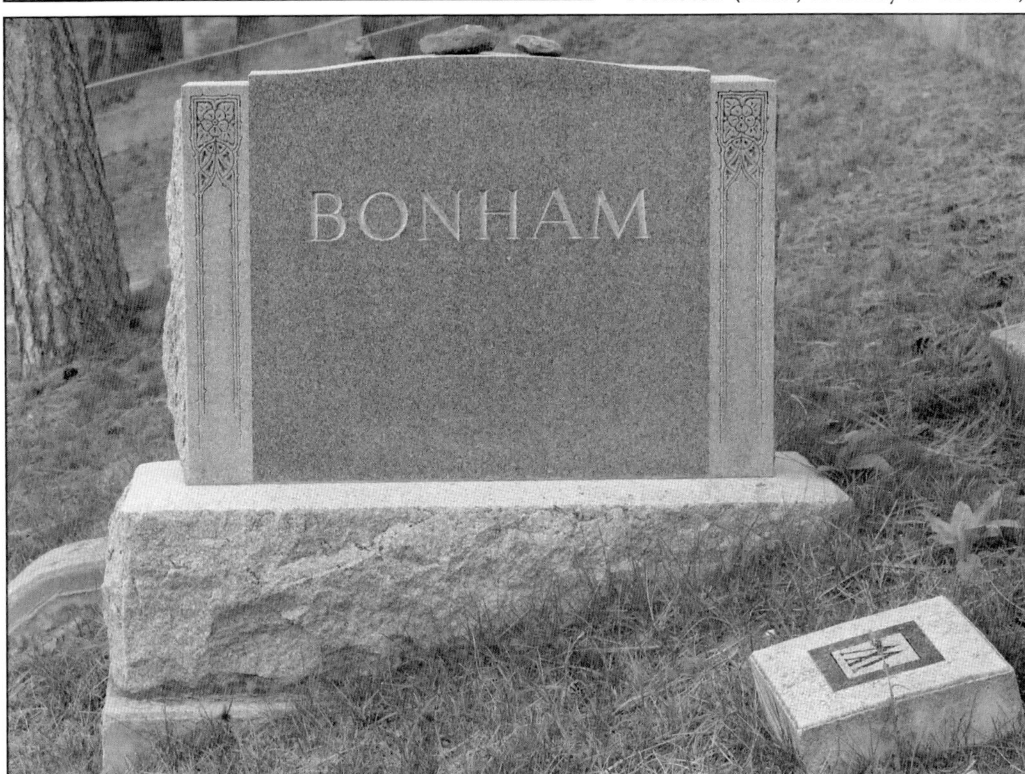

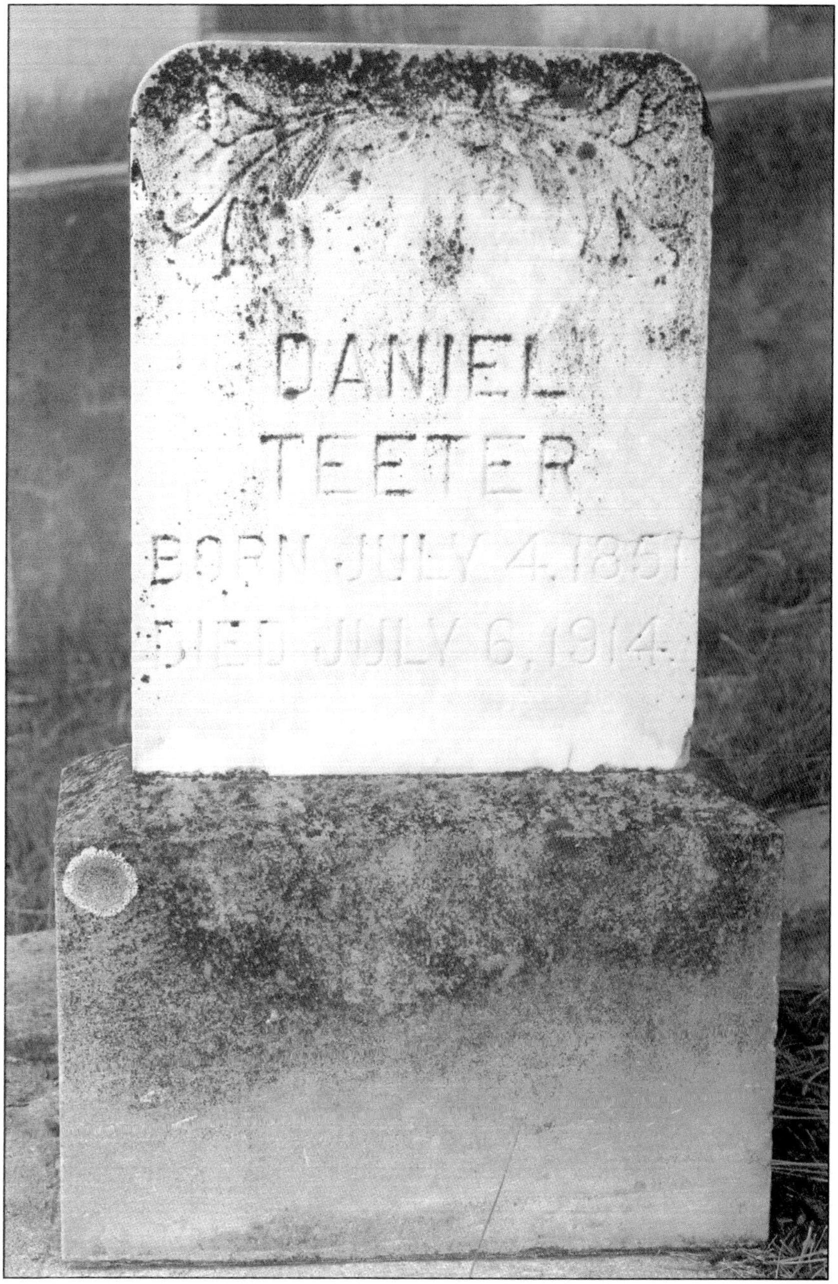

Daniel Teeter (1850–1914) came to the Black Hills in 1877. He became an accomplished mill wright and mill superintendent who ran numerous milling operations in Colorado, Nevada, Montana, South Dakota, and Africa. Newspapers referred to him as a "first class mine and mill man." In 1901, Teeter was hired by the English firm Ashanti Gold Fields Corporation, based out of Obuasi, West Africa (today's Ghana). Over time, the Ashanti Gold Fields Corporation became one of the nine largest gold-producing companies in the world. While in Africa, Teeter contracted blackwater fever, a severe form of malaria. In 1904, he returned to the United States to work for the Minnesota Mines Company in Maitland, South Dakota. Later, he set up milling operations in Nevada and Montana before returning to Central City. (Courtesy of CODA.)

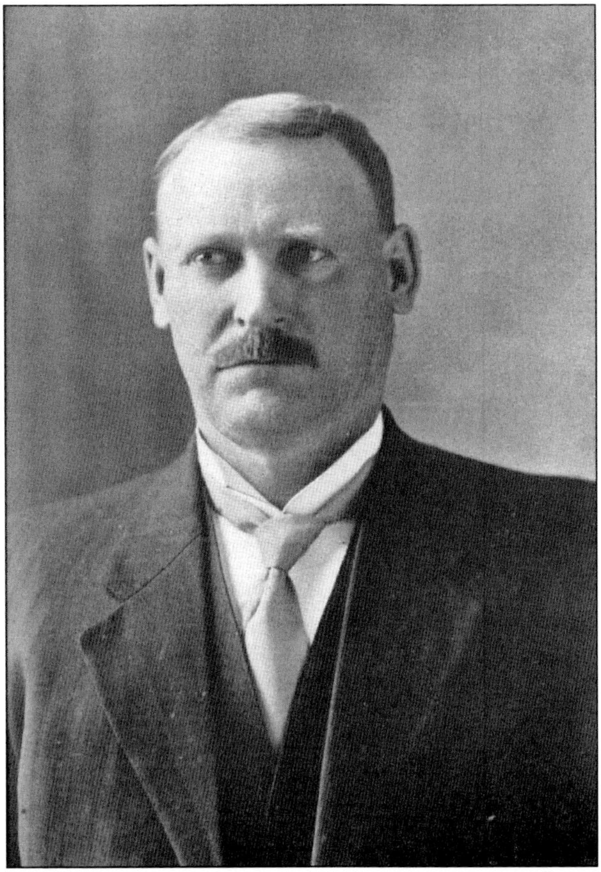

Norwegian immigrant Olaf Seim was born on September 20, 1866, in Bergen, Norway. At the age of 19, he immigrated to Lansing, Iowa, and later Watertown, South Dakota. In 1889, Seim arrived in Deadwood and established himself as a general contractor and later city alderman. One of Seim's more interesting financial endeavors was the acquisition and operation of a mine on the edge of Deadwood. His mine contained a high concentration of pyritic ore much needed in the smelting process. At the height of production, over 50 tons of pyritic ore was extracted daily and hauled to the Deadwood and Delaware smelter in Deadwood's First Ward. Seim's mine remained in operation until 1903 when pyritic ore was replaced by chlorination and cyanidation in the gold smelting process. (Both, courtesy of CODA.)

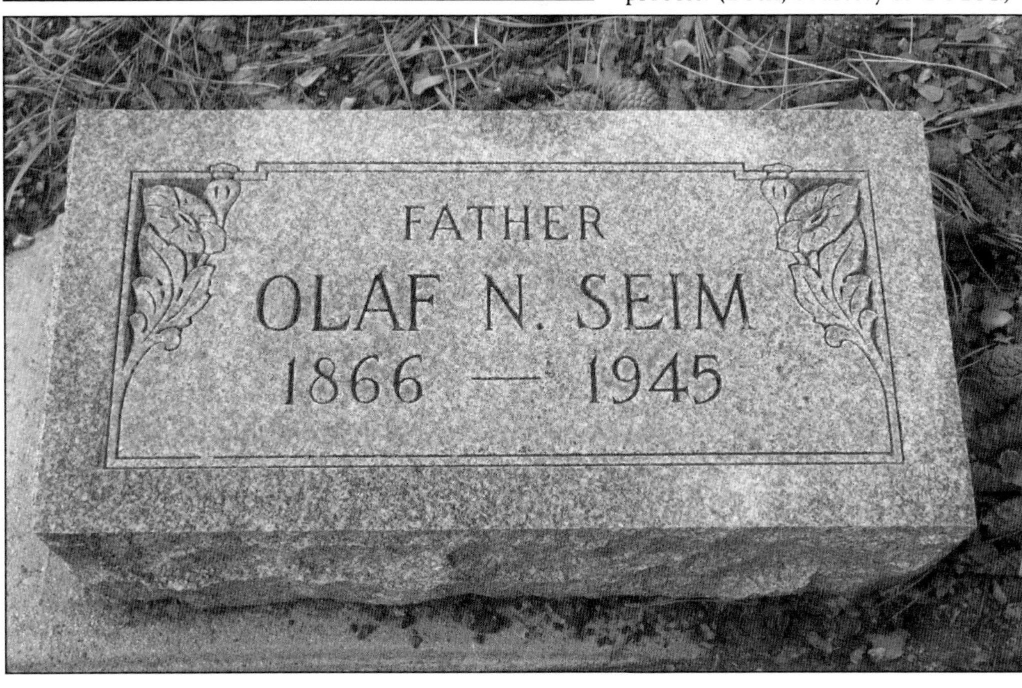

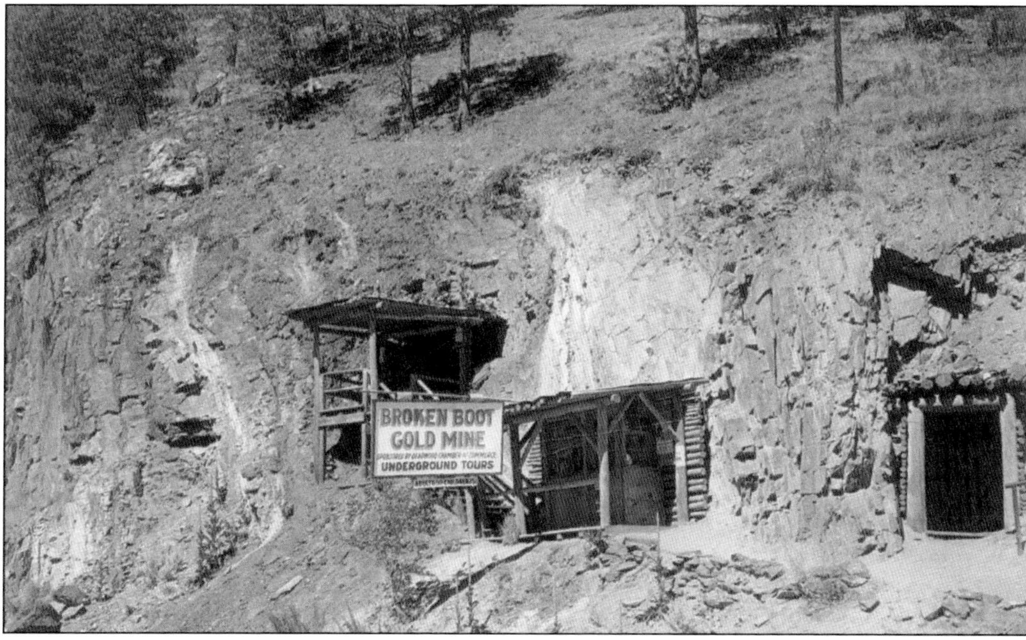

Ida Selma Hebert was the daughter of Olaf Seim. In March 1954, the Deadwood Chamber of Commerce partnered with Hebert and reopened the Seim Mine as a tourist attraction. It was renamed the Broken Boot Gold Mine after a discarded miner's boot was found in the mine. Before her death in 1986, Hebert deeded the Broken Boot Gold Mine to the Deadwood Chamber of Commerce. Today, over 20,000 tourists visit the Broken Boot each summer. (Both, courtesy of CODA.)

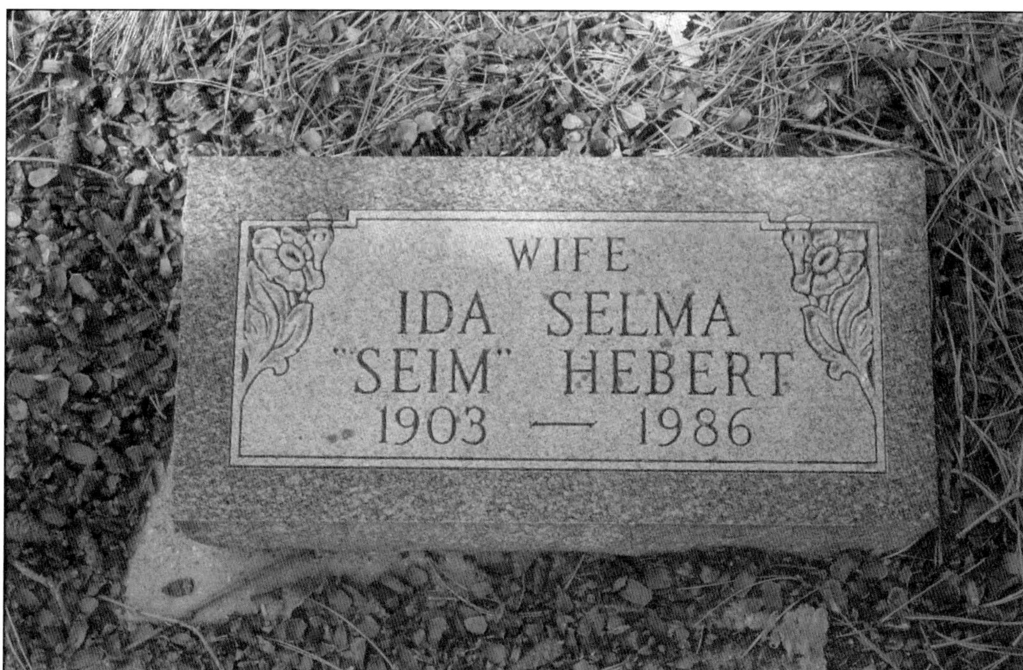

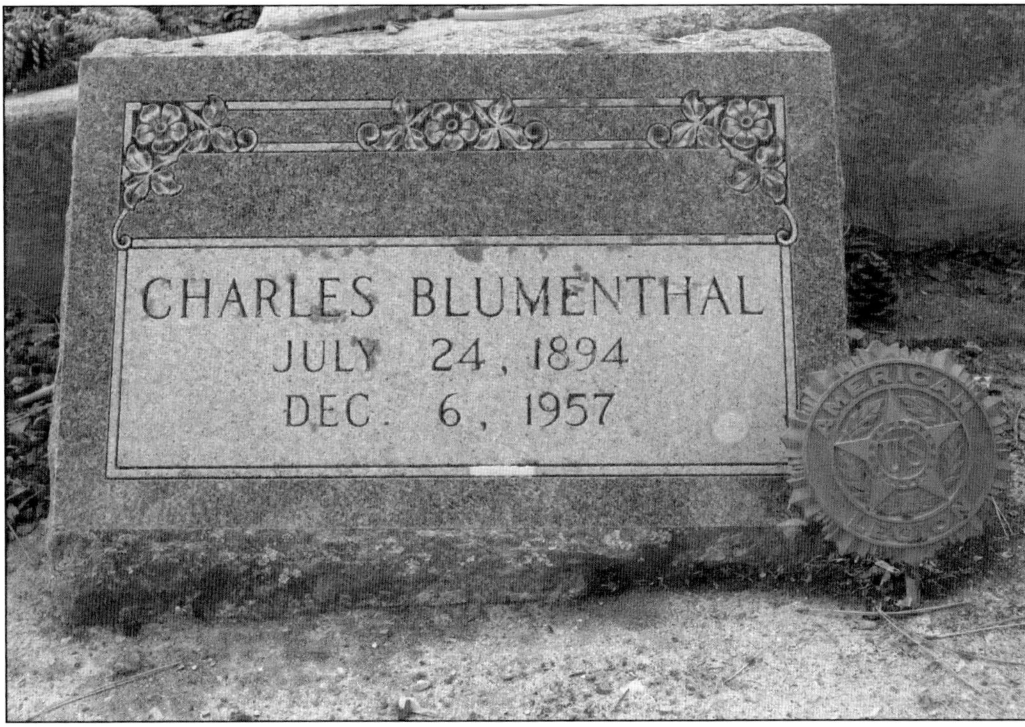

Charles Blumenthal was born in Deadwood. During his youth, he worked an assortment of jobs, including delivering milk and herding milk cows, delivering the *Deadwood Pioneer-Times*, and lighting and extinguishing the gas lamps along Deadwood's streets. From 1908 until 1917, he worked for Gus Kellar at Sasse's Meat Market before enlisting in World War I. Blumenthal was in Company B, 52nd Ammunition Train, Coast Artillery Corps in France. In 1935, he purchased Kellar's business and relocated it to Pluma. Blumenthal was a member of numerous organizations, including the Masons, Shriners, Elks, Eagles, American Legion, and Veterans of Foreign Wars. In 2014, construction workers, while excavating a utility trench along Cliff Street, unearthed a cast-iron gas lamp that may have been serviced by Blumenthal. (Both, courtesy of CODA.)

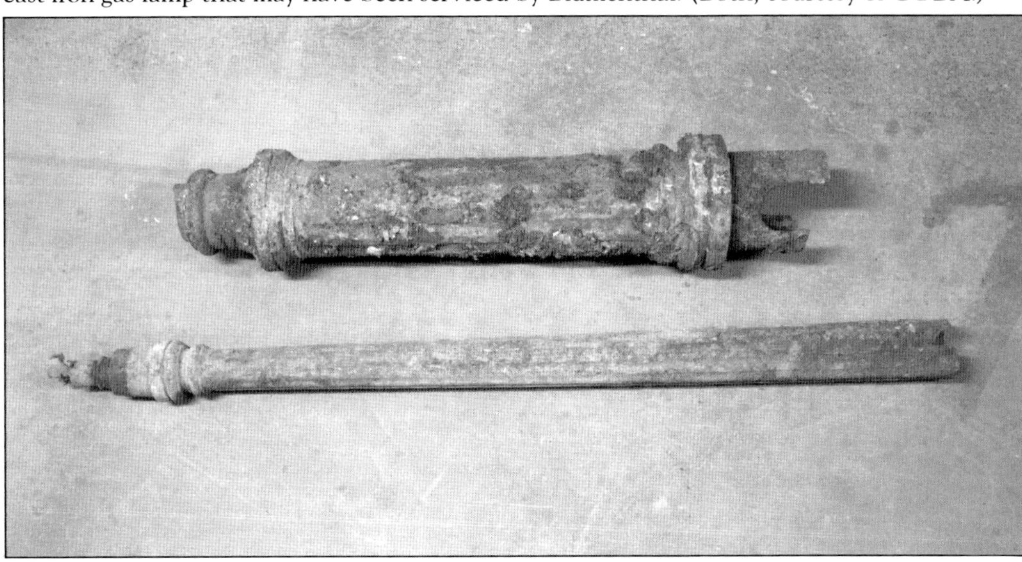

Willis Carlton Spindler was a good father and citizen and a friend to all who knew him. In 1900, he came to Deadwood with his wife, Nellie, and opened a restaurant on Main Street. He later sold the business and opened a dairy in Central City, where they delivered milk from house to house. Applying his knowledge about running a dairy, Spindler began purchasing played-out mining claims and converting them into farmland. This provided land for them to raise chickens, have a 30-head dairy farm, and grow vegetables that he supplied to the restaurants and grocery stores in Deadwood. In 2014, Spindler was honored on Deadwood's Wall of Fame for his contributions to the development of the city. (Right, courtesy of Adam Spindler; below, courtesy of CODA.)

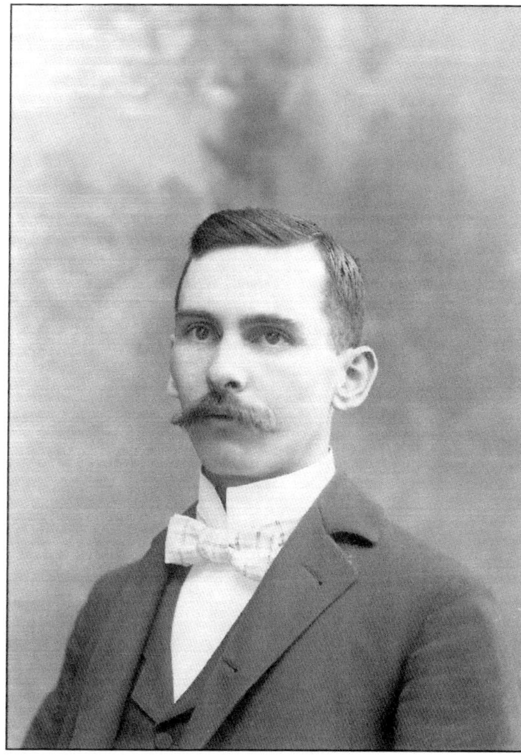

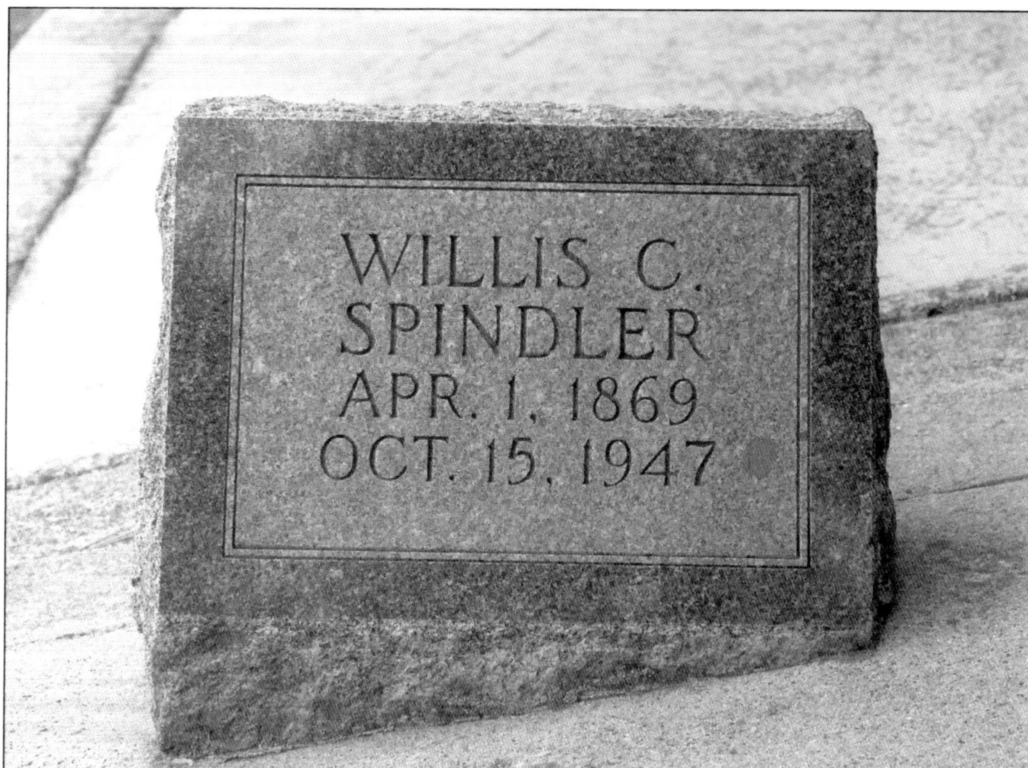

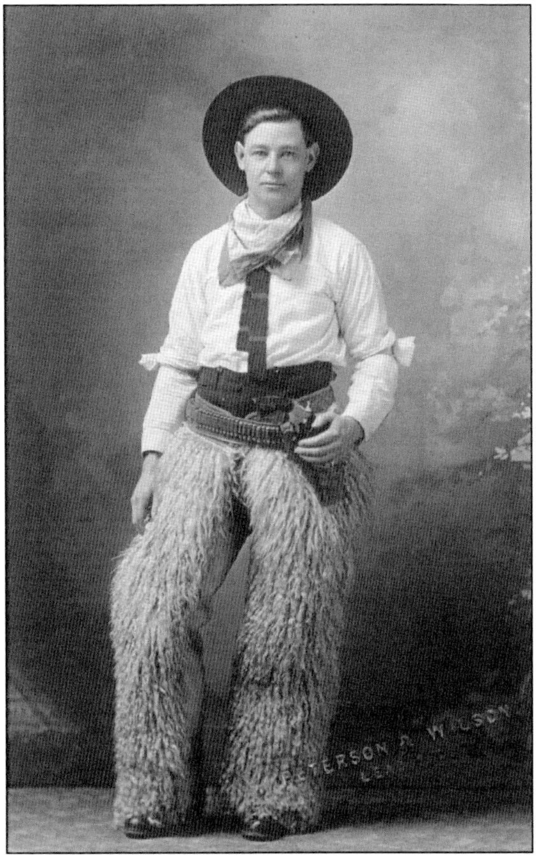

Andrew B. Mattley (August 9, 1890–May 26, 1959) was born in Hay Springs, Nebraska, and came to Deadwood at the age of 10. Twelve years later, Mattley purchased Kiser's Cleaning & Dye Works, located on Pine Street. He would become involved in local politics beginning in 1938, when he was elected a city alderman. In 1943, Mattley was elected mayor of Deadwood, a position he held until 1948. In 1992, Phyllis M. Palmer, daughter of Mattley, donated a small collection of ephemera to the Deadwood Historic Preservation Commission. Several of these items, including this photograph, reflect Mattley's life, business, and accomplishments in Deadwood. (Both, courtesy of CODA.)

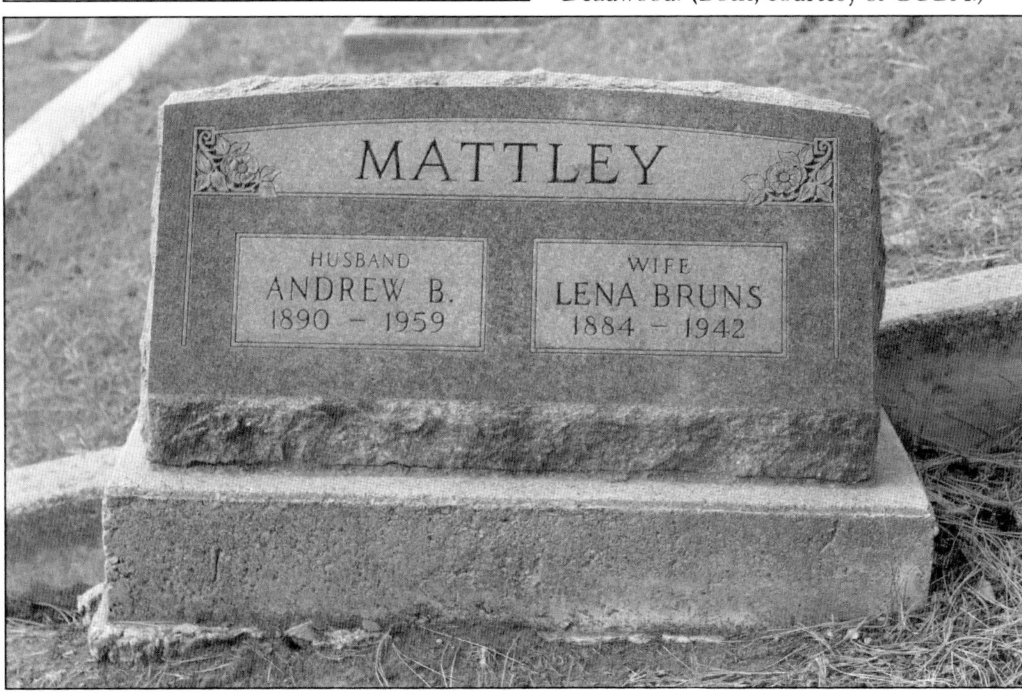

Five

Sections 5–9, Potters Fields, and Section A

On January 5, 1893, the City of Deadwood Board of Education conveyed the lands west of the original oval in Mount Moriah to the Deadwood Cemetery Association. This land, consisting of approximately 1.15 acres, is bordered by a steep cliff face historically known as Black Rocks. Buried within these sections are some of Deadwood's most prominent businessmen and civil servants. These sections also contain a diverse array of children's graves and funerary art. Section 6, located to the north, once contained the largest concentration of Chinese burials and a brick altar and burner used in funerary rituals, as discussed in chapter two.

Surrounding the original oval on the north, south, and east sides are potters fields. The North and South Potters Fields are original to the 1878 cemetery layout and contain approximately 525 burials. East Potters Field and Section A were added to the 1895 cemetery map but not used until after 1900, based on burial records. East Potters Field contains approximately 258 burials, including an infant section that dates from 1944. Section A, northwest of the original oval, contains approximately 174 burials that date from 1908 to 1936. Historically, many of the graves in the potters fields once contained wooden headboards. Today, these areas are primarily open expanses dotted with occasional permanent monuments.

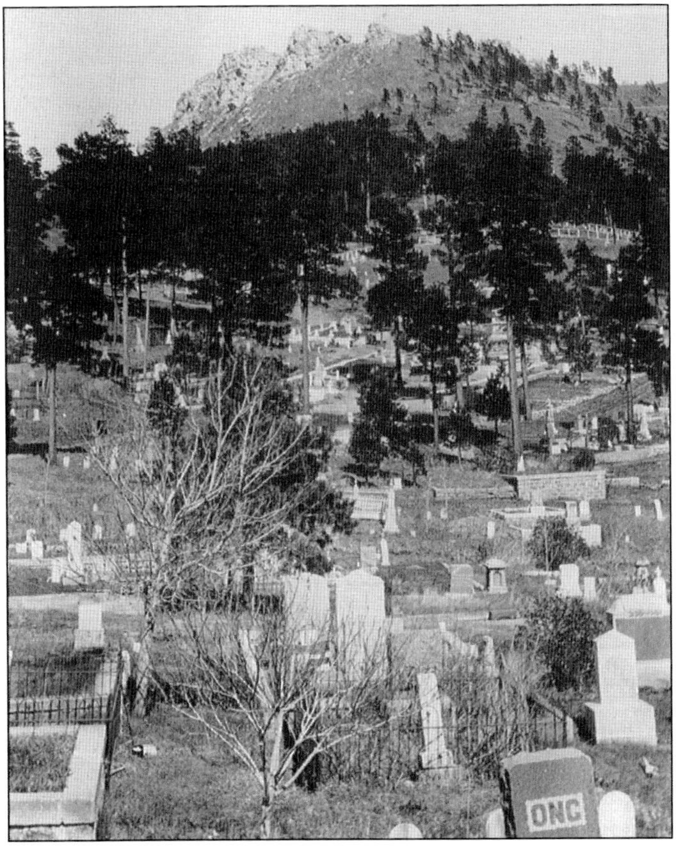

After its inception in January 1893, approximately 549 burials were interred in Sections 5 through 9. Cemetery sexton Charles Robinson, under the direction of the association, began planting nonnative trees throughout the cemetery, especially in these sections. The photograph at left, taken after 1909, records the openness of these sections. In contrast, amateur historian Charles Haas took an almost identical photograph in 1944. According to Haas's notes on the back, this image was taken near the flagpole, showing White Rocks in the background. The Ong monument is in the lower right corner of each photograph. (Left, courtesy of Deadwood History Inc., Adams Museum Collection; below, courtesy of CODA.)

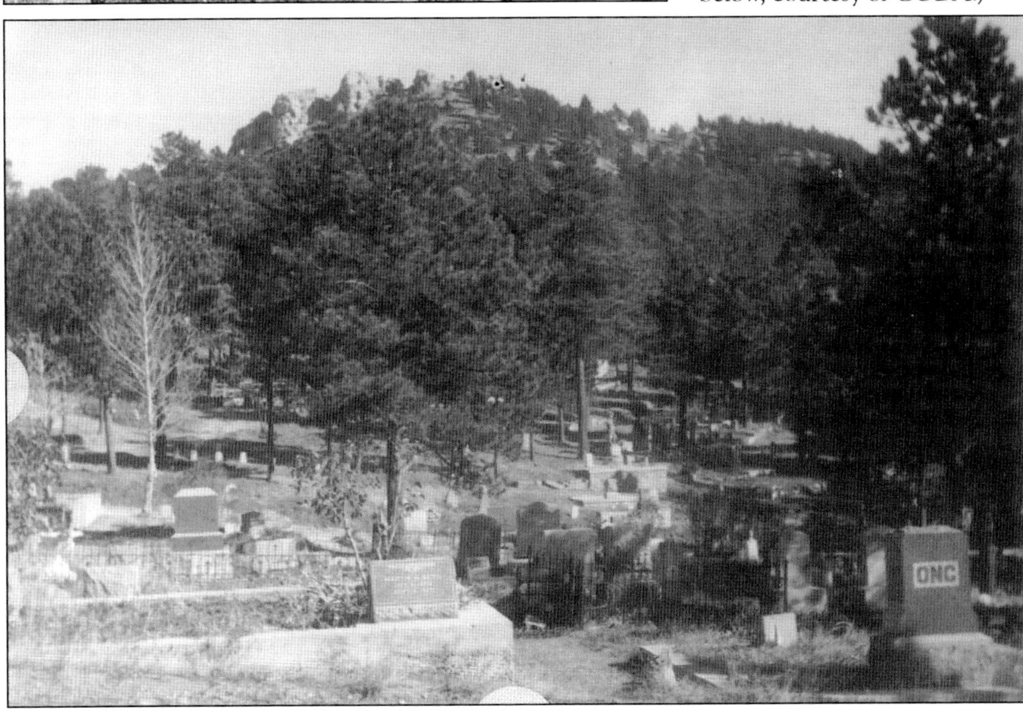

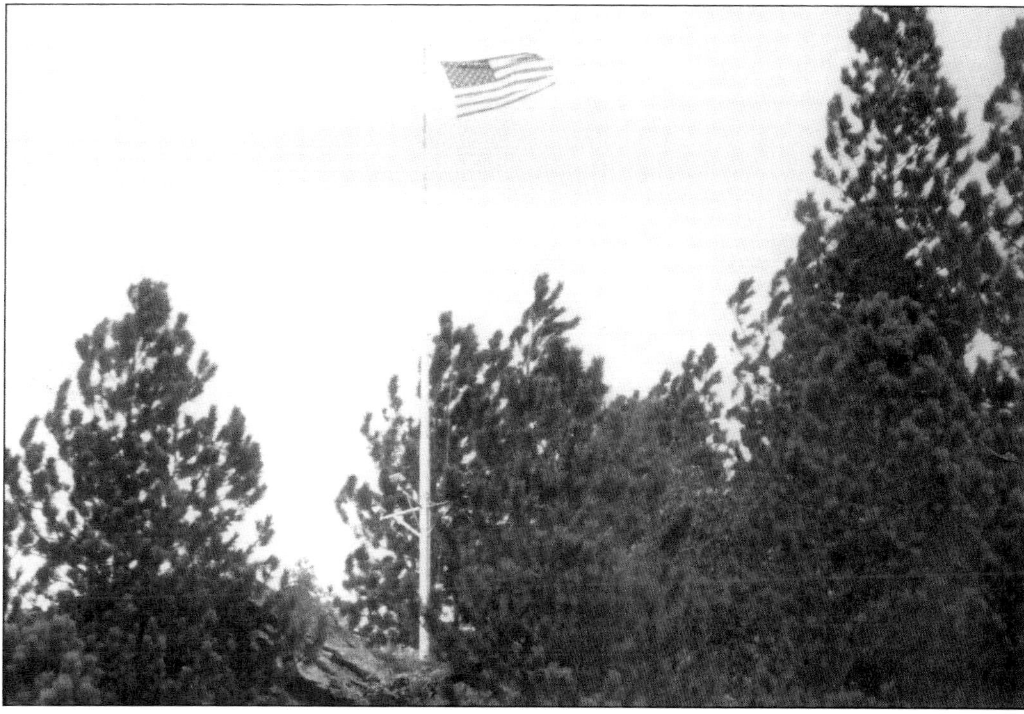

On April 6, 1917, the United States entered World War I, and Deadwood, with the rest of the country, became energized with patriotic fervor. Eighteen days after Congress declared war, Deadwood mayor Nathan Franklin requested that an illuminated American flag be placed on the cliff face in Mount Moriah Cemetery. Consolidated Power, the precursor to Black Hills Energy, installed electric lights to illuminate the flag 24 hours a day. After the war, the flag flew periodically from this location until the bombing of Pearl Harbor on December 7, 1941, and once again Old Glory was flown 24 hours a day. Deadwood has continued this long-standing tradition of flying the American flag 24 hours a day through today. Every year, the Deadwood VFW Post 5969 holds a Pearl Harbor remembrance ceremony at the flagpole. (Above, courtesy of Deadwood Public Library; below, courtesy of Vince Coyle Collection, CODA.)

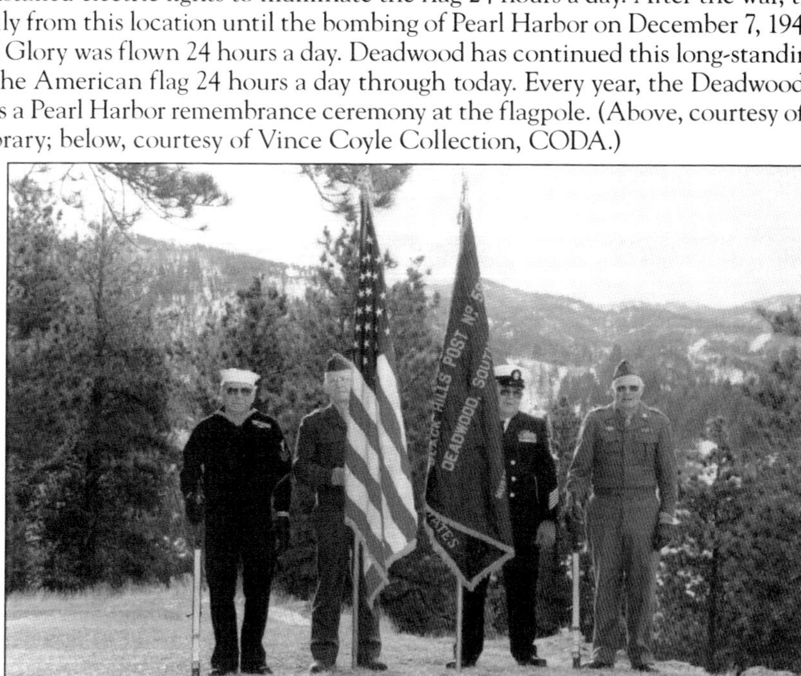

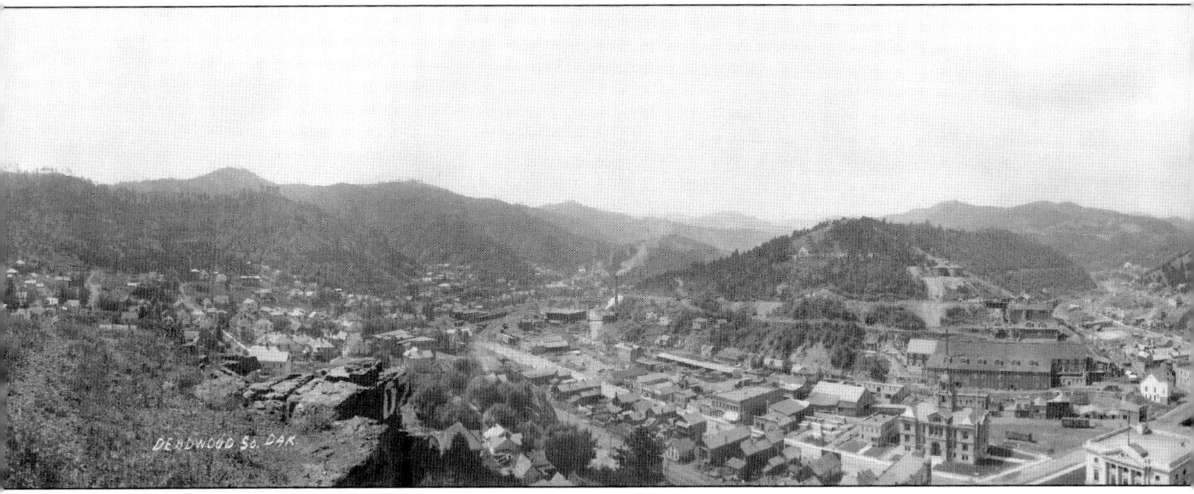

The natural overlook in Sections 5 through 9 of Mount Moriah Cemetery is probably one of the most photographed areas in Deadwood. Over the past 100 years, amateur and professional photographers have taken advantage of the 200-foot elevation difference and open expanse to capture amazing photographs of Deadwood's historic district. The overlook also provides a wonderful opportunity to stop and reflect upon Deadwood's built environment and its architectural features,

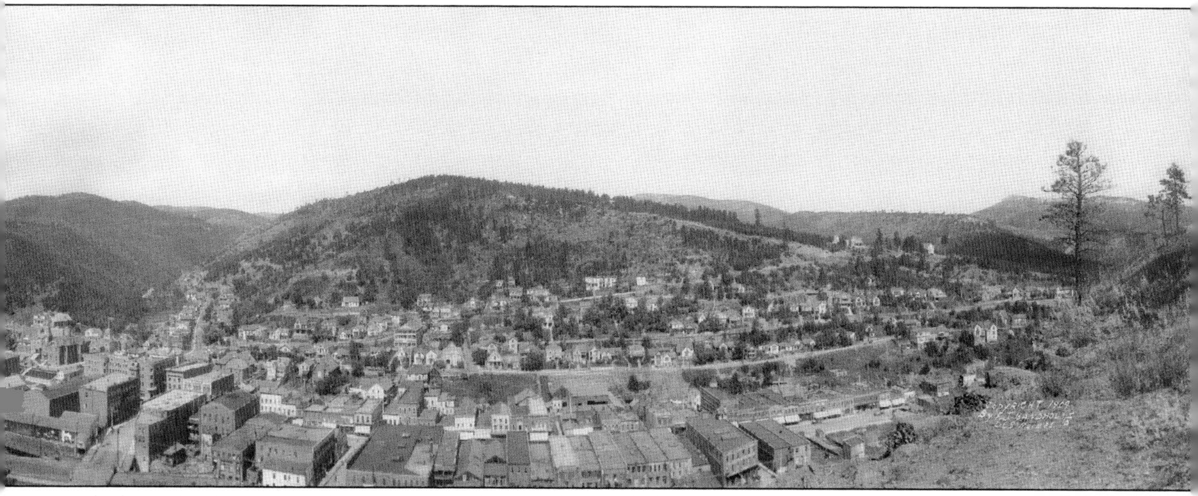

including the Lawrence County Courthouse, Federal Courthouse and Post Office, Homestake Slime Plant, Franklin Hotel, and Main Street. In the fall, many of the deciduous shrubs and trees that cling to the mountainside paint Deadwood Gulch in a plethora of vibrant colors. (Courtesy of Coburn Collection, CODA.)

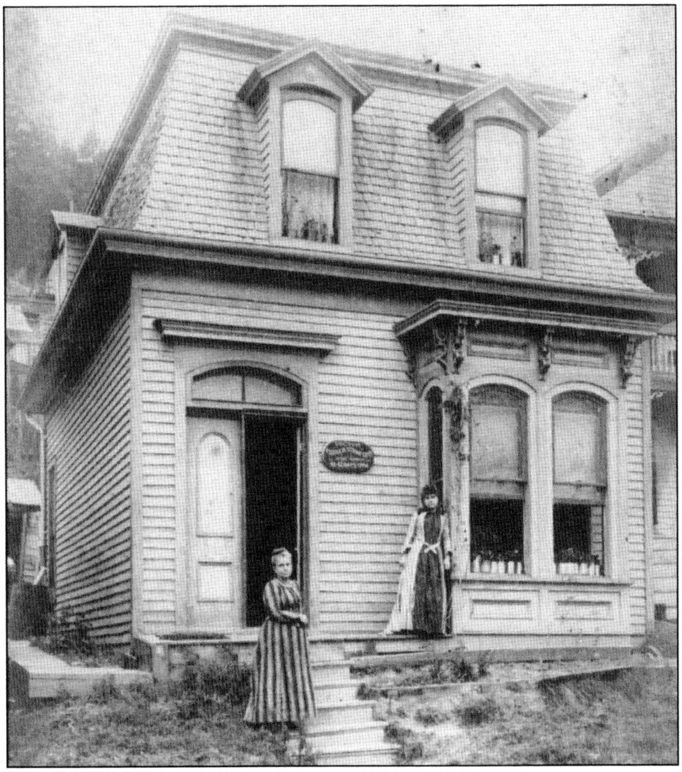

Dr. Flora (Hayward) Stanford was Deadwood's first female doctor. She was born in Trinity Bay, Newfoundland, aboard her father's ship. She taught at the Normal School in Buffalo, New York. While there, she married Valentine Stanford and relocated to Corry, Pennsylvania, where she raised two children. Upon the passing of her husband, Stanford moved to Massachusetts, where she graduated from Boston Medical School in 1878. Ten years later, Stanford opened a medical practice at 374 Williams Street in Deadwood. She was a member of the Woman's Relief Corps and Daughters of Rebekah. In 1900, she was elected to the Deadwood Board of Education but died shortly thereafter. In 2014, the Deadwood Historic Preservation Commission placed a granite marker on Stanford's unmarked grave, as part of the Cemetery Headstone Grant Program. (Above, courtesy of Deadwood Public Library; right, courtesy of CODA.)

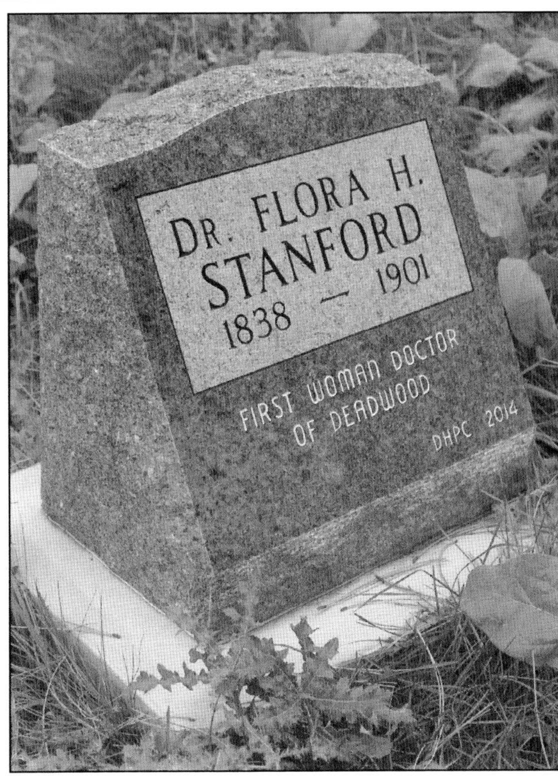

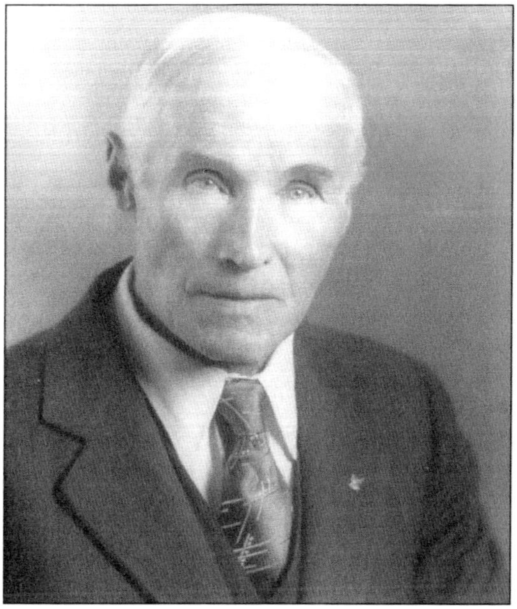

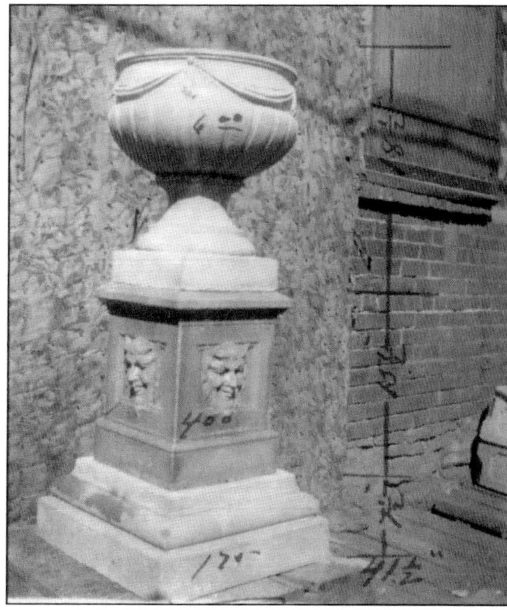

Lars Peter Shostrom was a master stone mason who helped build Deadwood with rock and concrete. Born in Sweden, Shostrom immigrated to the United States with his mother and younger siblings in 1883, settling in Des Moines, Iowa. Six years later, Shostrom moved west, eventually settling in Deadwood. While working for the Golden Reward Mining Company, Shostrom learned the masonry trade and eventually went into business for himself. His work can be found around the Lead-Deadwood area in numerous sidewalks, retaining walls, laid stone foundations, and the concrete urns and lawn vases that adorn graves in Mount Moriah Cemetery, including Martha "Calamity Jane" Canary and Dora Dufran. The face that appears on the urn base is the Greek god Pan, the god of sheep and shepherds. (Above, both courtesy of Keith Shostrom; below, courtesy of CODA.)

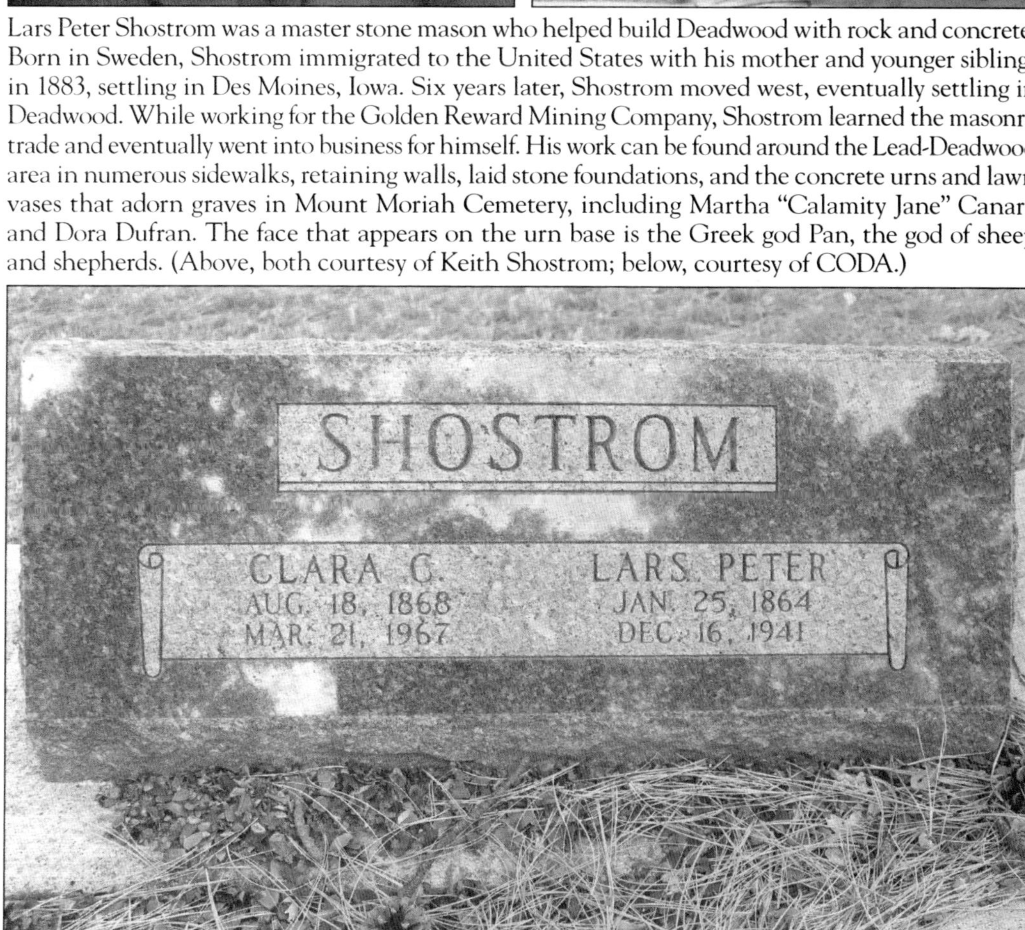

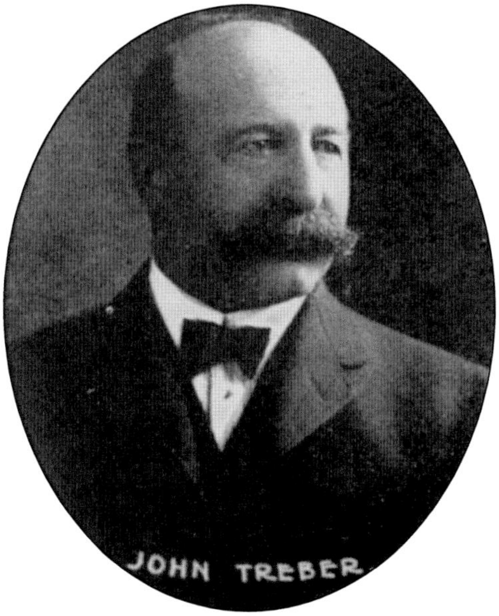

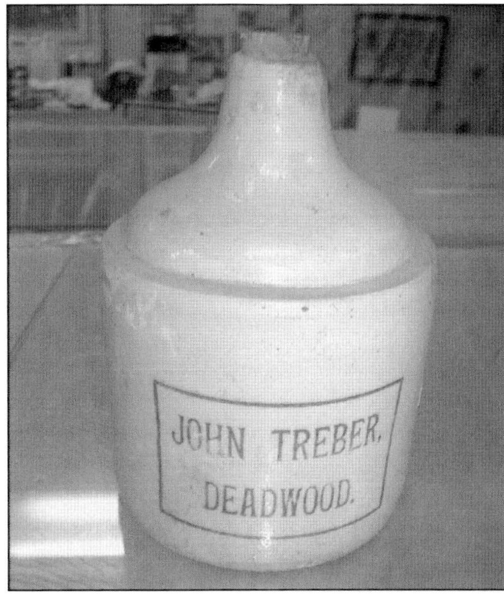

John Treber was a wholesale liquor and beer distributor for western South Dakota. Born on March 2, 1853, in Hochheim-on-the-Main, Germany, by age 21, he immigrated to the United States and settled in Leavenworth, Kansas, and later St. Louis, Missouri, where he worked as a brewer. In April 1877, Treber relocated to Deadwood and established a wholesale liquor business on Main Street. In the 1890s, Treber expanded his business to include a bottling works, warehouse, ice plant, and distribution center for Anheuser-Busch products. In addition to his businesses, he served on the Deadwood City Council for 24 years, was a member of the South Dakota State Legislature, and a member of Deadwood's Benevolent and Protective Order of Elks No. 508. (All, courtesy of CODA.)

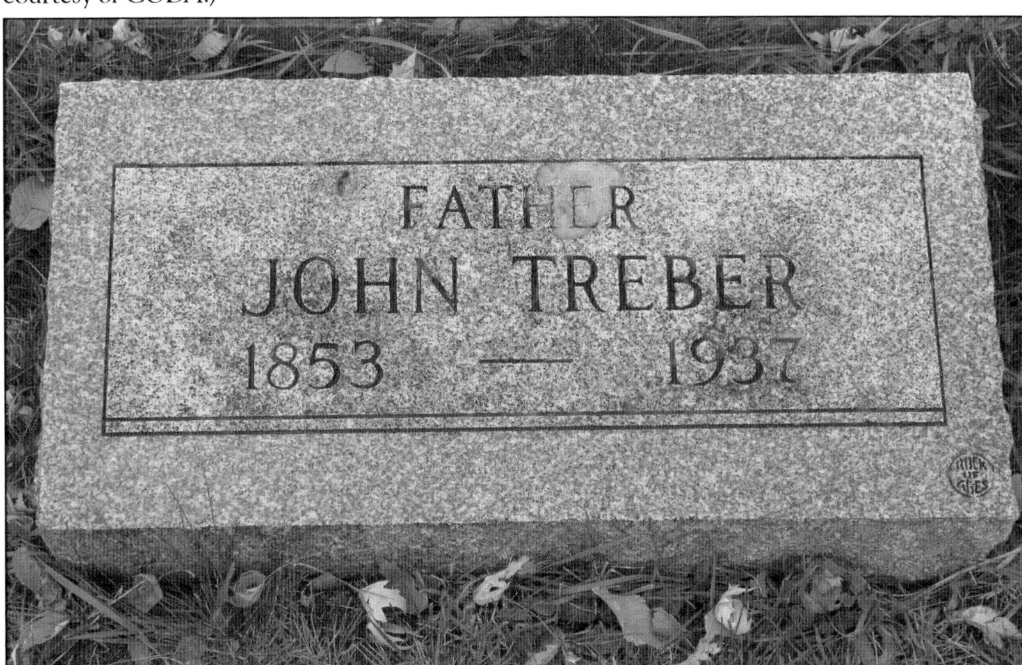

John Hunter (1845–1920) was the founder of the Fish & Hunter Company in Deadwood. Hunter was born in Canada and immigrated to Minnesota in 1865, where he worked as a blacksmith and sawyer in a lumber mill. In 1877, he left Minnesota and traveled to the Black Hills with a portable sawmill, one of the first in the northern Black Hills. Hunter's business flourished after the disastrous fire of September 26, 1879, which destroyed much of Deadwood Gulch. In 1891, he established the Fish & Hunter Company, a wholesale hardware and food distribution business. In his personal life, Hunter and his wife, Elizabeth (Weaver), had eight children; however, only two lived to adulthood. The photograph below, taken before 1900, shows John Hunter posing beside the family plot in Section 9. (Right, courtesy of CODA; below, courtesy of Deadwood Public Library.)

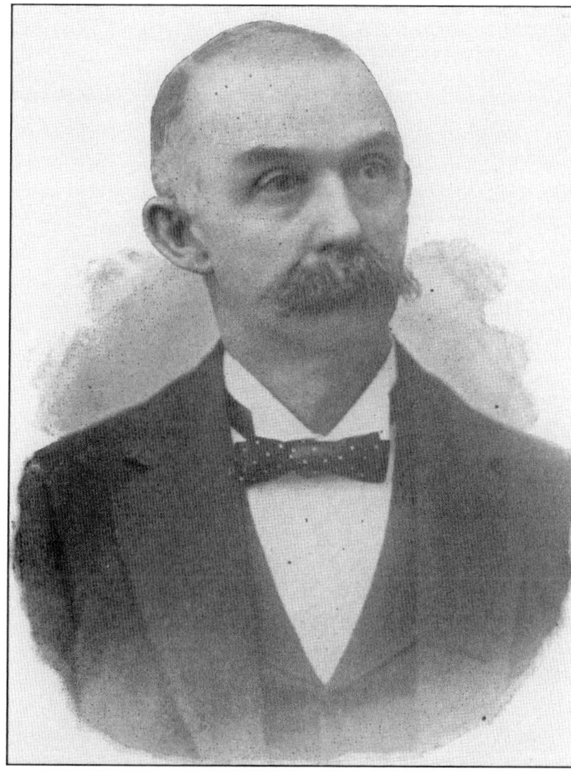

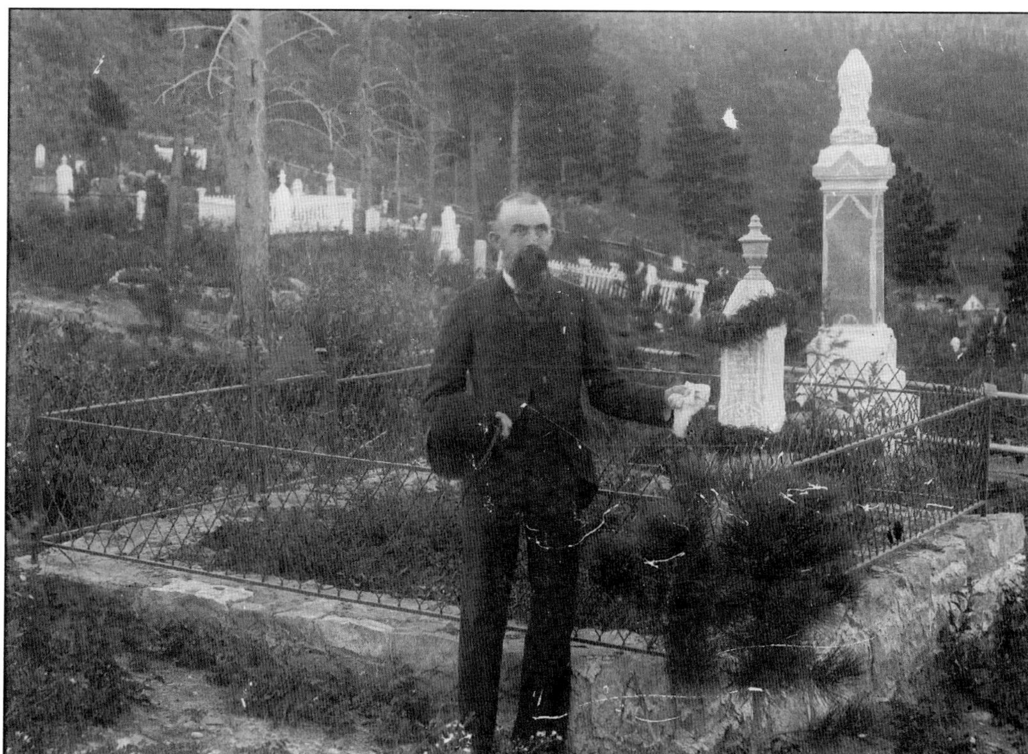

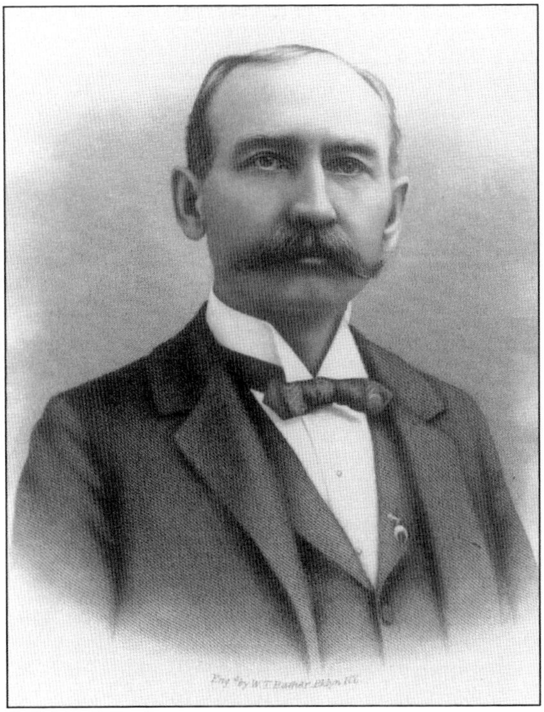

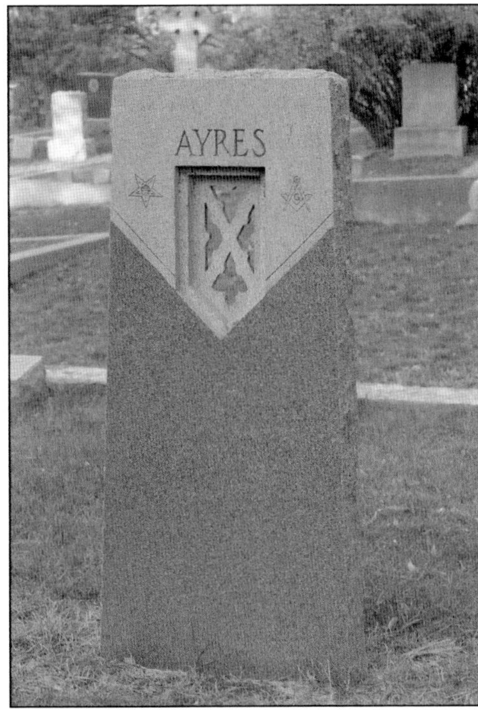

George Vincent Ayres was born in Wyoming County, Pennsylvania. In 1876, he came to the Black Hills and found employment at Richard C. Lake's hardware store in Deadwood. Five years later, Ayres purchased Lake's store, expanded the business, and ran it for the remainder of his life. In Freemasonry, Ayres served as the master of Deadwood Lodge No. 7, grand master of the Grand Lodge of Dakota in 1888, and, after statehood, the first grand master of the Grand Lodge of South Dakota in 1889. He was a charter member and past president of the Society of Black Hills Pioneers and served as city commissioner, county commissioner, and member of the South Dakota House of Representatives. He took an active role in supporting the development of the Lawrence County highways. (All, courtesy of CODA.)

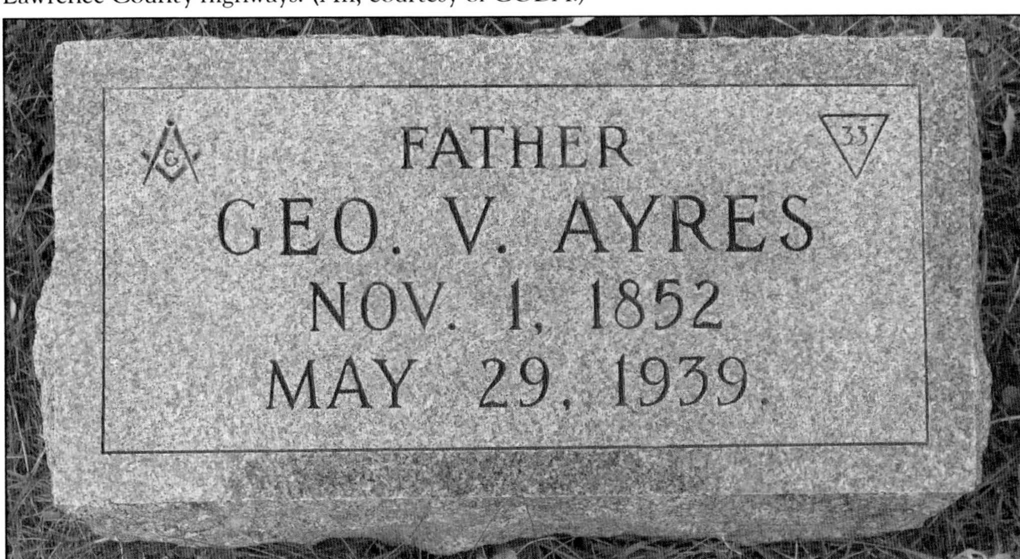

Frank S. Peck was born in Modoway, Missouri, and came to Deadwood with his parents in 1878. For 10 years, he received on-the-job training in civil engineering and helped survey government townsites in Fall River County and the northern border of South Dakota. In the 1890s, Peck served as the city engineer for Deadwood. During the national Good Roads Movement, Peck played a pivotal role in developing and paving many interconnecting roads and highways in Lawrence County. In 1921, the Lawrence County commissioners appointed Peck as the county road supervisor. During his tenure, he improved Spearfish Canyon Road, US Highway 85 from Lead to the Wyoming border, Boulder Canyon Road, and the Spearfish Road. (Right, courtesy of Deadwood History Inc., Adams Museum Collection; below, courtesy of CODA.)

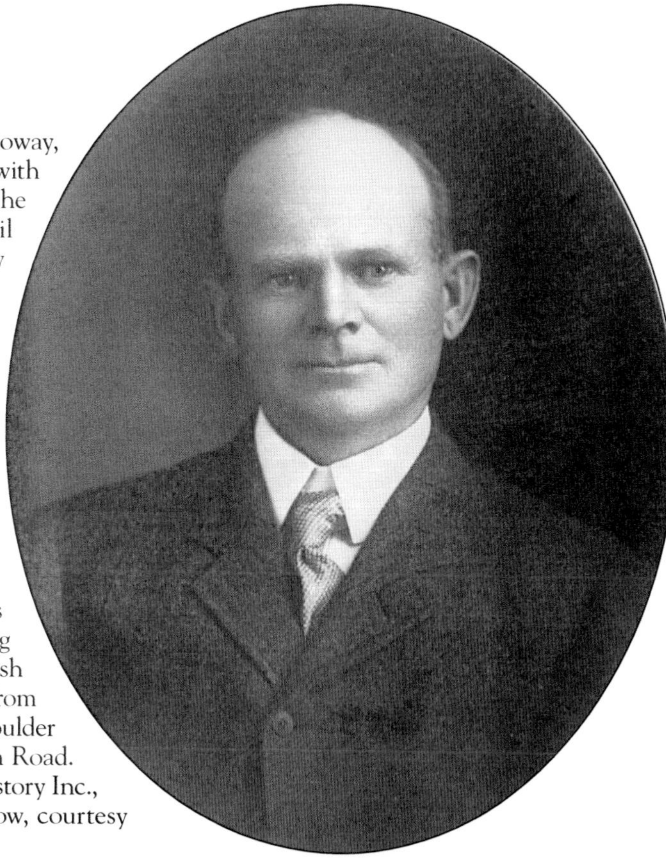

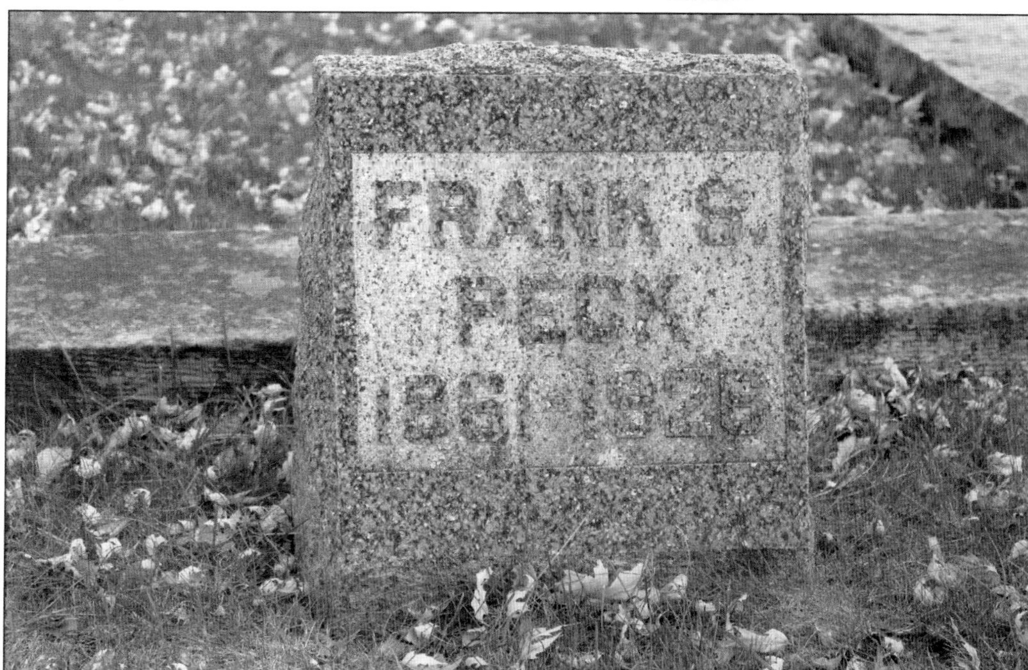

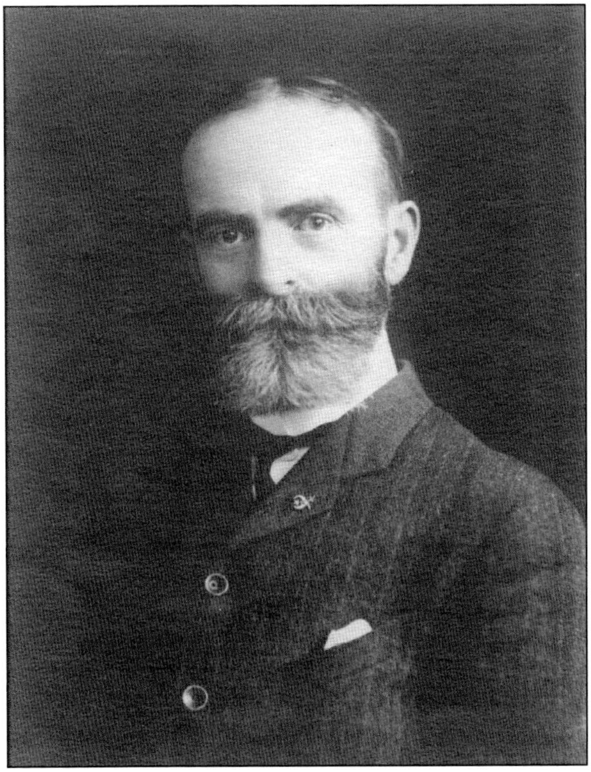

Samuel Wagner Russell (1857–1936) was a mine owner and businessman in Deadwood from 1898 to 1919. Born in Towanda, Pennsylvania, he graduated from Lehigh University in 1881. Seventeen years later, he acquired the Uncle Sam Mine, located near the town of Roubaix. In 1901, Russell helped organize the Black Hills Mining Men's Association and served as the chairman for the South Dakota Commission to the St. Louis World Fair in 1903–1904. After 1919, Russell moved to Sioux Falls and worked for Mutual Life Insurance as a special agent and statistician. The Russell monument is unique to Mount Moriah, as it is the only Celtic cross in the cemetery. The letters "IHS" in relief signify the first three letters of Jesus's name in the Greek alphabet: iota, eta, and sigma. (Left, courtesy of Deadwood Public Library; below, courtesy of CODA.)

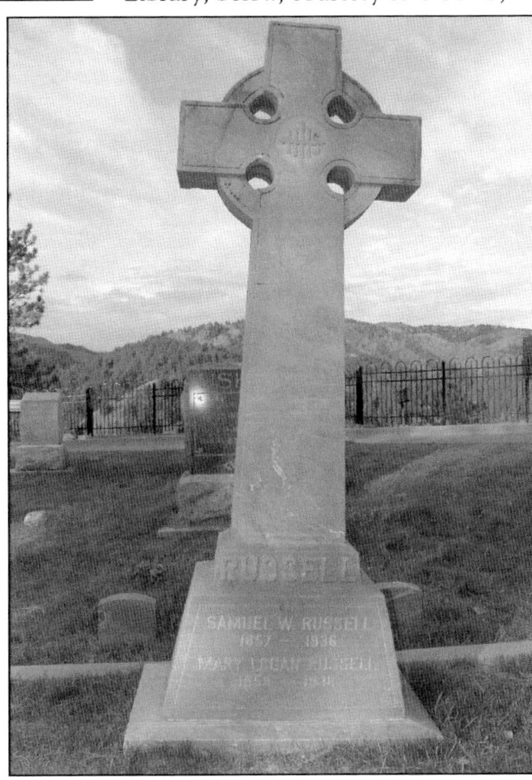

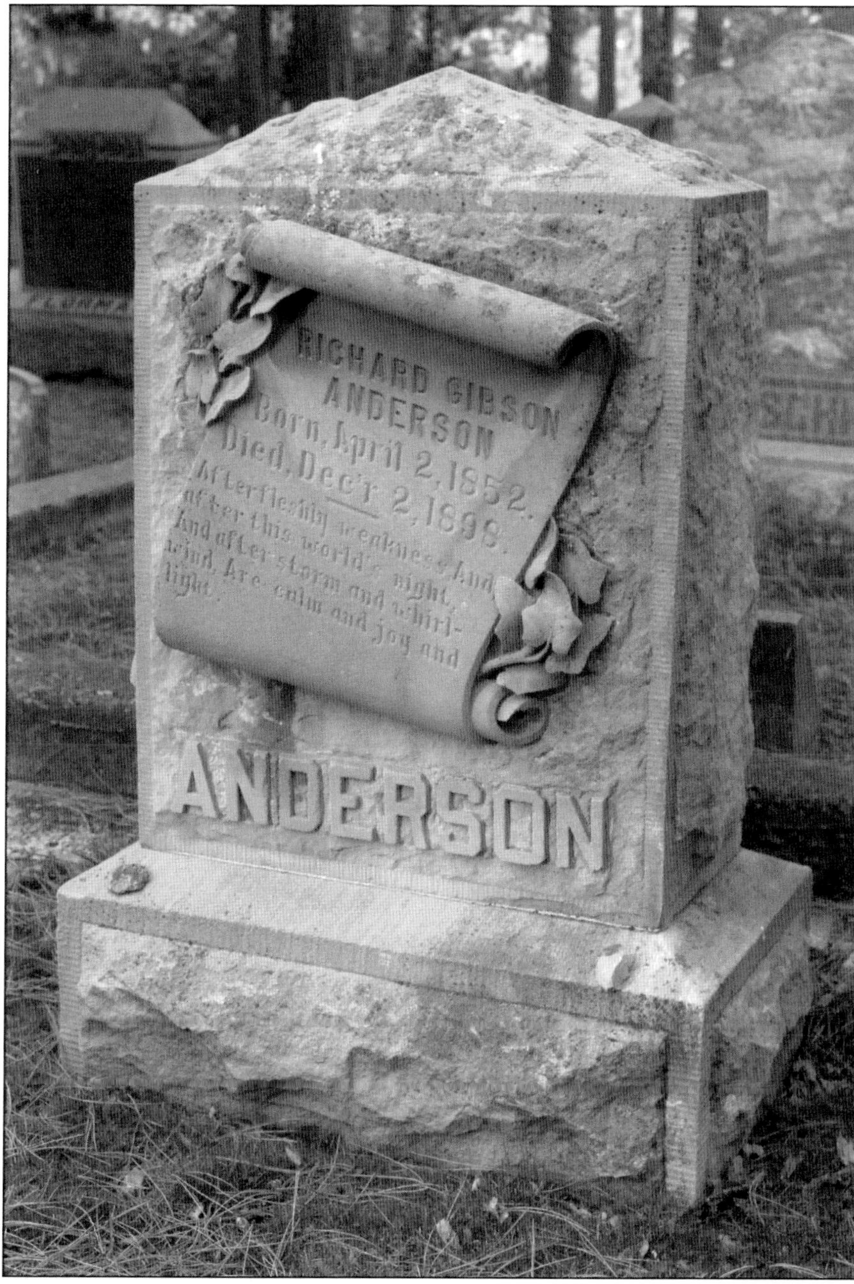

One of the more ornately carved markers in the cemetery is the sandstone memorial to Richard Gibson Anderson, who died on December 2, 1898. Born in South Carolina, his father, Gen. Richard H. Anderson, was a West Point graduate and served in the Confederate army during the Civil War. In 1877, Richard arrived in Deadwood Gulch and became a prominent civil and mining engineer. He went on to become the US deputy mineral surveyor for Dakota Territory and Wyoming. Several of his more significant projects included locating the railroad line near Hat Creek in 1884, platting the town of Whitewood in 1888, and platting the now nonexistent Scobey County, east of Meade County, South Dakota. His monument is adorned with a scroll and ivy, beautifully carved in relief. (Courtesy of CODA.)

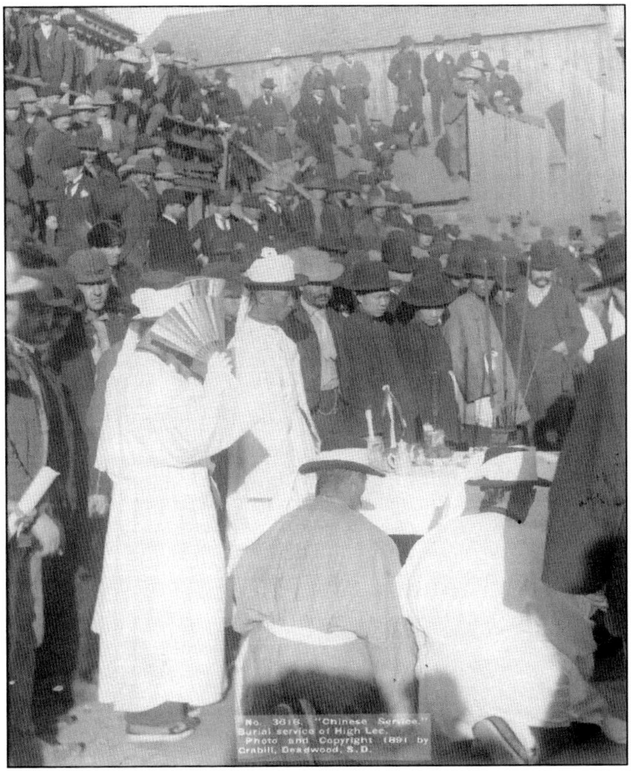

On September 1, 1878, Yung Set became the first recorded Chinese burial in Mount Moriah Cemetery. The local newspapers recorded this funeral in great length, describing the procession and eventual interment. Chinese religion and burial practices stemmed from an assortment of beliefs revolving around Taoism, Buddhism, Confucianism, and local folklore. In some instances, fireworks, a community band, and symbols were used to drive away lost or evil spirits. Taoist monks used flags to honor the dead and to keep the soul of the deceased and their mortal remains together until burial. In 1891, photographer John C.H. Grabill captured the funeral service for High Lee in Deadwood. The photograph below records an unidentified Chinese grave in Mount Moriah Cemetery. (Left, courtesy of Library of Congress; below, courtesy of CODA.)

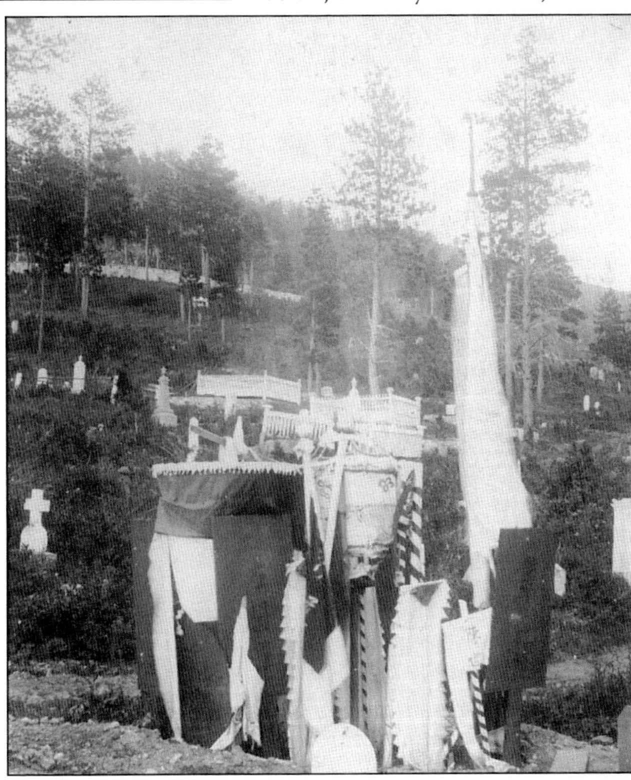

From 1878 until the 1920s, approximately 33 Chinese were buried in Mount Moriah Cemetery. Many of these graves once contained wooden headboards with painted Chinese characters. In 1944, amateur historian Charles Haas located and photographed two marble monuments in Section 6. Unfortunately, these markers have been removed from the cemetery. In 2016, staff from the Deadwood Historic Preservation Office hired the Genesee Valley Daoist Hermitage in Genesee Valley, Idaho, to translate the characters on these monuments using high-resolution photographs. The names that appeared on the monuments were Yu He Neng (May 4, 1914) and Chen Ying Fen. Unfortunately, neither of these names appeared in the Mount Moriah Ledger. (Both, courtesy of CODA.)

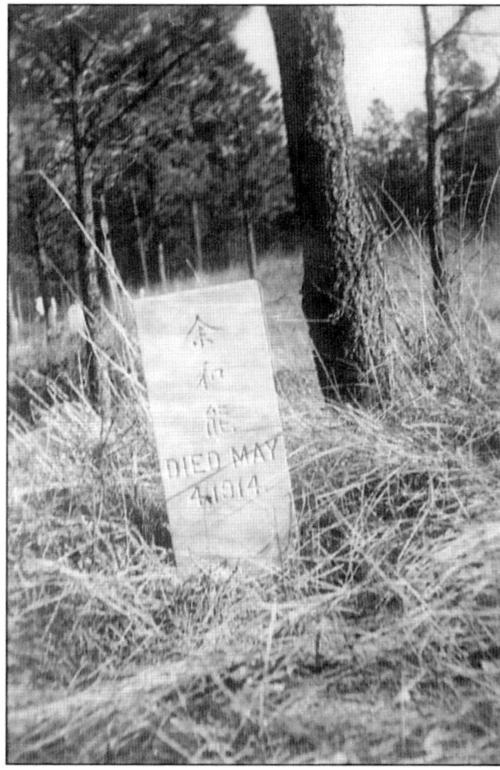

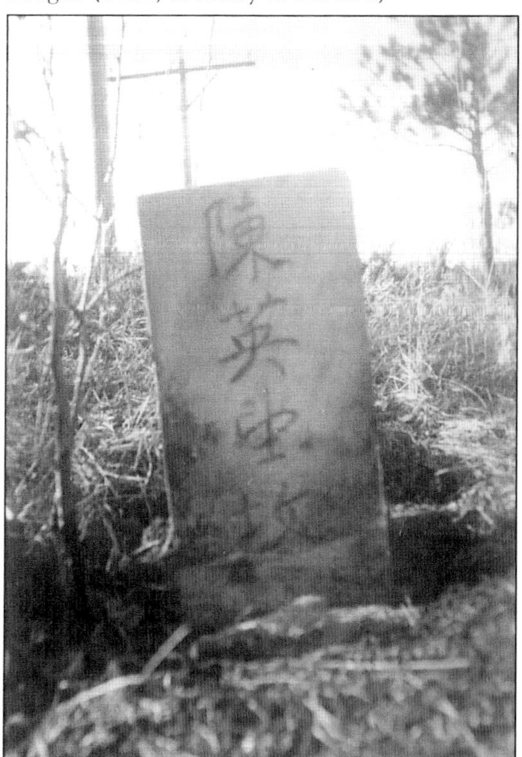

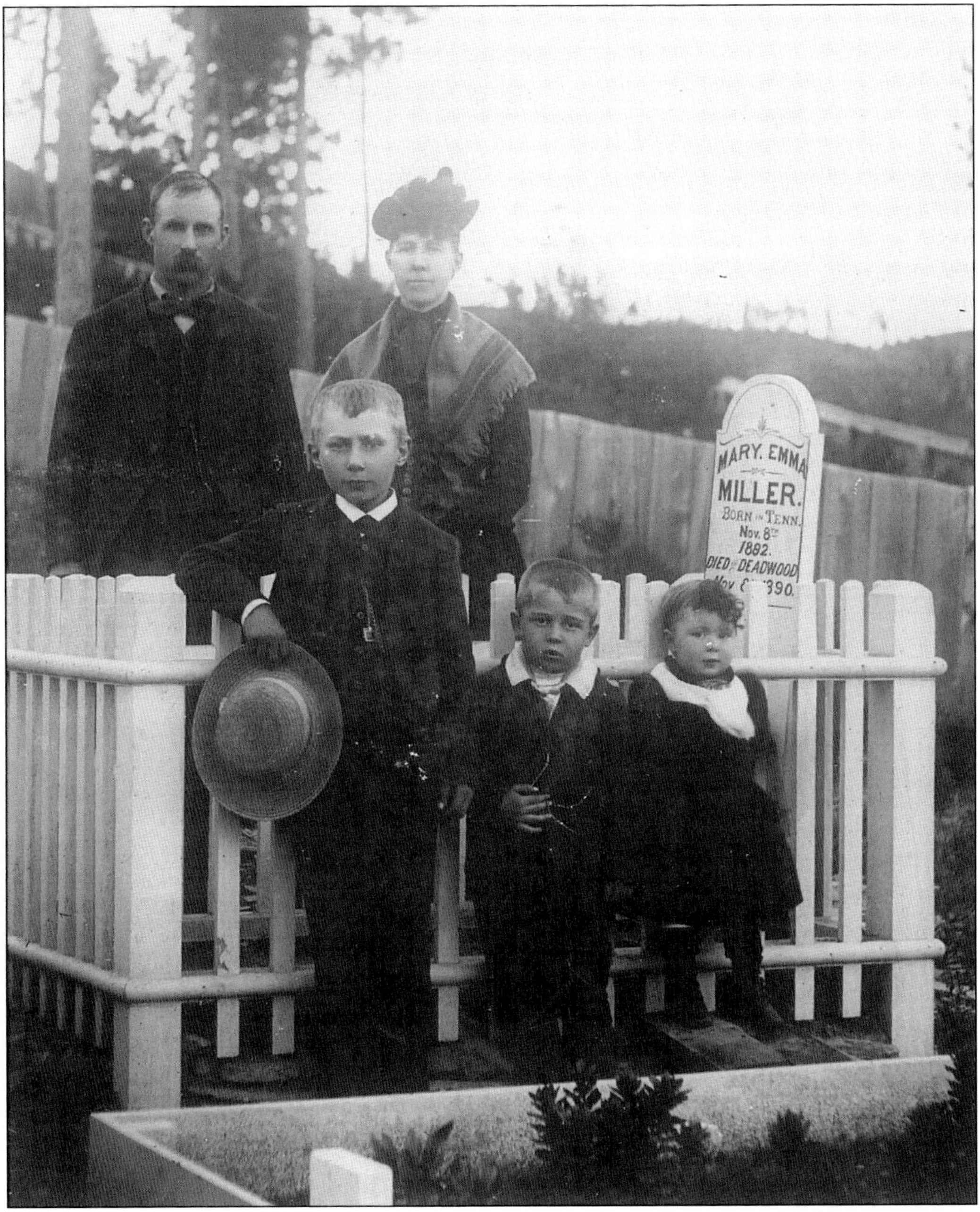

Infant and child fatalities were relatively common prior to the 20th century. Children were more susceptible to an assortment of communicable diseases caused by poor sanitation, lack of personal hygiene, or not having an adequate source of fresh water. Diphtheria, an acute infectious disease spread by airborne bacteria, frequently afflicted children. Local newspapers ran articles covering those with diphtheria, as in the case of Mary Emma Miller, who died of diphtheria on November 8, 1890. Two days prior to Mary Emma's death, the Miller family moved to Deadwood and all four children contracted the disease. By the time the authorities came to help, Mary Emma was dead. This cabinet card of the Miller family at her grave is a solemn reminder of the childhood diseases that once plagued Deadwood and Lawrence County. (Courtesy of CODA.)

Other diseases, including whooping cough, croup, pneumonia, and scarlet fever—coupled with accidents—also took their toll on the children of Lawrence County. Testaments to these premature deaths are found scattered throughout the cemetery in the form of monuments that contain lambs (Kenneth Sjogren), doves (Bella Michelson), or a small stump of a tree with all of the branches removed (Clark W. Woodbury). (All, courtesy of CODA.)

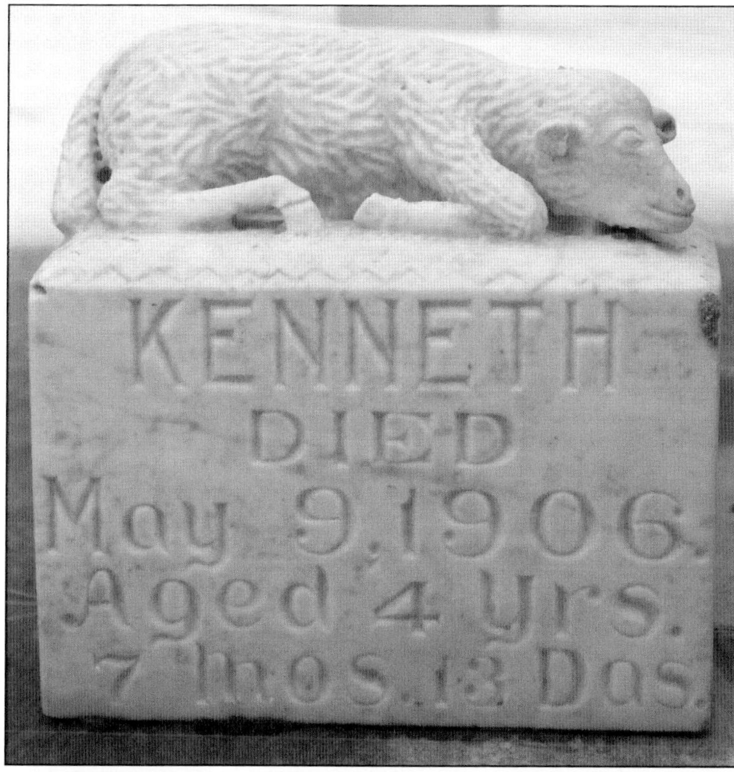

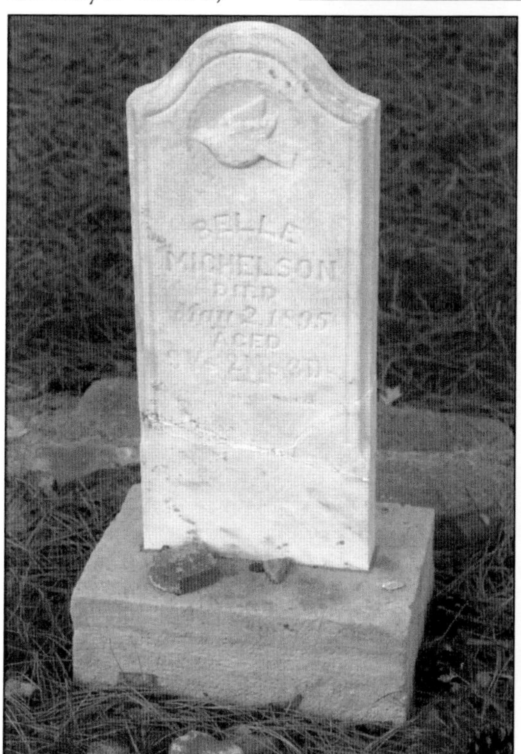

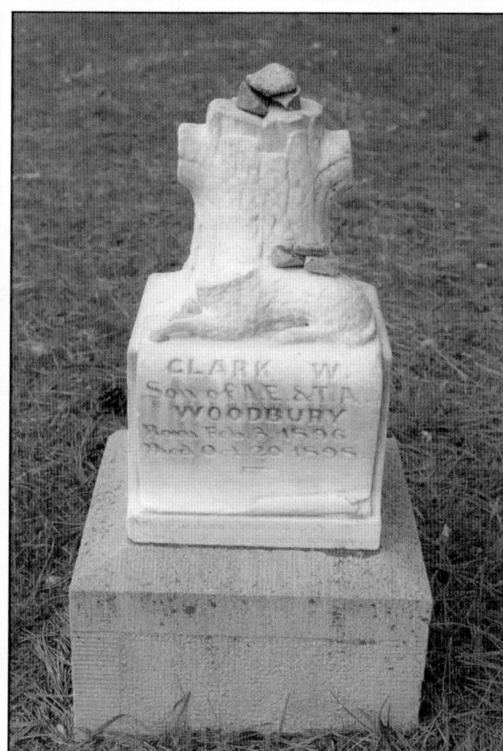

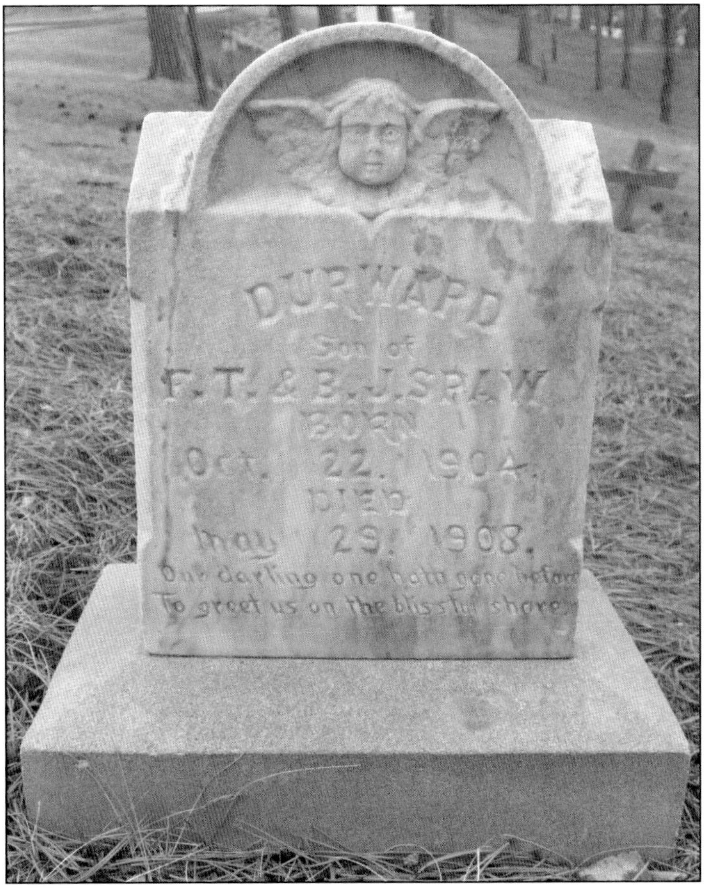

Durward Spaw (October 20, 1904–May 29, 1908) was the son of John W. and Laura E. Spaw, of White Owl, South Dakota. The Spaw family operated a store and post office 71 miles east of Deadwood. The Spaw monument contains a child's face with wings protruding from the side of the head. Known as a "soul effigy," this symbol has its roots in 16th century New England. Over three centuries, the symbol evolved from the skull and crossed bones to a human face with wings, and the name "death's head" was replaced with "soul effigy." By the mid-19th century, the soul effigy was replaced by winged cherubs. This is the only example of a soul effigy in Mount Moriah Cemetery. (Both, courtesy of CODA.)

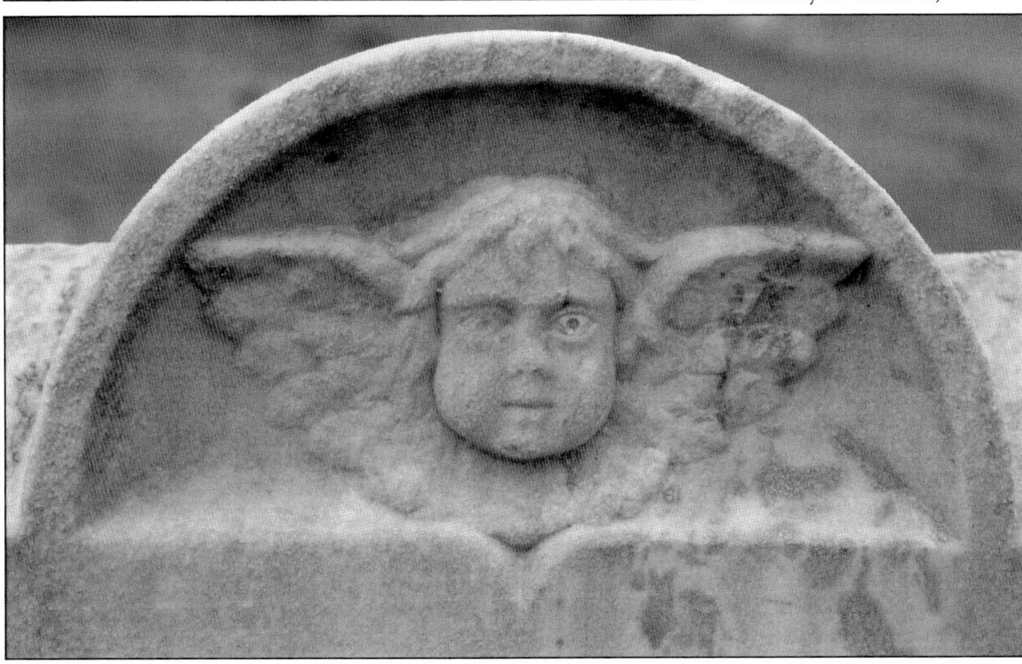

THE DEADWOOD HISTORIC PRESERVATION COMMISSION

The Deadwood Historic Preservation Commission's (DHPC) mission is to preserve, protect, and promote the rich and unique heritage of the city of Deadwood—a National Historic Landmark. The DHPC and Historic Preservation Office (HPO) fund educational and interpretive programs and report on the historical, architectural, archeological, and cultural significance of historic properties. The mission of the City of Deadwood Archives (CODA), an operation within the HPO, is to acquire, preserve, and interpret municipal and county records in accordance with historic preservation efforts in Deadwood and Lawrence County, South Dakota. To accomplish this, CODA acquires, identifies, inventories, and houses historic documents and artifacts of enduring and significant value pertaining to the history of Deadwood and Lawrence County. Since 1990, the DHPC and CODA have worked together to preserve, protect, and enhance the city's permanent collections.

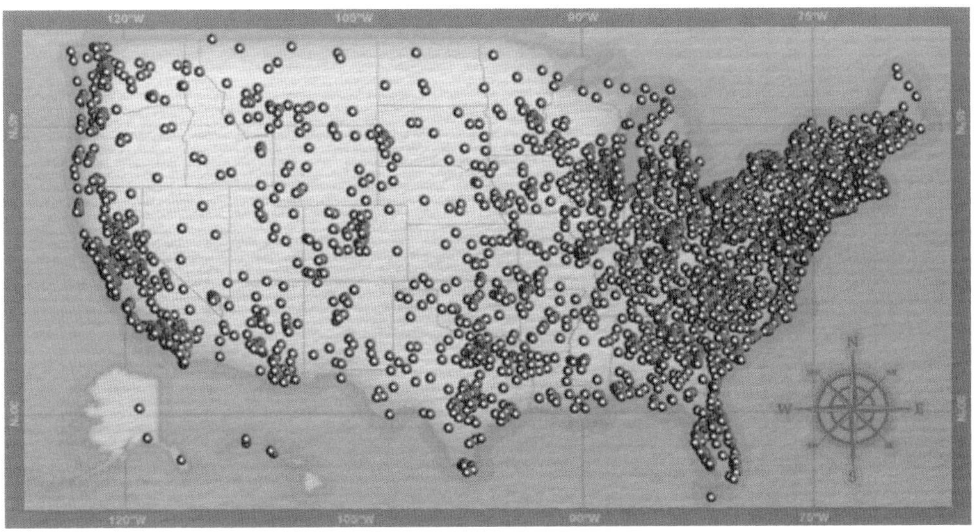